DATE DUE

DEMCO, INC. 38-2931

Issues in Education

View from the Other Side of the Room

Geraldine Coleman

BERGIN & GARVEY
Westport, Connecticut • London

Library of Congress Cataloging-in-Publication Data

Coleman, Geraldine.
   Issues in education : view from the other side of the room /
Geraldine Coleman.
     p. cm.
   Includes bibliographical references and index.
   ISBN 0–89789–634–3 (alk. paper)
   1. Educational change—United States. 2. Education—Social
aspects—United States. 3. Education—Parent participation—United
States. 4. Academic achievement—United States. 5. Motivation in
education—United States. 6. Teachers—United States–Attitudes.
7. School discipline—United States. I. Title.
LA217.2.C65 2001
   370′.973—dc21   98–38308

British Library Cataloguing in Publication Data is available.

Library of Congress Catalog Card Number: 98–38308

ISBN: 0–89789–634–3

First published in 2001

Bergin & Garvey, 88 Post Road West, Westport, CT 06881
An imprint of Greenwood Publishing Group Inc.
www.greenwood.com

Printed in the United States of America

The paper used in this book complies with the
Permanent Paper Standard issued by the National
Information Standards Organization (Z39.48–1984).

10 9 8 7 6 5 4 3 2 1

In loving memory of my niece, Jacqueline Laura Coleman, whose kind and gentle spirit touched my heart and enriched my life and will forever be remembered in the song of a robin, a gentle ocean breeze and the beauty of a sunset.

Contents

Acknowledgments

Rare is the individual who achieves formidable goals in the absence of caring others whose support, encouragement, and guidance serve as a beacon of hope and inspiration. This author is no exception. I am indebted to the many individuals who in some way large or small contributed to this work's coming to fruition. A very special thank you to my colleagues Cynthia Marshall and Judy Fox who contributed their very formidable data retrieval and research expertise in assisting me in locating resources; to Jane Wisniewski who assisted me in managing numerous resources; and to those colleagues who, formally or informally, shared their experiences with me.

A very special thank you to my sister and brother-in-law, Bernice and James Lloyd, who assumed many of my mundane yet essential daily responsibilities to allow me time to work on this project.

Introduction

In writing this book, I made a deliberate attempt not to get mired down in minutia and long historical details tracing the evolution of educational change and resultant issues. Rather my primary objective is to provide persons in some way connected to institutions of learning concrete and practical information to guide their practice.

The face of American education has changed over the decades. Its features have become more intricate and detailed. For most people, the days of the one-room schoolhouse where students were simply taught the fundamentals of reading, writing, and arithmetic are faded memories of a bygone era. In its physical, social, and philosophical structure, education has become a chameleon of sorts to conform to societal change. It has assumed a bureaucratic structure to accommodate its more global mission.

At the most fundamental level, no longer can its primary mission to transmit knowledge be accomplished without addressing the many extraneous variables that impact its ability to successfully fulfill its mandate. Changes in technology and the family, economy, and government (the basic foundation of our social structure), as well as increased ethnic and cultural diversity have not only impacted the changing role and function of education but have caused practitioners to examine more closely their methods and policies.

Technological advances have not only affected curriculum (what we teach) but also instruction (how we teach). It has necessitated a partnership between educational institutions and businesses to establish an ongoing dialogue regarding the needs of the workplace. Changes in the family structure have created the need for education institutions to assume some of the responsibilities traditionally held by parents—for example, health education, driver education, personal counseling, after-school care and programs. Our transformation from an agrarian to an industrial and now a technological society has similarly impacted education, ending the need for child labor and freeing children to reap the benefits of public education and providing them with marketable skills to successfully compete in today's workplace. To maintain our position as a world power, government has increased its involvement in education, establishing mandates to ensure that our students possess the academic skills necessary to maintain our presence in the world community. In effect, this book addresses, in part, some of the primary issues in education that have evolved as a result of changes in our basic social institutions.

This is an empirical study to the extent that it relies on practical experience rather than theory. While it incorporates a review of the extant research, it goes a step further, contextualizing it to allow those who are in some way connected with institutions of learning a clearer view of how research findings can impact their practice. In teacher-training institutions and at staff development meetings, education practitioners are bombarded with theory and the never-ending new trends in education, all in an effort to improve the efficacy of their practice. However, there is a paucity of literature that contextualizes research findings to reflect real-life educational experiences.

There are five underlying themes that reoccur throughout this book. They are: (1) education is a partnership; (2) perceptions and attitude dictate our behavior; (3) knowledge creates understanding and understanding creates change; (4) there are different ways of knowing, and educators must broaden their pedagogy to allow students to learn in ways amenable to their learning style; and (5) there are many extraneous variables that impact a student's educational experience.

Education does not take place in a vacuum. Home, school, and community must join together in a symbiotic relationship if this institution is to successfully carry out its mission transmitting knowledge and preparing our children to produce knowledge and become productive citizens and informed consumers. All must realize their vested interested in educating our children. They are all architects of the future. Working together they can lay a firm foundation upon which our children can build an appreciation of learning.

What has been lacking in the literature as well is simple, straight talk about how teachers, administrators, and parents perceive the educational process. Ultimately what matters is not so much the extant reality but one's perception of that reality. What matters is how one perceives a situation, and the only way to effect change is to first change or alter the perception. This holds true whether the issue is a student's lack of performance, an administrator's administrative style, or a teacher's classroom management. Our reactions to people, situations or events are colored by our perceptions. If a teacher's perception of students is positive, he or she will react to students positively. If administrators perceive that staff abuse privileges, they will react accordingly. If classroom teachers perceive that their students are incapable of the self-discipline required to engage in cooperative learning activities, they will react accordingly. It is irrelevant whether or not their perceptions are on target, because ultimately unless they can be convinced otherwise, they will base their behavior on their perception of the individual or situation.

Veteran teachers, student-teachers, administrators, and parents can learn much from this book to improve the efficacy of their practice. Hopefully, it will place them in a position to momentarily stand on the outside and look in. It will afford them the opportunity to really hear what the other side has to say and understand how the persons on it construct meaning from their experiences. Having acquired this knowledge, then and only then can they meet on common ground to fulfill their mission of educating students.

Additionally, this book seeks to call increased attention to the need to educate the whole child, taking into consideration the many extraneous variables that impact children's worldview and, more specifically, their view of the role of education in their lives. It also addresses the importance of acknowledging the variety of ways in which students know and learn.

These five underlying themes are woven throughout six chapters. They are parental involvement, academic achievement and motivation, teacher attitude, discipline, and school and the social order. These variables are among the most significant issues in education today. They define our practice and form the measuring stick of success.

In Chapter 1, the discourse centers around establishing the importance of the role of the parent in education. Education starts at home. Parents are the first and most influential teachers with whom children come in contact. Through the socialization process, they lay the foundation upon which children build the social skills necessary to function appropriately in secondary groups. In this chapter, primary consideration is given to a discussion of the impact of the value parents place on education on student attitude toward school and academic success. It elaborates on ways in which parents convey the importance of education to children. Understanding that education, at its best, is grounded in a partnership between home, school, and community, the discussion turns to ways in which the school can increase parental involvement. The chapter concludes with an in-depth look at the varied communication styles parents employ when interacting with school officials and how their style impacts student attitude in general and, more specifically, their attitude toward school and school officials.

Chapter 2 has as a major focus academic achievement. The discourse centers around a discussion of the variables that impact student achievement. It identifies such variables as a relevant and academically challenging curriculum , that engage the student, classroom environments conducive to learning, teacher attitude, parental involvement and expectations, proper academic placement and student attendance as the building blocks of academic achievement. This chapter also discusses the evolution of state initiatives designed to improve academic achievement.

Chapter 3 examines the role of motivation in academic success. Attention is given to the sources of motivation and an in-depth look at the roles of teachers, parents, and students in motivation.

Chapter 4 examines the role of the teacher in the education process. The use of the word "process" is deliberate, for it attests that educating children does not conform to a cookie-cutter formula. Humans are very complex beings, alike yet each uniquely different. Consequently, cookie-cutter formulas for educating children fall short of meeting the needs of all of these unique beings. Educators must, therefore, continuously and consistently explore new ways to meet the varied needs of children in the classroom. This cannot be accomplished in one fell swoop.

In this chapter special attention is given to the impact of teacher attitude toward students and to their role as educators on student performance. It also identifies various teacher interactional styles that drive the dynamics of what transpires in the classroom. It reflects on the need for teachers to be more introspective, assessing their role in the success or failure of students. In the final analysis, educators must commit to more closely scrutinizing their personal and professional attitudes, methods, and strategies to improve the efficacy of their practice and reach children.

Chapter 5 examines increased concerns over student discipline in schools across America from elementary to high school. The types of disciplinary problems seen in schools today are not as sophomoric as a generation ago. Smoking cigarettes in the restroom and playing hooky have given way to more serious concerns such as gross insubordination and disrespect to staff, drug and alcohol use, academic dishonesty, fighting, theft, and intimidation. Many would contend that this phenomenon is just a sign of the times. They would assert that it is a by-product of students being constantly bombarded via the media with images of violence, sending the message that the way to settle disputes is with the use of force.

These kinds of problems are symptomatic of a society that sends conflicting messages about drug use and alcohol consumption, on one hand glamorizing it and on the other condemning it. Movie stars, rock stars, and others in high profile occupations portray a lifestyle appealing to youth. However, when the use of alcohol and drugs is commonly associated with such individuals these practices, by association, may be construed as acceptable by young adults. They are simply emulating their role models. Similarly, when lead stories in newspapers and magazines reveal cheating scandals and other illicit activities perpetrated by government officials at all levels, the message to our youth is clear. The lack of civil decorum in government chambers, sometimes erupting in physical brawls, etches an indelible mark on the minds of our youth. Fighting among players on major league teams is regularly broadcast on the evening news. Given this social commentary, the aggressive behavior of our children in school should not come as a total surprise.

This chapter also takes a look at common behavior problems and explores some of the reasons why students misbehave. It goes a step further, however, in examining how teacher behavior affects discipline in the classroom and in offering concrete measures teachers can take to create classroom environments where discipline problems occur infrequently.

Chapter 6 addresses the issue of social change and how it has impacted educational institutions, forcing schools to broaden their scope. This chapter has as a focal point how social problems affect student learning and achievement. It addresses such social issues as single-parent homes, peer pressure, gangs and violence, teen pregnancy, poverty, and many other issues. It calls into clear focus the need to attend to and educate the whole child. Many students today come to school bearing a facade that masks deep psychological and emotional scars that negatively affect their ability to learn and function appropriately in an educational setting. It is not always easy to follow the rules and concentrate on your studies when your intellectual faculties are being weighted down by low self-esteem, hunger, fear, and a sense of hopelessness.

This chapter attempts to show educators a different perspective, so that behaviors, typically viewed as errant acquire new meaning and change the manner in which they interact with students. It stresses the need for educators to focus more on being proactive rather than reactive, to be supportive rather than punitive, and to go beyond responding to the symptoms to discover the cause. It does not advocate eradicating consequences as a means of behavior modification. It does advocate seeking the cause and providing support to end the cycle of deviant behavior.

This book takes a more humanistic approach to the discourse on issues in education. It offers a candid expression of ideas, observations, perceptions, and experiences based on research findings, on the experiences of veteran educators, and on this author's twenty-eight years in the field. There has been no attempt at political correctness that would mask free expression or distort the interpretation of personal experiences. Hopefully, for those not in some way connected with institutions of learning, it will provide greater insight into what it means to be a teacher, student or parent of school-age children. For teachers, students, and parents, it will create greater understanding of the role of the other and reinforce the need to work collectively to fulfill a common mission.

The scenarios described in the book are true, and I am sure reflect the extant reality for educational institutions across the nation. At the very least, it will stimulate a dialogue for further discussion and culminate in increased awareness and understanding of the issues and the development of personal and institutional action plans for change.

Chapter 1

Parental Involvement

That parents are the most important influence in a child's life is axiomatic. The nature of the bond forged between parent and child forms the essence of their being. Parents are the quintessential role models. Their established behavior patterns, what they do and say, leave an indelible mark on the child. It is, therefore, ironic that while we require a license, as a symbol of competency or readiness, to get married, drive a car or practice many occupations, there is no prerequisite for parenthood, except reaching puberty. For the most important role a human being can assume— being responsible for the care and well-being of a child—there is absolutely no prescriptive social prerequisite to validate competency or readiness to assume that role. The lack of a social prerequisite suggests that, culturally, we operate under the assumption that parenting skills evolve naturally. The alarming statistics on child abuse, neglect, juvenile delinquency, and the number of children in foster care however, attest to a different reality.

THE IMPORTANCE OF BONDING

At the most fundamental level, parental involvement starts with bonding with the child during infancy. Numerous studies have shown the importance of human touch and interaction (McNichol, 1998). The classic cases of feral children (those raised in the wild by animals) have shown they adopt the behavior and mannerisms of the species on whom they depend for survival. Similarly, studies of children raised in orphanages have revealed that limited physical contact with adults in the form of caressing, cuddling, and being spoken to negatively impacts mental and social development (Ragland & Saxon, 1985).

The importance of bonding, between "parent" and child, in the sensory, physical, social, and emotional development of children has come center stage with the relatively new phenomenon of foreign adoptions by American couples. This phenomenon was precipitated in 1990 by the social and political upheaval in Eastern bloc countries which left many children orphaned or abandoned (Saul, 1997a; 1997b). A shortage of Caucasian babies sought by infertile American couples and the host countries' less stringent policies for foreign adoption led many couples to Eastern Europe in hopes of building the perfect family. For many of these couples, their dream would take on nightmarish proportions, as the harsh reality of the devastating impact of institutionalization on children surfaced.

Unlike orphanages in many other countries, the severely understaffed facilities in Eastern Europe resulted in children being warehoused, left to lie in cribs all day or to roam aimlessly with virtually no sustained and meaningful interaction with their adult caretakers. As more and more couples began to experience problems with these children, a pattern was noted which led to questioning why so many of the children from these countries had problems. Adoptive parents found themselves in a futile struggle to bond with children seemingly trapped in a world of implacable behavior. These children screamed, engaged in behaviors inconsistent with the social context, flew into rages, engaged in masochistic and sadistic behaviors, stiffened when being held, and did not like being touched. Some of the children suffered symptoms of fetal alcohol syndrome, autism, and other developmental problems. No amount of love the adoptive parents could lavish upon them seem to turn the tide (Saul, 1997a; 1997b).

As parents sought professional help, the impact of institutionalization on the children became evident. By one estimate, 30 to 40 percent of children from foreign institutions will have moderate problems that include learning disabilities. Most startling, however, is that 20 percent will be severely impaired with such problems as autism, retardation, fetal alcohol syndrome, and attachment disorder. Attachment disorder syndrome refers to the inability to bond with others as a result of the lack of sensory development that evolves from human contact and interaction deprivation. In other words, these children were deprived of the necessary stimuli to learn and develop appropriate sensory responses (Saul, 1997a; 1997b). These findings raise interesting speculation regarding the social/psychological impact on children who have spent years since birth in the foster care system being moved frequently from one placement to another.

In effect, positive, meaningful contact between parent and child is essential to good physical, mental, and social development of children. As children grow, they depend less on parents to perform basic tasks for them such as feeding, bathing, dressing, etc. As the boundary of their world expands beyond the home, first bringing them into contact with the school (the institution where next to home they will spend the largest percentage of their time), the importance of parental involvement does not wane.

The importance of the role of the school and its success in fulfilling its mission to educate children is bolstered by active parental involvement that begins at birth. This chapter sheds light on just how important it is for parents to become active participants in the education of their children and to forge a supportive and cooperative relationship with school officials.

REASONS FOR LACK OF PARENTAL INVOLVEMENT

Most research acknowledges a sharp decline in parent involvement in school between elementary and middle school (Henderson, 1998). Given the very powerful impact of parental involvement and student achievement, this is an issue that warrants further consideration.

Ladson-Billings (1994) gives some viable reasons why parents, particularly the working class, may not get involved in the education of their children. Among variables she mentions are: with busing many students attend schools located far from their homes and parents lack transportation to school meetings; in many families both parents must work; and many parents are intimidated by the school. Others attribute the decline in parental involvement as children grow older to change in schools, schools farther away from home, larger schools, and the greater number of teachers each child will have in a given day. At the high school level, parents may be driven away by lack of understanding of the system (Henderson, 1998).

However, others would instead focus on those parents who labor under the same conditions or circumstance and yet are involved in their children's education. The question becomes, What is the difference that makes the difference? The answer invariably lies in the value that is placed on education and the degree of sacrifice and personal commitment one is willing to make to support one's values. This is not to suggest that there are not certain circumstances that prevent parents from becoming actively involved in their child's education, but it does encourage examining with greater acuity the reasons parents give. The bottom line is, first is the parent making an effort to be involved, that is, to resolve the circumstances that are preventing involvement, and second, has the school made an effort to study the issue, to determine causes, and to assist parents with solutions.

Some underlying causes for a lack of parental support may be grounded in more global social issues. For example, in many inner cities hopelessness shrouds the community ("Psychology Profession Fails," 1998). Hopelessness breeds apathy and submission to one's condition.

The power of attitudes of hopelessness and helplessness in determining success and failure cannot be overstated and is documented in research. Bruno Bettelheim (1960), himself a Nazi concentration camp survivor, observed that many prisoners were so consumed by feelings of helplessness that they became as walking corpses. Similarly, Seligman (1974) describes the reaction of a Vietnam Prisoner of War (POW) who was able to adapt to the atrocities of his condition on the promise of an impending release. However, when the appointed time arrived and his release was not preeminent, he lapsed into a severe depression and died. When he lost hope, he lost the will to live, to continue to struggle to survive. Seligman (1989) focused on the concept of learned helplessness. In a laboratory experiment he placed a dog in a shuttle box. Shortly after he activated a light to go on at the same time the dog received a shock. Soon a different dog learned to immediately jump to the other side when the light was activated. In a previous experiment the dog was restrained by a harness and unable to move and subjected to a number of shocks (Overmier & Seligman, 1967). When the dog was placed in a shuttle box with an obvious means of escaping the shock, when the light was activated the dog responded by crouching, howling, and whining. There was no attempt to escape. In effect, the dog had previously learned that attempts to escape its circumstance were futile and, feeling helpless, made no further attempts to escape (Seligman, 1989). Similar effects were observed among humans when they were subjected to punishment they could not prevent or predict (Fox & Oakes, 1984). What we learn from these studies is that helplessness is a psychological state that evolves when there is a sense of loss of control over events or circumstances in one's life (Seligman, 1989).

Therefore, the larger question becomes, How do we restore hope? How can we make the inhabitants of our inner cities believe the American Dream is attainable? Once this is accomplished, the importance of education becomes clear. But until children see that education is a means to an end, educators will be hard pressed to teach, and the fruit will die on the vine.

REACHING THE HARD-TO-REACH PARENT

A major concern of many schools is how to reach the hard-to-reach parents. For many, parents circumstances prohibit involvement in their child's schooling. They may be single parents who cannot afford child care to attend school meetings; professionals with long work hours; parents who speak only limited English and are frustrated by their inability to effectively communicate; parents who shy away from interacting with school officials because of lack of proper clothing or education, or who live in crime-infested neighborhoods, and fear coming out at night. Whatever the reason, parental involvement is a significant variable in academic success. Therefore, the real issue becomes how to reach the hard-to-reach parent.

Schools that have taken the matter seriously have developed action plans for change. Here are five strategies that teachers, administrators and schools have used that have made a difference (Gutloff, 1997).

Meet Parents on Their Turf

A school parent coordinator drops by the neighborhood recreation center to play basketball with the residents or goes door to door. As a common problem is disconnected phones, this provides the opportunity for a more personalized face-to-face contact. The coordinator may talk to parents about discipline or other problems, inform them of activities, or give them other pertinent information about what is happening at school. The key to the home visit strategy is to establish trust and an ongoing relationship with parents. However, this may not be a viable strategy in communities with high crime rates. At no point should staff members feel their personal safety is being compromised.

Make Schools Parent Friendly

Create a school atmosphere that increases the parent's comfort level. Create a comfortable area where parents can meet with teachers. Train staff not to interact with parents in an officious manner. Limit bureaucratic red tape as much as possible. Guard against talking down to parents, and greet them with a smile. The parent who may feel intimidated by better educated teachers and staff, or receives public assistance, etc., should be treated with the same respect as parents whose background more closely approximates that of the middle-class teachers who teach their children.

Bridge the Language Gap

In schools with a wide range of immigrant groups, issues of ethnic and cultural diversity are a priority. The first challenge is to break the language barrier. Many schools have responded by using software programs that record phone messages in many different languages, printing important correspondence relative to the school in the languages represented by the student population, hiring support staff to serve as translators, and hiring bilingual teachers.

Involve Parents in Decision Making

In 1968, James Comer, who presently is the director of the Yale Child Study Center School Development Program, began pioneer work in the area of parent-school partnerships. Out of his work developed a model for the inclusion of parents in the school decision-making process, called the Comer model. It "encourages schools to create governance management teams composed of parents, teachers, support staff and mental health officials." This group works collectively to develop goals and establish academic and social standards for the school. This clearly gives parents a vested interest in their children's education. It increases parental commitment and support for school policies and practices.

Comer points out, however, that to draw parents into the fold requires effort on the part of the staff to build trust, and that once this trust is established, parents must be given roles and responsibilities of substance that directly impact their child's learning. Parents can be asked to serve on specialized committees ranging from the less formal discipline, strategic planning, textbook review, principal's' advisory council, etc., to the more formal and politically based organizations such as the local school councils in Chicago, Illinois.

Help Parents Help Their Children

One way to involve parents in their children's education is to train them to assist their children with schoolwork. Many parents feel they lack the necessary skills to effectively do this. For the past three years, The National Education Association's Center for the Revitalization of Urban Education has been providing parents with the assistance they need by training parents how to create effective learning environments in their homes. Additionally, they provided training for parents on how to resolve conflict in the home. Other programs train parents to help their children develop self-confidence, self-esteem, and motivation. The key to the success of these programs is that they provide consistency by training parents to reinforce what is being taught at school (pp. 4-5).

What follows are additional strategies to increase parental involvement:

- Require report card pick-up so that parents must come to the school to pick up report cards. This provides an immediate opportunity for dialogue to discuss any problems evinced by the actual grades.
- Encourage phone contact, with counselors calling home to discuss the student's program of study, and teachers calling home to inform parents of problems or potential problems.
- Offer GED, ESL, or adult education classes for parents in the evening. The focus here is on increasing the parent's self-esteem. This will also bring them into the school to establish a level of familiarity and comfort with this setting.
- Form parent groups and specifically invite parents to participate. Parents with special skills can be invited to serve as tutors or in other capacities. Particularly at the elementary level, parents should be invited to assist in the classroom.
- Create shared learning experiences. One school held a spaghetti dinner to bring together teachers, parents, and at-risk students. Another school offered free lunch coupons to students whose parents attended each biannual meeting for students enrolled in a special remedial reading program.

An administrator shared this scenario from a parent meeting. It clearly brings into focus the need for all who impact student learning to look for ways they can make a difference and to refrain from placing the onus of responsibility on others.

One father sitting in the audience commented that he was angry after reading the dismal performance of students in math and science based on the Illinois Goal Assessment Program test (the test at that time administered to students at certain grade levels in the State of Illinois) and wanted to know what the school was going to do about it. He suggested that students weren't learning because teachers weren't teaching, and the curriculum was inappropriate. He was operating on the premise that if teachers teach, kids will learn and test scores will increase.

Another father, in attendance, along with his spouse and son, pointed out that while the school had a population of well over one thousand students, only ten parents were at the meeting. Here lies the problem. A mother commented that parents have abdicated their responsibility: they must reclaim responsibility for their children and their performance in school; they must make an effort to connect with the school. The father who initiated the debate countered that most students come from families where both parents work. Without exception, the other parents commented that this was not a viable excuse. The real issue, they shared, was the value parents place on education and where they set their priorities. This was a particularly interesting perspective that tended not to be characteristic of just the parents in attendance. In a series of articles run by a major metropolitan newspaper, when students, administrators and parents were posed the question of why students are not performing academically, teachers were not given as the primary reason. Students placed the onus of responsibility on students and parents on parents (Mitchell, 1996).

COMMUNICATING THE VALUE OF EDUCATION

For the most part, students who are successful in school have parents who are very supportive and have placed a high value on education. Contrary to what many may think, the supportive parent does not necessarily have to be well educated. Most important is the value the parent places on education and the willingness of the parent to behave in ways that consistently reinforce that value (Clark 1983). Parents send this message to their children in many ways such as:

Reading to and in the Presence of Children

In 1994, approximately 27,400 students in fourth, eighth, and twelfth grade were given a reading assessment by the U.S. Office of Education. The target population included students from public as well as nonpublic schools. As part of the study, students were asked to provide information about home support for reading, as evinced from the presence of magazines, newspapers and encyclopedias in the home, as well as homes that had twenty-five or more books. The study revealed a positive correlation between reading proficiency and the variety of literary materials in the home. That is, the more types of literary materials in the home, the higher the student's reading proficiency (Shields, 1996).

Instilling in children the value of education and interest in learning is a process that can actually take place during infancy. In a study of the development of language skills conducted by Peter W. Jusczyk of Johns Hopkins University, it was concluded that infants as young as eight months old are cognitively able to hear and remember words. The researchers tape recorded stories that were played to eight-month-olds daily for a period of ten days. Two weeks later, the infants were tested for word recognition. Words were read to the infants from two lists. One list contained thirty-six words from the stories, and the other contained similar words that were not found in the stories. To test for word recognition, the infants were placed between two speakers, each equipped with a light. The lights were used to get the infant's attention, and then the words were read through the speaker. Using data from earlier research that revealed infants tend to look toward the source of sounds that interest them and when they lose interest look away, researchers found that the infants in their study listened significantly longer to the lists of words from the stories even after a two-week lapse between their first hearing of the story, suggesting that infants do remember sounds (Recer, 1997).

These research findings provide strong support to the importance of parents reading to children during infancy. According to Jusczyk, "Reading to children at such an early age, even if they don't seem to understand, can start the process of learning language" (Recer, p. 3). In the process, the child is gathering information about sound patterns of words, and how words are formed, thereby enhancing the development of speech.

Consequently, parents must understand the importance of reading to their children in not only strengthening the bond between parent and child but also laying the foundation for the development of good language skills and an appreciation for learning.

Asking Children What They Have Learned in School Each Day

Typically, if a parent asks a child how was school today, the answer will invariably be "fine." Unless the parent follows up with additional probing questions, no further information will be volunteered. Therefore, to encourage an open dialogue regarding school, perhaps a more appropriate question would be "What did you learn in school today?" The question is specific and requires a specific response. Additionally, it will provide the parent with a clearer perspective of the educational setting and the curriculum.

Attending Parent Teacher Conference Days

This sends a clear message to the child that the parent's interest in his education is genuine. It is indicative of the parent's desire for direct communication with school officials, and it provides parents with an opportunity to experience first hand the educational setting and get a feel for the attitude and demeanor of staff members. It is here that parents' perception of the school is formed, invalidated, or validated. Parental perception may foster or hinder support for the school. Parent-teacher conference days also provide the foundation upon which parents and teachers can build relationships. Once relationships have been established, issues involving the student's academic performance or behavior can be discussed on more amicable terms as each party feels the other has the child's best interest in mind.

Attending Performances/Activities/Athletic Events the Child Is Involved In

A parent's attendance at school events in which the child is participating validates the parent's sense of pride in the child and support of activities that are of interest to the child. It also establishes the importance of the child in the parent's life. It establishes the child, and his/her accomplishments and interest as a priority. It lends support to the child's effort to achieve goals. This is particularly noteworthy for the child who sits on the bench week after week and never experiences actual play in the game yet can peruse the crowd and see his/her parents cheering the team to victory. To this child it sends a clear message of support in having made the team. The underlying message is a sense of pride and support for each accomplishment, no matter how small. This kind of parental support is conducive to increased self-esteem, determination, and the ability to take risk without fear of failing. "Anyone will invest in a sure success, but aren't we grateful when someone supports us when we were somewhat of a risk?" (Jakes, 1994).

From the student perspective, participation in such activities can be a determining factor in the direction they take. Participation in extracurricular activities is an essential part of the school experience, providing opportunities for personal and social growth and development and creative expression in a relaxed environment. Such programs provide numerous opportunities for students to develop leadership, and decision-making and communication skills, while working collectively to achieve goals. Participation in sports and other school activities has been credited with repelling the lure of gangs or other socially unacceptable behaviors.

On a larger scale, community involvement in staffing and developing after-school programs for students culminates in positive returns for both students and the community. The latchkey generation was ushered in with the increased number of households in which both parents work. Consequently, children and young adults are often unsupervised for the period between the time that school is dismissed and parents return home. This unsupervised time can have negative repercussions for the community, with increases in loitering, vandalism and, in general, time that is not spent in pursuit of some constructive activity. Many communities have attempted to address this problem with the institution of after-school activities for elementary students. Most programs provide a variety of activities for students, as well as a study period to complete homework. Many community park districts have developed similar programs consisting of intramural sports teams, mentoring programs, and tutoring sessions.

For students in economically depressed areas with high crime rates and gang activity, the reach of such programs extends well beyond supervision. For many of these students home is not a happy place, therefore such programs provide an extended period in which children can feel safe and develop relationships with caring adults. Caring teachers and coaches should take time to talk to and forge a relationship with that student who forever seems to be hanging around school well after hours and is not a part of any organized after school activity (Coleman, 1996). Sometimes, there is a story hoping to be told. Once the relationship has been established and the foundation of trust laid, well-kept secrets can be exposed and support systems put into place.

Volunteering

Definitions of volunteerism have changed over time and have conformed to changes in extant social problems and the social climate (Ilsley, 1990). Definitions have ranged from action derived from emotional commitment, to rational choice, to a response to pragmatic concerns characteristic of the Progressive Movement (Dewey, 1916). Volunteerism is the definitive statement of commitment to our beliefs and values. When parents volunteer for school functions, it establishes the importance of education in the familial value system. It also provides the parents an opportunity to not only observe firsthand educational and extracurricular processes but also assume an active role. When parents feel they have a vested interest in the school, their level of commitment will increase. Some school officials may find it necessary to clearly define the role of parents as volunteers. Parents must understand the extent to which district policy and state mandates govern the decision-making process. Volunteerism in this regard creates greater understanding of the constraints sometimes imposed on educational institutions.

A case in point was a group of parents at a parent meeting calling for the ouster of disruptive students. However, parents who regularly attend such meetings were cognizant of mandated due process hearings and, in some states, special disposition for students classified as requiring special education. At the legislative level, where local school councils or school boards operate, the issue of abuse of power may be called into question. Charges of parents vying for positions on councils and boards to carry out personal vendettas can create some dissonance in the system, particularly if the charges are grounded in fact. For the most part, however, parents who serve are committed to providing a quality education for all students and devote numerous man-hours in the process.

Assisting the Child with Homework

What better way to fully comprehend what is required of students and simultaneously experience firsthand the curriculum offered by the school? Assisting students with homework in the early grades is not as problematic for most parents as when they reach high school. Many parents may find algebra, trigonometry, calculus, and physics shadowy figures of a bygone era (i.e., their high school years). This dilemma, ironically, may afford the school an opportunity to connect with parents; particularly those who are actively involved in their child's schooling. One innovative response at the elementary school level is to allow parents to attend school with their child. In so doing, parents would acquire the necessary skills to enhance their child's performance; they would experience, firsthand, the challenge to the teacher in meeting the varied needs of students, and the presence of additional adults in some classrooms would be efficacious in creating a learning environment where more individualized instruction could take place. This response is not without potential negative side effects. However, depending upon the situation, it may be worthwhile to weigh the positive returns against the side effects. This program would also afford parents with limited skills and acknowledge the opportunity to learn by assisting their child and, in the process, strengthen the bond between parent and child (Sun, 1996).

Following up on Information the Child May Share Regarding Events at School

Proof to the child of the parent's genuine concern about school and his/her responsibilities is when what they say is backed by action. To assist school authorities in maintaining their credibility and dispel any misconceptions or break in communication, parents are well advised to call school officials regarding information about which they may have questions or concerns. It is damaging to the reputation and agenda of the school and parents when action is taken by one or the other that is not grounded in fact.

Reviewing the Child's Report Card with Him/Her and Providing Feedback

The importance of school is again reinforced when parents discuss with the child his/her academic performance. This provides the parents with information regarding the child's academic strengths and weaknesses and guides their interaction with appropriate school officials. In instances that warrant contact for remediation, parents are brought into contact with various support staff and may become familiar with various programs to assist the child. It should be noted that poor academic performance may be a manifestation of problems unrelated to intellectual ability. Report cards, therefore, may serve as red flags of other deeper issues with which the child is struggling. Both parents and school officials are cautioned against a perfunctory assessment of the reason for poor academic performance. Poor academic performance may warrant the involvement of the school psychologist, nurse, substance abuse counselor, social worker, or speech pathologist in addition to the traditional role of the counselor.

The teacher should take the initiative in contacting parents and support staff when changes in student behavior is noted. This initial step will set the process of assessment and remediation in motion. Parents, typically, are appreciative when teachers make a personal contact, particularly at the first sign of trouble. Such contacts can provide each party with valuable information that may assist in pinpointing the problem. This mutual expression of concern builds a solid foundation upon which teachers and parents can work together to get the student back on track. Education is truly a partnership.

Asking about the Curriculum and Extracurricular Activities before Enrolling Students

In many instances parents may feel intimidated by territory that is unfamiliar to them. Consequently, there may be the tendency to trust the professionals to make decisions regarding curriculum. School officials therefore, must encourage parents to not only review the curriculum put provide input. In this regard, parents can be a valuable resource. Being removed from the theory, practice, and professional jargon, parents can provide a purist perspective on education. They can shed light on the question, Is the education my child is receiving adequately preparing him or her for the real world? Who is in a better position than they— inextricably bound to the world of work themselves,—to assess the fit between what is taught in school and the knowledge and skills both academic and social to successfully compete in a global economy?

Educational naysayers may lament that parents' limited knowledge of the complexities of the educational process may result in unrealistic expectations. Even if that were the case, the most important outcome is that it opens the door for dialogue and provides parents with information to enhance their understanding of the curriculum. Conversely, such dialogue may force educational institutions to make the curriculum more culturally relevant, particularly in the case of minority students.

Clearly Articulating Their Expectations Regarding Academic Achievement and Behavior

The debate continues to rage. Teachers blame parents for students' lack of academic achievement and parents blame the teachers. When the dust clears, what remains is this: teachers and parents must work together to ensure academic success. Communication between the home and school is a vital part of this endeavor. Overwhelmed with paperwork, some teachers find it difficult to make repeated phone calls to a student's home. Their level of frustration is heightened in communities where a large percentage of students don't have phones or where parents are inaccessible while at work. Parents sometimes don't understand that the many responsibilities of a teacher, when multiplied by thirty students, makes it virtually impossible to inform the parent of every problem. Yet, this is a common expectation. Consequently, phone contacts or requests for parent conferences are often used as a last resort when other efforts have failed. Even in some middle-class communities where both parents work, getting parents involved can be problematic.

Parents must stress respect for adult authority and insist that behavior problems will not be tolerated. They should discuss with their children how to deal with perceived problems with teachers or other school staff members. A good plan of action is, as a first step, to instruct the child to discuss the matter with the parent(s) who will then contact the appropriate school authority and schedule a parent/teacher conference with the student to discuss the issue. Students should be discouraged from becoming confrontational.

Teachers sometimes feel they don't have the support of parents. *Who's Who Among America's Teachers* recently conducted a survey of 2,733 of the nation's top teachers. The majority of those surveyed felt that parents failed to provide the moral leadership necessary for children to learn. Compared to ten years ago, of the teachers surveyed 73 percent felt that parents are less willing to spend time with their children; 69 percent viewed parents as less moral and 41 percent felt parents expect less from their children. Based on these statistics it is not surprising that these teachers perceived a decline in student dedication, ethics, and lifestyle. They unequivocally cite parents for the decline (Hancock, 1998).

PARENT COMMUNICATION STYLES

The communication style parents use when interacting with school officials may impact student attitudes toward school and school officials. Based on my experiences, what follows is a description of modal communication styles parents engage when interacting with school officials:

Sherman Tank

This parent does not want to hear an explanation. Whenever a problem arises, the Sherman Tank Parent rolls in full force and immediately begins the attack. The assault continues full force and no one else can get a word in edgewise. Efforts to interject objective data are dismissed as fruitless attempts to distort the facts. The Sherman Tank Parent will tell you in no uncertain terms, "My child does not lie." Frequently, this parent will point out that the teacher is at fault for having provoked the student into insubordinate behavior. "Had she/he not spoken to Johnny in that tone of voice, he never would have said that to him/her." The underlying message is he got what he deserves.

As the assault continues, Johnny becomes a mere bystander watching the action. Under these circumstances, the teacher, the dean, the administrator becomes the problem and not Johnny. This person's motives or behavior is being called into question, not Johnny's.

Virtually every veteran administrator has probably had a Sherman Tank parent roll into his/her office. Consider this scenario. Two female students were engaged in an ongoing feud that started in the community and needless to say spilled over into the school. As the tension between the two escalated, each felt her safety was in jeopardy. One day, for reasons unknown, things reached the breaking point, culminating in one student spraying the other in the face with some unknown substance. Rather than reporting the incident, the victim left the building and informed her guardian. The guardian, accompanied by the student and another adult relative, entered the building and proceeded down the hall in pursuit of the perpetrator until they were intercepted. This was a guardian out of control and only after being faced with being forcibly removed from the building did this guardian gather enough composure to sit in the office to discuss the matter, that is, to hear both sides of the matter.

Exceptionally strong interpersonal communication skills are required of those who must interact with a Sherman Tank Parent. The most effective measure is to follow the adage that sometimes the best action to take is no action. Let the parent's rage dissipate by allowing the parent to vent until he/she has said everything he or she wants to say. As the school official begins to present the facts of the case, if the parent interrupts, the school official should be assertive and demand the parent remain quiet and listen.

See, Hear, and Speak No Evil

This parent behaves in a manner that supports the child in refusing to accept culpability for his/her actions. They generally attribute the child's errant behavior to others. Sowell (1997) was very blunt in assessing them: "We all know the kind of parent whose child is never wrong. It was the other kid's fault, the teacher's fault, the policeman's fault. Someday, it may be the executioner's fault" (p. 20). He alludes to the damage and long-term consequences incurred by children whose parents refuse to require them to accept responsibility for their actions. These children will find it extremely difficult to see the error of their ways, as parents consistently send messages, by virtue of their unconditional support, that validates the child's behavior. According to Sowell, "One of the worst things you can do to a human being is to exempt him from criticism and find excuses for whatever he does" (p. 20).

Unlike the Sherman Tank parent, the See, Hear, and Speak No Evil parent is not as aggressive or vociferous in defending the child. However, this parent will maintain their position that the child is innocent. Their firm belief in the child's innocence is often grounded in the fact that the child has been taught strong values, and therefore it is inconceivable to the parent that the child might be guilty of the rule infraction. The parent often underestimates the power of peer pressure and seems unaware that children, when not directly under the parent's control or scrutiny, may engage in behaviors that betray the values taught at home. Unfortunately, some students take advantage of the situation. Being assured of the parents' unconditional support, this student may feel invincible and continue to engage in behaviors that will result in disciplinary action. The See, Hear, and Speak No Evil Parent will often say, "He doesn't do things like that"; "He doesn't use that kind of language"; "I know he didn't say that"; "He's not violent, he wouldn't hit another child"; "What he said sounds like that, but wasn't what you said."

Richard came to class wearing his coat, which was against school policy. When the teacher refused him admission to class and instructed him to return to his locker and put his coat away, he responded with a few expletives. Needless to say, the teacher wrote a disciplinary referral, as Richard proceeded down the hall. A short time later but during the same class period, Richard materialized outside of the building and ended up talking to a student through the window of the classroom he should have been in. The teacher, noticing his presence, approached Richard again but he just walked away. This incident was added to the referral. When the dean finally caught up with Richard and disciplined him for his behavior, his mother met with the dean to challenge the disciplinary action. The gist of her position was this:

Richard, she contended, did not use profanity in responding to the teacher because he doesn't use that kind of language. Since the teacher could not recall verbatim every single word that was said, she must have misunderstood Richard's comments. The teacher was called in and, in the mother's presence, reiterated that she was not mistaken regarding his use of profanity. The mother persisted that Richard would not do that. The conversation then led to the matter of his being outside of the building and approaching the very class he should have been in to talk with students. Richard's mother indicated that he was outside waiting for her to pick him up. When it was explained to her that by Richard's own admission he had to go out of his way to end up at the classroom window talking to another student, his mother responded that the student had beckoned to Richard; therefore he couldn't possibly avoid the student and simply went to see what he wanted. The question was raised as to why would Richard want to continue to call attention to himself when in the act of breaking yet another rule. The mother held to her original position. The disciplinary action was appealed to a superior and sustained. The parent then carried the appeal further. When they too upheld the disciplinary action, she vowed to take the matter before the school board. It is interesting to note that at no time did the parent question Richard regarding any of his actions. In fact, Richard had very little to say in defense of his actions except that he wasn't guilty and he was outside the school (two hours before his actual dismissal) waiting for his mother to pick him up.

Unfortunately, See, Hear, and Speak No Evil parent are so sure of the efficacy of his/her parenting skills, they are unable to objectively and logically review the facts. In some instances, they may attempt to infuse race or gender issues, stating that the staff member is prejudiced.

In dealing with the See, Hear, and Speak No Evil parent, the school representative must be persistent in focusing the discourse on the facts in the case and refuse to be baited by issues of race or gender. After having restated the facts of the case and calling in others, if necessary, to verify the facts, continued discussion will be uneventful and the parent should be referred to a superior to continue the appeal. This parent is likely to take full advantage of the appeal process.

Diplomatic Negotiator

The Diplomatic Negotiator's interaction with the school representative is characterized by respect for position. This parent understands the need for rules and regulations and accepts that there will be consequences for infractions. This parent is often calm and will sit patiently while the particulars are being stated but will then present a rebuttal calling into question the interpretation of the child's action by the school official. The tone of interaction between the parent and school official is precise, ordered and not antagonistic. This parent will ask probing questions in an attempt to find support for their position. If satisfied with the school representative's response to these questions, he/she will accept the school's decision.

At this point, the parent will engage in the process of negotiating the penalty. He/she will call into question the value of suspension or any punishment that removes the child from the classroom and suggest imposing a punishment him/herself. Depending upon the severity of the infraction, the school official may allow the parent to handle the matter. For more serious infractions, the school official may impose a penalty consistent with school policy. The official may explain to the parent that to remain credible the school must apply uniform penalties. Needless to say this position is always open to challenge with parents citing the need for humanity in dealing with students.

A student was suspended for calling the teacher a name but claims, "I didn't say b____, I said witch." The teacher insists that the student's response was clear and audible and unequivocally directed at her. The student contends that she was talking about someone else and her mother had rallied in her defense. The teacher explained that no one else was involved in the events that led up to the gross disrespect and insubordination. Therefore, the student's explanation was not valid. The teacher reviewed in detail what had transpired. Still, the mother was not persuaded.

The matter was appealed to a superior. After having discussed the matter with the teacher, and the dean and questioning the student, the administrator concurred that the facts as presented by the teacher were credible. The parent once again repeated that her daughter was not referring to the teacher. As this student did not have prior incidents of this type of behavior, the suspension stood but the number of days was slightly reduced.

The mother asked the student to have a seat in the outer office, while she continued her discussion with the administrator. What transpired took the administrator totally by surprise, given how vehemently the mother had supported her daughter's account only moments before. She said, "I know she probably said what the teacher said she said. I'll take care of her at home." One would question, what if anything did this student learn? Why didn't the mother expect this student to take responsibility for her actions? Why couldn't the mother say in front of the student what she shared with the administrator? Will the mother on her own turf, confront the student and administer some type of discipline?

Accountability: Do the Crime, Pay the Time Parent

These parents know their child well. When given a scenario by the school official and after listening to the facts carefully, they will make the determination as to whether or not the accusation is within the realm of possibility. During the conference they may make such statements as, "I know its possible that you did that because this is a problem that we frequently have had to deal with at home." This parent stresses accountability. They will allow the child to present evidence to the contrary. If the child's argument is not convincing, the parent tells the child in no uncertain terms that he/she will have to suffer the consequences for his/her actions. They may even require the child to offer an apology. This parent may also impose their own brand of punishment, in addition, by grounding the student or taking away other privileges.

At first glance, and to the casual observer, it may appear that the accountability parent is not supportive of the child. Quite the contrary is true. This parent teaches the child values by insisting that they accept responsibility for their actions. The child is encouraged to examine not only his/her actions but their motives and to learn to think before taking action. The accountability parent will take time to discuss with the child ways to prevent such situations from occurring again. The accountability parent will most often have values that are closely aligned with the school and is supportive of the school's efforts to maintain an educational environment that is conducive to learning.

High school seniors are often caught in the turbulent man/child, woman/child world. There are times when they insist on being treated as full-fledged adults, and there are other times when feeling particularly vulnerable, they seek the comfort and protection of parents. Heather was encountered in the halls on a day she obviously had no doubts about her adult status. Previously, she had had an encounter with the dean and another staff member about wearing her jacket in school despite numerous previous warnings. Another administrator encountered her, unaware that she had just previously been reprimanded about the jacket and told to put it in her locker. True to her reputation, Heather began the debate. Consequently, she was brought to the office of administrator who then telephoned her parents to discuss the problem.

The mother was most cooperative and agreed that her daughter's attitude had been a problem of late and asked to speak to her. Heather snatched the phone from the administrator's hand with such force that it fell and broke. What started out as a simple reprimand and using a technique that usually worked well (students hate to have you call their parents and be required to explained why they are in the office) now turned into a suspension for insubordination. Using another phone, the mother was contacted again, and it was explained how they happened to be so rudely interrupted. The mother responded, "Heather, has a temper and of late she seems to feel that rules are not intended for her. I'm not going to stand for it. You do what you have to do and I'm going to do what I have to do. I apologize for her behavior." She asked that Heather be put back on the phone. Heather rolled her eyes in her head, held the phone about a foot away from her ear, and when her mother finished the conversation gave the phone back to the administrator.

Her mother did come in but only to make Heather apologize for her behavior. In subsequent conversations, she explained her efforts in attempting to teach Heather the necessity of learning to follow the rules (whether she liked them or not), respect for adult authority, how to deal with conflict, and the importance of accepting responsibility for your actions.

Lethargic/Disinterested Parent

This parent exhibits no interest in the guilt or innocence of the child and tends to accept the charges brought against the child. Ironically, the children of such parents may not even attempt to defend themselves. The parent's attitude is do what you have to do, so that I can go home.

A young man had experienced many problems, academic and behavioral, while in school. As a result, he was sent to live with his mother, since his parents were divorced. The mother, pursuing her career in another state, seemed to feel inconvenienced by the child's presence. Ultimately, the young man was sent back to live with his father. When both parents showed up to reenroll the student, it was quite obvious that the relationship between the parents was strained and that they both considered the young man a burden. A conversation was had about the young man, in his presence, but as if he were not there. Needless to say, he resumed his studies at the school with continued academic and behavioral problems. What kind of support can you offer a student who feels unwanted by his own parents?

The Impatient Parent

This parent is always in a hurry and never seems to have time to deal with issues of his/her child's schooling. Body language is one of nervous energy. Interactions with the impatient parent is scattered with, "How long is this going to take?" "I don't have time to come to the school, can we do this by phone?" "Can he take care of it himself?" Is it really necessary for me to come in?" Sometimes the impatient parent is well intentioned. He/she may be a single parent overwhelmed with the responsibilities of child care and the demands of a job. In other instances, he/she may be parents who has narrowly defined parental responsibility as providing for the necessities, that is, food, clothing, and shelter and nothing else. This parent is devoid of a very important element of parenting—nurturing. Regardless of the parent's intent, the message sent to the child is clear: "You are not a priority; your education is not a priority."

According to one observer, this message was never so clear as during registration for the new school year. A mother brought her son to school to register him. He was a returning student. However, school was already in progress. They were about a week or so late. Everything about his demeanor suggested that he was not infected with the enthusiasm of returning to school and meeting with old friends, that is so characteristic of many students after the long summer vacation. He was sullen and disinterested. His mother was clearly annoyed by the need to wait in line with other parents registering students late and, upon reaching the head of the line, being presented with the typical paperwork required for registration. Clearly frustrated she commented, "After I do this, can he finish the rest of this on his own?" The question becomes how successful this young man will be given the apparent lack of motivation and parental support.

One of the most vivid memories of my youth goes back to my junior year in high school. I was about to be inducted into the National Honor Society. It was the policy at my high school that inductees were not told whether or not they had been selected. However, the inductees' parents were notified and invited to the induction ceremony that consisted of an all-school assembly during the school day. My father worked as a burner in a steel mill and after work often did odd jobs. I have very vivid memories of how hard he worked to take care of his family, but he always had time for me and my siblings. I can't ever remember my dad missing work due to illness. I knew that he frequently suffered with a bad back. This was always evident upon his trips to the drugstore to get a back plaster. Mom would nurse his back, and regardless of how he felt, he was back at work the next day.

On the day of the induction ceremony, my class was seated in the balcony. After being seated, I scanned the crowd of parents seated in chairs on the gym floor. I thought I had a good chance of being inducted, so the search for my mom was going to be my confirmation. I say mom because I never knew my dad to miss a day of work. While scanning the crowd, my eye caught the image of someone who looked like my dad. A second more studied look confirmed that it was my dad, dressed up and sitting proudly next to my mom. I couldn't believe it, because I had seen him leave the house for work as he always did just before I left to catch my bus. But there he sat, my dad! WOW! The man who never missed a day of work took time to see me inducted into the National Honor Society. I don't think I need to tell you the message embodied in my dad's presence that day over thirty years ago.

Parents must be mindful of the messages they send to their children regarding the importance of education. Most important, they must be aware that the message can be conveyed in any number of ways by word, deed and action. Counselors can assist here by opening the lines of communication with the parent to inform them of the importance of their involvement. They can assist the parent with suggestions on how to provide the necessary support to enhance academic achievement.

The Intimidator

The intimidator is devoid of appropriate social behavior. This parent enters into a dialogue with school officials with direct verbal threats against school officials or whomever they deem the offending party.

Consider this scenario. A student attacked another student with a knife-like instrument, causing a wound that required stitches. What was ironic was that the confrontation was sparked because each (claiming not to know each other or having had any prior contact) didn't like the way the other looked at him— called "mad-dogging or mean-mugging." The mother of the weapon-wielding student responded immediately to the school's call to report to the dean's office to discuss the incident. The mother listened attentively to the dean's account of what had transpired and was most understanding. Her focus was not so much the event that led up to the attack but the fact her son was inextricably involved, was found in possession of the weapon and admitted his involvement.

The father arrives while the conference is still in progress. He enters with these remarks, "Where's the other boy? I want the other boy. Jake is not violent, he wouldn't do anything like this. I want the other boy." Ironic, yes? Prior to entering the conference, the father had no specifics regarding the incident. Yet, not only did he assume his son's innocence, he wanted revenge on the student his son assaulted. With the mother's prodding, the father was admonished to contain his emotions and listen to the facts. The son's admission of guilt should have quelled the father's wrath but not so. The father continually repeated that Jake was not violent and the other boy must have done something to him. It didn't matter that by Jake's own admission the incident erupted over the way the other boy looked at him.

Not only might intimidators threaten their children's adversary, they may even go so far as to pose physical or verbal threats against the school officials handling the matter. Attempts to communicate with this kind of parent are usually emotionally charged as the parent postures and peppers the exchange with expletives.

As a footnote, the reader's attention is called to the fact that much of the conflict between students quickly escalates to more serious infractions because of students' inability to control their rage. This seems to be a problem not confined to the hallowed halls of academia. A recent TV special addressed the issue of highway rage, that is, motorists getting frustrated and angry, cutting each other off in traffic, and, at the most extreme, shooting their traffic adversaries (Baldacci, 1997). Similarly, airlines have adopted more stringent policies for dealing with disruptive passengers. What is the fundamental cause of this rage that seems to have our society in its grip? Some contend that TV violence is a major contributing factor. Children learn that physical confrontation is an acceptable means of resolving conflict.

Some schools have responded with the institution of peer mediation programs. In some schools, when students find themselves embroiled in a potentially inflammatory situation, they can request peer mediation in hopes of de-escalating the conflict and preventing a physical confrontation. The conflict between the two parties is mediated by a student specifically trained for this role. This process has met with such success in the schools that some communities have instituted peer hearing panels of sorts to hear cases of teens charged with minor offenses. Other communities have established panels consisting of community residents to hear cases and settle disputes between neighbors to curtail police intervention. The message is clear. We must teach youth how to resolve conflict without resorting to violence. In the process, we also teach them to think about their actions and examine their role in the evolution of the conflict.

The Cocoon—The Overprotective Parent

The over protective parent is driven by a desire to shield the child from the normal challenges encountered as one advances through life. Whether it is attending to the child's basic needs or interpersonal relationships, the parent takes control and assume responsibility. In extreme cases, this hold on the child may extend through the adult years.

This parent makes virtually every decision for the child, including issues as mundane as what to wear or eat or what activities to participate in. Children of the overprotective parent are typically not given choices or allowed to perform certain basic tasks for themselves such as preparing their breakfast, washing clothes, or even walking to school alone or with their peers.

Each stage of life should be accompanied by an increased level of comfort and confidence garnered from trial and error experiences as we interact with others in our environment. As a result of incessant parental intervention, children of overprotective parents may feel vulnerable, intimidated, afraid, or put upon because they lack the social survival skills learned through interacting with others (Hatty, 1998).

Children of overprotective parents may be given a distorted sense of their importance in larger secondary group settings, expecting that everyone will respond to their needs and desires as their parents have. The emotional issues that come to bear as a result are particularly evident when the child begins school. Consider the parents of a high school student who stage an all-out challenge of the rule that denies their child bus service because the student has to walk less than a mile through a residential area that poses no threat of gangs or traffic safety hazard to get to the neighborhood school, or the parents who request a parent conference when their child's feelings were hurt because he/she did not make the cheerleading squad or basketball team. Others allow children to stay home for any minor physical complaint, or challenge the school nurse for not notifying them when a child falls and scrapes a knee. The list is endless. Overprotective parents may challenge school staff when they perceive the child's feelings were hurt by the manner in which someone spoke to them, making it perfectly clear it is not so much what was said to the child but how it was said, the tone of voice. The interpretation, of course, is very subjective.

Taken to the extreme, the overprotective parent's behavior takes on a more pathological dimension. "The fear of not being needed motivates many controlling parents to perpetuate this sense of powerlessness in their children. . . . So much of a controlling parent's identity is tied up in the parental role that he or she feels betrayed and abandoned when the child becomes independent" (Forward, 1989, p. 49). Similarly, Mones (1991) journeyed into that obscure world of children who murder their parents as a result of extreme mental, physical, or sexual abuse. He observed that the pathological nature of the relationship between parent and child is grounded in the parent's perception that "no boundary exists between themselves and their children—for them their son or daughter is an extra limb or just another object that belongs to them, like a piece of furniture" (p. 13). There is a sense of entitlement, granting them complete control over the child. He further contends that these parents believe the "child exists solely to satisfy their needs and desires and thus is raised to have no independent identity" (p. 13).

Nothing has a greater impact upon the developing self than the nature of the relationship forged between parent and child. Everything the parent says or does will reverberate through the child's life. How the child feels about himself/herself and the world in which he/she lives is colored by this most fundamental human bond. Parents must understand the need to allow children to make mistakes, take risks (that do not hold the potential to be life threatening), and accept responsibility for their actions, if they are to develop into physically and mentally healthy adults. For some parents, this means accepting that they cannot usurp the child's identity to fulfill their personal needs and desires.

In the final analysis, the parent's communication style may impact the student's attitude toward the school and school officials. The parent models behaviors that validate for the student acceptable patterns of interaction with school officials and impact student behavior and attitude toward school officials and school in general. The parent's communication style also provides the school with valuable information to assist in identifying the source of the student's problems. In many instances, the old adage ,the apple doesn't fall far from the tree, is borne out. For example, students aren't likely to accept responsibility for their actions when parents, despite the facts, defend them. Parents who threaten and use abusive language in interacting with school officials should not be taken by surprise when their child relates to staff in similar fashion. Similarly, parents who show a lack of interest in their child's education can expect children who are not likely to see the value of education or to strive for academic success. Parents, therefore, must be mindful of the hidden language of the manner in which they interact with school staff.

DEALING WITH THE INCOMPETENT TEACHER

Parents may encounter during their child's school-age years teachers whose level of competency is questionable. This oftentimes creates a dilemma for parents as they are questioning someone whom it is assumed has acquired a level of mastery of the subject matter and teaching skills that qualifies them to do what they are doing—teach. However, we have all encountered teachers (hopefully few in number) who fail to make the grade. These are teachers who clearly have not mastered the subject matter, are unable to provide instruction in ways that are meaningful to students, and/or do not have a firm grasp of classroom management strategies to create an environment that is conducive to learning. We are not talking about parents who simply disagree with a teacher's method.

Because of tenure, it is often difficult to dismiss weak teachers. Approximately 80 percent of teachers in the United States are tenured. Teachers receive tenure after two or three years of service. In some states, less than 2 percent of tenured teachers are dismissed annually for incompetency. The original intent of tenure was to provide job protection for teachers. It was a safeguard against being dismissed for capricious reasons such as personal vendettas, political activism, race, gender, religious affiliation etc. Ironically, while well intentioned, it provided an extra layer of insulation, making it difficult to dismiss incompetent teachers. There are those who contend that tenure has outlived its purpose, as all U.S. workers are privileged to civil rights protection against unjustified dismissal. However, teacher union officials present a counter argument based on the premise that school boards, or small groups of parents, or community leaders motivated by personal vendettas or philosophical differences may still attempt to dismiss competent teachers (Fischer, 1997; Hancock, 1998).

The level of concern over this issue is evinced by its inclusion among issues discussed by President Bill Clinton at the 1996 governors' National Education Summit. The President called for a fair process for determining incompetent teachers. Challenging tenure can be a long laborious process. Most states give tenured teachers a year to improve and provide them with supervision. The process involves detailed documentation. Should the teacher fail to improve, the principal can take measures to dismiss him/her. The teacher can appeal the decision. However, because of time and financial constraints (contested dismissals may take anywhere from one to three years at a cost of $70,000 to $200,000 in legal fees, for the school district, depending upon the state) there is often hesitancy to move to dismiss a teacher. During this process, the teacher receives full salary (Hancock, 1998).

What then is the solution? The solution is for principals and board members to deny tenure to weak teachers and for teachers' unions to take a stand against members of the profession who are incompetent. As various states look more closely at tenure, they have developed some innovative policies. For example, in September of 1997 the local teachers' union in Rochester, New York, approved a measure that affords parents a role in overall teacher evaluation. Parents rate teachers on, among other things, communication skills, respect for parents, and the ability to assign meaningful homework. Massachusetts, Oklahoma, Colorado, and New Mexico have eliminated tenure. New Jersey, New York, and Florida, while taking less drastic measures, are nonetheless contemplating the use of renewable contracts. Missouri and Indiana have opted to increase the number of years of required service from three to five before awarding tenure. Michigan, Oklahoma, Florida, and Texas have reduced the amount of time for teachers at risk of dismissal to improve their performance from one year to three months. Only time will tell how effective these measures are in weeding out incompetent teachers (Hancock, 1998).

Meanwhile, what can parents do to ensure their children receive a quality education at the hands of competent teachers? Hancock (1998) suggests a variety of steps parents can take to call attention to the issue:

Get to know the teacher and if possible volunteer in the classroom.
Document observations.
Talk to the teacher about the problems.
Address concerns with the principal.
Network—talk with other parents or go to the school board (p. 144).

Parents should not underestimate the integral role they play in the academic success of their children. This is a sustained responsibility, one that should not terminate or wane with the increased independence of the child during elementary and secondary school ("Parents Remain," 1997; Noonan, 1998).

The most valuable gift parents can give to their child is their time. In terms of the impact this will have on every aspect of a child's life, it supercedes the efforts of many parents who attempt to compensate by plying their children with material things. Dr. Mike Litow, through his work counseling students who have been labelled troublemakers and underachievers and whose clients range from children of CEOs to housing project residents, found great affirmation in this precept. He made the following observation: "I see too many people who want to phone in their parenting. They spend more time in line to buy Beanie Babies than they will spend helping their kid with homework, or talking to their kid" (Mitchell, 1998).

In regard to interaction with school authorities, parents must learn to exercise their right to ask questions and demand answers of the educational community without timidity. They must set high expectations for their children, teachers, and themselves. Ultimately, the relationship the parent forges with the school will set the climate for the student's attitude toward school and school staff. Consequently, parental support of the school's efforts becomes a significant factor in determining the nature of the student's educational experience.

Chapter 2

Academic Achievement

Educational institutions are centered around the dissemination of knowledge. As knowledge continues to expand at a phenomenal rate, educational institutions have broadened their focus, placing less emphasis on memorization and greater emphasis on teaching critical thinking skills, researching the various ways in which students know and learn, and developing amenable teaching strategies. The measure of their success in fulfilling their mission is commensurate with the level of academic proficiency attained by the students they serve. Consequently, student academic achievement is an issue of major proportions in the field of education. In attempts to identify reasons for lack of achievement, educators who are myopic in their vision of the problem tend to focus too narrowly on the student as the primary cause. Those who take a more global perspective get a more accurate view of the extant reality, acknowledging the multiplicity of variables that impact academic achievement. There are a number of extraneous variables that affect academic achievement, all of which should be considered in our efforts to improve student learning outcomes.

FACTORS THAT AFFECT ACADEMIC ACHIEVEMENT

Socioeconomic Status

Kleinman, et al. (1998) compiled data and reported the results from a series of surveys conducted in nine states and the District of Columbia by the Community Childhood Hunger Identification Project (CCHIP). The purpose of the study was to examine the relationship between hunger and variables reflecting the psychosocial functioning of low-income, school-age children. The study revealed that children from families that experience recurring periods of hunger or insufficient food were more predisposed to exhibit behavioral, emotional, and academic problems based on a standardized measure of psychosocial dysfunction than their counterparts from the same low-income community who did not experience hunger or insufficient food. Clark (1983) found the determining factor in the academic success of black children was the quality of family lifestyle rather than their socioeconomic status.

I prefaced this section with this data to highlight the importance of the fact that while there is a positive correlation between socioeconomic status and school achievement, the education practitioner must be more global in interpreting exactly what this means. Socioeconomic status and its implications for education are complex and far-reaching. Serious consideration must be given to examining how numerous extraneous variables interact to impact socioeconomic status and student learning outcomes. Simply being poor does not portend academic failure.

While statistics show higher performance on standardized tests for students from more affluent communities, caution is advised in using this information to define the academic potential of students from poor communities. In some areas in the State of Illinois, the practice of publishing school report cards (which among other information provide data on student performance on standardized tests) often send a misleading message to the public. Based on these scores, certain positive or negative assumptions are made about the ability level of students. Numbers do not tell the whole story. These numbers only have meaning if one is comparing fairly homogeneous groups. Unfortunately, this is not the case.

There are obvious disparities between the lifestyle and life chances of upper-middle-and lower-class students that for many result in different learning outcomes. In the mid-1960s, James Coleman addressed the issue of educational achievement and inequality of educational opportunity. His first and successive findings were reported in the noted Coleman Report in 1966 and 1981. Three decades since he first delved into this issue, inequities remain exacerbated by increased needs of the workplace for highly skilled workers (Coleman, 1990).

It has become increasingly evident that while much has changed, much remains the same. While the gap in average achievement based on race, gender, and ethnicity has narrowed since 1960, the higher dropout rate for blacks and Hispanics and statistics on the declining enrollment of Black students in college suggest that there is yet much to be done to close the gap. Coleman also noted indications of a widening differential in educational outcomes between inner city versus suburban and public versus private schools and schools with predominantly white versus minority populations (Coleman, 1990). He is not alone in this assessment of educational disparities.

Attendees at a conference held at Kennedy-King College in Chicago in February of 1997 also addressed the issue of educational inequality. They pointed to inequity of educational funding as a contributing factor, noting that equitable funding and the issue of higher academic standards are not mutually exclusive. Disparities in per pupil expenditures in a confined geographical area may range, as in one case, from $5,000 to $15,000. The irony is that many jails spend considerably more to keep an inmate (Ihejirika, 1997). In 1996, Education Trust, a watchdog group, made a most disturbing finding. They noted that not only is the gap between academic achievement between whites and blacks widening after a long period of narrowing, today minority students are more likely than their white peers to be taught by teachers who are unqualified in their fields. The Rev. Jesse Jackson, who attended the conference, observed an "opportunity gap and a funding equity gap based on property tax funding." He further asserted that inner-city schools today are worse off than in 1954 when the United States Supreme Court ruled against school segregation (Ihejirika, 1997). This can, in part, be attributed to demographic shifts.

Initially, the shift showed a pattern of white flight from the city to the suburbs. As minorities began to move in increasing numbers to the suburbs, there was another population shift evincing a pattern of white flight from the suburbs to outlying areas or to more pricey upscale communities. This pattern of population movement has resulted in the resegregation of many communities and consequently of the educational institutions that serve these communities. The exodus has resulted in the erosion of the middle-class tax base (Brownstein, 1997). The dire implications for school districts whose funding is tied to property taxes is clear.

Many financially strapped school districts have tried to deal with the issue of inadequate educational funding. Some have turned to referendums, which are often difficult to pass because they result in increased property or other taxes, and many residents already feel overburdened with taxation. Michigan, with property taxes above the national average and a sales tax below the national average, sought a solution calling for lowering property tax and increasing sales and cigarette taxes. In any event, most would concur that school reform does not provide for adequate funding for education. Many suburban districts in Michigan with cash surpluses feel restricted in their efforts "as reform unfairly bars them from tapping their wealth to keep pace with rising costs" (Rodriguez, 1997, p. 6).

Additionally, educational institutions have undergone a paradigm shift in their definition of the variables that make for quality schools. In the past, school quality was measured by inputs such as quality of the infrastructure, level of degrees earned by teachers, and the more traditional per pupil expenditure. The recent emphasis on establishing academic standards at the national level is indicative of a paradigm shift using such outputs as performance on standardized tests as a measure of school quality. Coleman suggests that this paradigm shift was orchestrated to divert attention from seeking answers to some fundamental questions about educational equality. He contends that this paradigm shift avoids a critical analysis of how inputs and outputs interact to impact educational achievement and opportunity (Coleman, 1990).

Therefore, the conclusions drawn about schools based on these scores are erroneous, for they do not take into consideration the numerous extraneous variables that impact test scores and often serve to perpetuate stereotypes regarding certain ethnic groups or communities. In drawing conclusions about schools based on the school report card, consideration should be given to such variables as the proportion of students receiving public assistance, the number of students in foster care, mobility rates, level of proficiency at the time of admission, funding, and educational equity. All of these variables collectively interact to impact the overall performance level of schools. This is not to say that students who fall into these categories are not capable of academic success. It does, however, attest to the types of conditions or circumstances that place these students at a disadvantage and impede academic success. Similarly, it does not exempt teachers and administrators from seeking ways to decrease the learning gap between these students and their counterparts in more economically affluent areas.

There is another dark side to the publication of school report cards without explaining the variables that impact scores and warning the reader to exercise caution in drawing conclusions from this data. As parents, educators, and community leaders grapple with the problem of low test scores and often engage in public debate on the issue, they must keep in mind the effect overly negative verbiage may have on students and teachers (Lawrence & Houlihan-Skilton, 1998). Is it possible that students may come to internalize this assessment of their intellectual ability? The well intentioned must guard against turning the issue into a self-fulfilling prophecy by being insensitive to how the manner in which they approach the problem impacts a student's perception of self. It also turns a negative indictment against teachers who may not be operating on a level playing field with their colleagues from more affluent areas. Many teachers and administrators in schools that are grappling with low test scores are doing an exemplary job under the circumstances and continue to explore programs and policies to close the learning gap. The question becomes, Is it fair to use school report cards as a reflection of their effort? To close the learning gap reflected in school report cards will require time and more than effort on the part of schools and teachers. At a more global level, it will require a political and sociological construct to examine and seek solutions to the source of the problem.

In interpreting the scores on the school report card, the focus should be on the level of improvement from year to year and not the raw score. Movement in this area should be the measure of the school's success in increasing academic performance. At another level, one must consider that the narrowly defined cognitive focus of standardized tests does not acknowledge or give credence to the concept of multiple intelligences. These tests attempt to predict success or level of academic proficiency based on those ways of knowing sanctioned by traditional pedagogy, that is, linguistic or logical-mathematical intelligences.

These tests are generally geared to the experiences and life chances of the dominant culture. That cultural, racial, and gender bias is an issue in testing can be attested to by the initiative to reconstruct many standardized tests. All too often, there is the tendency to, erroneously, equate the level of performance on standardized tests to intelligence.

These issues give rise to the need to reassess assessment. Many colleges have taken the first step by placing less emphasis on test scores in determining admissions. One college that no longer uses test scores as a criterion for admission has noted such scores are very subjective. Their philosophy is grounded in the belief that there is more to getting on in the world than being able to process data. "There is a need for individuals with ability and interest in reading analytically, in integrating knowledge and skills and their ability to express themselves" (Marcus, 1998, p. 6A). Some post-secondary institutions specifically geared to advancing the development of the more non-traditional intelligences such are art institutes, music academies, and other proprietary schools.

Transiency

For schools with high rates of mobility, the issue of academic achievement is exacerbated by a lack of a uniform curriculum and performance standard. As students, for whatever reason, move from school to school, the absence of a uniform set of learning goals, objectives, performance standards, and assessment instruments, makes it increasingly difficult for them to follow the flow of things and maintain their academic equilibrium. It is here that the differences in school districts and city versus suburban curriculums become all too apparent.

The Journal of American Medical Association published a 1993 study that confirmed the detrimental effect of student mobility. The study found that children who move frequently are 50 to 100 percent more likely to have to repeat a grade, and experience delayed growth or development, behavior problems, and learning disabilities (Gutloff, February 1998, p. 4). While schools cannot prevent the social circumstances that give rise to the problem, there are strategies that can be put into play to soften the impact of mobility on students. The National Education Association proposes strategies to address the problem at the classroom, school and district level. They are (Gutloff, February 1998, p. 4-5):

In the classroom. Teachers can prepare the class for the arrival of new students and enlist the class's help in assisting them to get acclimated. I am reminded of a devastating house fire in my community a number of years ago that resulted in one of the local grade school students being severely disfigured. After months of treatment and prior to her return to school, the children in the school were called together in an assembly, and the school staff and health professionals explained the student's appearance, her needs, and what other students could do to help her. I am told the reception this child received upon her return to school was phenomenal.

Teachers can:

- Get background information. Many of these students will arrive at their new school without academic records to assist with proper placement. Consequently, it is recommended that school authorities talk with parents or contact someone from their former school for information.
- Find out what the student already knows. Start by giving the new student the assignments the class is presently working on. This will help in assessing what the student knows.
- Make connections. Coming into a new school can be racked with apprehension and foreboding for many students. This is particularly true for students who are highly mobile. Consequently, teachers should make a concerted effort to make students feel welcome and accepted. This can be accomplished by asking them about their hobbies, the place where they used to live etc. One teacher gave her new students a small care package.

In school.
Schools can:

- Form welcoming committees. Welcoming committees can be composed of students from various organizations in the school. At my high school one year, the student council assumed this responsibility. On the first day of school, these students wore badges identifying themselves as student helpers. When they encountered a freshman or new student looking lost, they would offer their assistance with such things as finding classes, and various offices or unlocking lockers. The guidance department also uses student aides to walk new students (who enter during the school year) through their class schedule.
- Create after-school clubs. One school in Michigan that serves children of migrant workers found that when these students return to the area of the crop season many have lost any academic gains made during their initial enrollment for the school year. One teacher responded by forming an after-school club just for these students. Using a buddy system, older students helped their newly returned peers with academic needs. The program also effectively heightened cultural awareness and sensitivity.

In the district. Worcester, Massachusetts, is representative of many communities that experience high student turnover rates. In this community 30 percent of their 24,000 students change schools each year. In other schools, the turnover rate is as high as 70 percent. What can be done to ameliorate a problem of such virulent proportions? The community of Worcester formed a partnership with the local department of social services and other community groups and formulated the Mobility Action Plan. The plan called for a mobility tracking system, a software program that tracks the number of students that enter and leave the school throughout the year. Offices were equipped with fax machines, making possible immediate access to records from the previous school. Additionally, the school district registration process was centralized so that school officials could be alerted when a student was moving for a second or third time. Ten schools adopted standard textbooks to ensure uniformity of subject matter covered as students moved from school to school. The community also used grant money to provide taxi service so that students who had to move during the year because of foster home reassignment could continue their studies without having to change schools. Through funding from another grant, the school secured the services of a case-worker whose responsibility was to work with the families of mobile students.

Attendance

Students cannot learn if they are not in school. In areas where educational funding is based on attendance rates, the issue of school attendance becomes more global. The attendance rates in many inner-city schools are dismal. A colleague teaching in an inner-city school commented that at least half of her class was absent on a daily basis. Needless to say, there is a high positive correlation between school attendance and academic achievement.

While schools have acknowledged the problem, there seems to be a paucity of innovative response. Typical responses have consisted of telephone calls or letters to the home and, in areas with financial resources, truant officers deployed to the homes of truants. In an effort to get parents involved, some schools suspend students for chronic truancy until the parent appears to discuss the matter with school officials. The American Heritage Dictionary defines a truant as one who is absent without permission, especially from school. This simplistic definition of truancy betrays the complexity of the problem. Too often our analysis does not go beyond a superficial assessment that a student has missed too many days of school, and it is our obligation to notify the parent of the problem.

As educators we must deconstruct the issue. We must go beyond the perfunctory role of the attendance office in recording absences and notifying parents so that we can confront the causes of the problem. To do otherwise is akin to treating the symptom and not the disease. Those in positions of authority must allocate more time to examining the reasons for poor attendance. It is only after this has been accomplished that we can seriously look at solutions. It is much too easy to attribute truancy to lack of interest in school.

While this may be the case in some instances, this attitude prevents the practitioner from recognizing the multifaceted nature of the problem.

While truancy was once defined as an all-day absence, some schools are experiencing a growing problem with students who cut classes during the school day. These students avoid classes for reasons such as failure to complete homework assignments, lack of preparation for a quiz or test, problems with other students in the class, or dislike of the subject matter or teacher. They take refuge in the restroom, lunchroom, library, or gym, or they leave the campus, preferring areas that are crowded or not well structured or supervised to provide them with some anonymity (O'Donnell, 1997).

A study conducted by the University of Chicago that broadens the scope of the traditional definition of truancy to include class cuts challenges our perception of the typical truant. The study's author, Melissa Roderick, points out that truancy is viewed as acceptable behavior by even the good students. She found that cutting classes is exacerbated in schools with large student populations where there is neither adequate adult supervision, or an orderly school environment with a sense of community. In one large metropolitan school system, the study found that for the 1995–96 school year, "40 percent of ninth graders who miss a month or more of classes each semester are attending school, but cutting classes" (O'Donnell, 1997, p. 10). The study further revealed that half of the city's freshmen missed two or more weeks of instruction in at least one major subject in the first semester. The picture grows dimmer. Even when the attendance pattern of the high achieving ninth graders was examined, the study found that 42 percent missed two or more weeks of instruction in a primary subject area by the time they completed ninth grade. While it is frequently assumed that students will cut what is perceived by many as the most difficult classes, such as math or science, the study found this not to be a determining factor in class cutting (O'Donnell, 1997).

While the statistics are alarming, they should not be used to issue an indictment of large city-school systems. Many suburban school districts also must deal with this issue at some level. The causes suggest plausible solutions that will require additional funding to follow up on truants and to hire adult supervisors. Other suggestions include increased communication with parents; counseling and, tutoring programs, and reviews by teachers of their instructional methodology.

Additionally, there must be some feasible consequence for students who cut classes. Phone calls home, detentions, etc. may be effective preventive measures for students who are not chronic truants. Some systems resort to suspensions for chronic truants. The irony, however, is that in doing so, we reward the very behavior we are trying to eradicate. Perhaps a better solution would be to require that these students spend time in counseling with the school social worker, counselor, or outside support group. If this fails, schools could require a parent conference before the student would be allowed to return to school after each all-day unexcused absence. Then, there are those parents who allow students not to attend school or do not send them to school regularly for any number of nonvalid reasons: student doesn't feel well (minor complaints), student doesn't have clean clothes, parent couldn't get the student out of bed, parent didn't get up on time to get the student off to school, etc. In extreme cases, some school districts with truant officers have taken parents to court over this issue to stress the gravity of the problem. Because of the widespread repercussions of attendance problems, this topic will be revisited in Chapter 5.

Home Responsibilities and Circumstances

Many students have been thrust into the role of miniature adult. They may be responsible for caring for a disabled or infirm parent or getting younger siblings off to school and caring for them until parents return home from work. Others are required by parents to remain home to care for younger siblings when they are ill and unable to attend school or the regular baby-sitter doesn't show. Still others are left to fend for themselves and younger siblings when drug or alcohol addicted parents lose sight of their responsibilities. It is not uncommon to hear national news reports of six-year-olds being left alone to care for younger siblings, most often as a result of flagrant parental neglect induced by parental drug dependency. In a society where many families are only one paycheck away from poverty, some sacrifices have to be made and often it is the child's education. For many educators, coming from middle-class backgrounds, such conditions are inconceivable. Yet, for many students this is their reality and educators must understand this to effectively assist them. These are just a few of the conditions under which children must live out their daily existence.

In Carl's case, the events unfolded as follows. The administrator was informed by the school social worker via a coach of an athlete who had not registered for school. The student had attended the school the previous year. The social worker pursued the matter and discovered that a change in the family's circumstances had left the student alone to care for a disabled parent.

In another instance, there was nothing unusual or that stood out about Gregory. He didn't have the best grades, but he wasn't failing either. He attended class every day, didn't have much to say in class or to his classmates. Because he wasn't a student leader or exceptional academically or athletically and was not a behavior problem, he didn't call attention to himself. Perhaps the signs were always there but as the saying goes, the squeaky wheel gets the oil. Gregory was not a squeaky wheel, and the signals were missed by most of his teachers. The first sign was the change in his appearance. He started attending school with a disheveled look, and his attendance pattern changed. Gregory was referred to the guidance counselor, who learned that he had been abandoned by his parents and was living in a tree house.

In a similar incident, a parent inquired as to the process for enrolling her son in school. She indicated that he had previously attended the school but had decided he wanted to live with his father in a neighboring community. The father lost the house and moved on but left the student behind. Eventually, according to the mother, the utilities were disconnected and the house boarded up but the student continued to inhabit the residence. The obvious question to the parent was, "How could you not know he was homeless?" She continued, stating that he continued to attend school and was eating and bathing at a friend's house. Only after the authorities learned of the situation was the mother notified and the student returned to the parent. Obviously, there is much to this story that remains untold, and until that is known we can only leave to conjecture this student's motivation to live under such conditions.

The message to the educator is clear. Many students today come to class with very heavy burdens that impact their academic success and perception of the world. Their anger and frustration can easily become displaced or funnelled into socially unacceptable behaviors. Consequently, there is a need for educators to learn to accept students where they are, get to really know them, and then take them to where we want them to be. Educators need to look beyond behaviors to discover cause. Armored with an understanding of a student's circumstance will make dealing with (not accepting) the sometimes errant behavior more palatable. This is not an easy task, particularly for educators who work in gang- and crime-infested communities and for whom school feels more like a war zone than a place where they feel they can make a difference. Nevertheless, it will take understanding to bridge the gap.

Fear of Success

As ironic as it may seem, given that by nature humans strive for recognition, there are some individuals who fear success. Tresemer (1977) studied this phenomenon and identified three reasons why individuals may avoid success. Individuals may avoid success for the following reasons:

(1) fear that success may require the individual to reassess their view of themselves
(2) fear of being rejected
(3) fear that their ability would not meet the extra demands created by success

These are concerns so compelling for some individuals as to stifle their motivation to improve their performance or position in life. It creates a resistance to change. Particularly for adolescents caught in the throes of establishing their own identity while grappling with their need for acceptance by their peers, this type of change can tip the balance. Many students resist accepting recognition for their effort simply because they don't want to be viewed as different or set apart from their peers. As ludicrous as this may seem from the adult perspective, it is a very real and compelling issue for adolescents. As they relate to their teachers and parents, some students are driven by the adage "of those to whom much is given, much is required." Consequently, there is the fear that to do well will only increase the expectations that others, particularly significant others, have of them. For many adolescents this need or sense of obligation to live up to the expectations of others produces stress.

Therefore, a lack of success, for some, insulates the individual from circumstances that will inevitably produce stress. Certainly, as parents and educators assess the reasons for poor academic performance, the fear of success must be given serious consideration. Hopefully, from this assessment strategies can be developed to alleviate the fear of success and assist students in realizing their full potential.

Lack of Interest

For students who have not met with academic success or otherwise have been made to feel like social outcasts, interest in learning is easily abated. The level of our self-esteem is in part predicted on the measure of our successes. Except for those on a deliberate path of self-destruction, it is human nature to avoid situations and circumstances that bring us face to face with physical danger or threaten our psychological well-being. The task for the educator is to set about discovering the reason for lack of interest in school.

Perhaps the student has been academically misplaced requiring diagnostic testing. After seeking private counseling, one parent learned her son's behavior problems "stemmed from a lack of self-esteem due to an undiscovered learning disability" (Mitchell, 1998, p. 33). Under these circumstances, cutting class or acting out may be an expression of frustration and the embarrassment of being unable to compete on equal terms with one's peers. At another level, it may be that the cognitive connection is not being made because schools and educators are not addressing the varied learning styles of students. Information is not presented in ways that are meaningful to the student, and most important students are not permitted to express themselves, in the educational setting, in ways that are meaningful to them. "Students who find their culture and learning styles reflected in both the substance and the organization of the instructional program are more likely to be motivated and less likely to be disruptive" (Kuykendall, 1992, p. 36).

Similarly, Bruner (1996) directs attention to the need to make education more responsive to the needs of students. This can be accomplished in a number of ways but most notably by making instruction less teacher centered and more student centered. He advocates "discovery learning," a method that stresses active participation. This makes learning more engaging for the learner, enhancing interest. He further calls attention to the importance of cultural considerations in the educational process. He acknowledges the role of culture in shaping minds and in understanding how individuals construct reality, their perception of the world around them and their self-concept.

Hale-Benson (1982) also addresses the role of culture in shaping cognitive development, the way children approach academic tasks, and their behavior in traditional educational settings. Equipped with a firm grasp of the role of culture in learning, teachers working in schools with diverse student populations can better meet the needs of all of their students. Consequently, making learning relevant by considering the cultural context from which the learner constructs reality can enhance student interest and motivation.

In my own practice, as a former teacher of African American history, the tradition of having an African naming ceremony, giving all students an African name a few weeks into the term, made a lasting impression on students. I started by going to a local bookstore and purchasing a book on African names. Students were assigned names a few weeks into the term to afford me an opportunity to identify their individual personality traits and in general learn more about them and their aspirations. Each student was then, in a formal ceremony, assigned a name based on this information. They were given the meaning of their name and its region of origin. All of this was preceded by a discussion of the significance "name" in the African culture. They were informed of their responsibility to live up to the meaning that the name held. Just how grand an impression this tradition had on my students became increasingly clear to me, as over the years when I encountered former students, they would tell me their African name. Even more impressive was that most could tell me the name's meaning. Clearly, this instilled in them a sense of pride in their own being.

Success or failure impact self-esteem. In schools we too often place more emphasis on the end result than the process. How much improvement students have made and not whether or not they have reached the ultimate goal should be the measure of success. For the student who has repeatedly failed to achieve mastery, the attitude becomes why bother, if they perceive the goal is impossible to reach within the allotted time frame. Rewarding increments of improvement is more motivating than making an assessment based on the final result. Schools don't allow time for students to discover solutions to problems. Classrooms are structured so that activities must be played out in a prescribed manner and in a specific time frame.

As this standoff between traditional pedagogy and acknowledgment of individual differences in learning styles continues, both teacher and student lose ground. Some teachers may deem students uninterested and unteachable, while students may respond by being disruptive or simply dropping out. Sometimes, as educators, in responding to the behavior and not searching deeper for the reasons for it, we miss clues and look in the wrong places for answers. For example, sometimes test scores can provide some clues. If test scores reveal that a ninth grader is reading at the fourth grade level, one can reasonably assume the child will experience difficulty in classes that require extensive reading. The most obvious response is simply to talk to child and ask what there is about the class or school he/she doesn't like. Calling parents or talking to the school social worker or counselor, might reveal family crisis as the root of the problem. Consider the foster child recently enrolled in school. Before outgrowing the system, many of these children will have called many places home. Consequently, from their perspective, nothing in life is permanent. Why form attachments; in fact, doing so will only make the next move more painful than the previous one. What's the point of doing one's best in a temporary situation? For many of these children, academic success is made even more problematic by the wide range of curriculums and expectations they face as they are moved from one educational setting to the next. The lack of continuity leaves learning gaps that are difficult to fill. Lack of interest in school springs from many sources. Consequently, educators must look beyond the typical student-centered explanations and examine their own practice and other variables that impact student interest in school and learning.

Lack of Parental Support

Bloom (1985) studied top American concert pianists, sculptors, Olympic swimmers, mathematicians, research neurologists, and tennis players in an effort to find out what it takes to achieve extraordinary success. The results of the study revealed that contrary to popular belief, the success of these individuals was not attributed to innate ability but to drive and determination. The study further revealed that this drive and determination stemmed from parents who exposed these individuals to the activities in which they excelled as children just for fun. There was a direct correlation between the extent of recognition the children received and their increased interest and pursuit of the activity. This in turn led to parents lending even greater support and securing experts to assist the children with additional coaching and instruction. The children responded by spending even more time cultivating their talents until they reached extraordinary performance levels.

It can be a challenge to motivate students from home environments where emotional and sometimes physical needs are not being met, particularly if there has been a long-standing pattern of such neglect. If students enter school being made to feel that they are not special or, worse yet, that they are not worthy of being made to feel special the educator who is caring and intuitive enough to sense this has to first repair the damage in order to reach the child. Educators who narrowly define their purpose are doomed to failure in reaching kids. Whether we like it or not, we live in a society where many families are dysfunctional, leaving kids psychologically and physically vulnerable. Where families fail, schools have had to pick up the slack. The professions of school social worker, social psychologist, school substance abuse counselor, and school police liaisons attest to the expanded role the school now assumes in the life of students.

Perhaps, as we discuss such issues, the reader has formed a mental image of students sitting in classrooms in dilapidated inner-city schools. Not so, the poor do not hold a monopoly on emotional and physical abandonment of children. The student from the wealthiest of suburbs, who seemingly has all the trappings of wealth and privilege, can also feel alone and worthless. All parents must remember that the greatest gift they can give their children is their time (Mitchell, 1998). Plying children with material things is no substitute for parental love and affection. Perhaps here lies the answer to the rebellious rich kid phenomenon. Why would a kid who has everything consistently get into trouble? Negative behavior gets attention and negative attention is attention nevertheless. Oftentimes, such behavior is a cry for help. Once again, educators are admonished to look beyond the behavior to seek its source.

Preoccupation with Fads or Lack of Necessities

Unfortunately, we live in a society where one's worth and social standing are often measured by material possessions. Even young children are often preoccupied with designer label clothing. By the time children reach the teen years, this issue has taken on mammoth proportions. Even for students in economically depressed areas, the "right gym shoes, jeans, haircut or gold chains" can be the determining factor in acceptance into certain peer groups. Consequently, for some students who, for financial reasons, are unable to meet the "dress code," ridicule, taunting, or ostracism by their peers is a common occurrence. In extreme cases, these students may even avoid coming to school altogether or resort to criminal behavior to acquire these much sought after commodities. Urban newspapers frequently carry stories of students being mugged, shot, or robbed for their clothing.

As innocuous as it may seem, many contend that the issue of clothing can negatively impact the learning environment. National support for this position was evinced in President Clinton's 1996 State of the Union address, in which he expressed his support of school uniform policies (Atkins & Schlosberg, 1996). Many schools in urban areas and some suburbs have instituted uniform dress codes. Many others across the nation are seriously contemplating adopting such policies. Schools that have a uniform dress code contend that the policy has many advantages and has reaped many positive outcomes, reporting that it:

1. Limits socioeconomic distinctions as manifested in student dress and incumbent patterns of interaction that can dictate the nature of social relationships with others;
2. Detracts from the preoccupation with clothes to redirect students' attention to institutional purpose, that is, learning;
3. Contributes to a safer school environment as it serves to limit theft and aggressive behavior engendered in students forcibly or surreptitiously taking items of clothing from other students;
4. Relieves many parents of the financial burden of having to sacrifice to purchase the latest clothing items for their children to prevent them from feeling like social outcasts;
5. Eliminates symbols of gang affiliation such as certain colors or types of clothing;
6. Eliminates the time many parents expend in debating with students over what to wear to school and the appropriateness of certain types of clothing;
7. Improves academic achievement;
8. Promotes school pride, symbolizing affiliation with a group and conformity to its goals;
9. Improves student decorum and decreases the number of fights and other disciplinary problems (Atkins & Schlosberg, 1996).

While there has been a paucity of research to give empirical credibility to the positive anecdotal reports of uniform dress codes, many schools are nevertheless impressed with the reported results (LaPoint, Holloman & Alleyne, 1993). Despite the positive effects, some parents still object to the policy and because of this, some districts have been reluctant to tackle the issue. Those who oppose the policy frequently cite the infringement of the right of individual choice. For these individuals the larger issue is a perceived fundamental disregard for the democratic principle of freedom of choice. Others view it as the gradual encroachment of government into their private lives. However, one must consider that students hail from families with a wide range of values and beliefs. What might be considered acceptable dress for one group may be deemed highly inappropriate for another. Consequently, there is a need for institutions of learning to establish some standards. At another level, opponents contend that uniform dress codes deprive students of the opportunity to engage in the normal adolescent behaviors purposed to define their identity such as experimenting with various clothing, hairstyles, etc. (LaPoint et al., 1993).

Work Responsibilities

Some students must work to assist the family financially. Some work to earn money for college that would otherwise be a dream deferred. Many others work to acquire nonessentials such as cars, clothes, and electronic equipment. Regardless of the reason, when work tops the list of priorities, school performance often suffers. For many students, if the financial rewards of work are, in their estimation, substantial, school may cease to be a priority. Students who are employed full time often find that they lack the energy required to meet the challenges of academia. They may be unfocused, unable to sustain adequate periods of concentration, irritable, distracted, and prone to falling asleep in class. Those who work a late shift may frequently miss school or early classes. In many areas, students age fifteen and under are required to obtain special work permits issued by the school. The permits also require a parent signature and limit the number of hours per week a student can work. Students are discouraged from working full-time jobs.

However, there is a market for teenage workers and, as long as that market persists, teens will seek employment to satisfy their basic needs or desires. Teen workers are basically employed at stores in malls, fast food establishments, supermarkets, and restaurants. Such businesses prefer teenage employees for the economic incentive they provide. Because they are primarily hired as part-timers, their wages are low, and there are no benefits such as pension or medical insurance (McNamee, 1997, p. 19).

While teen employment is touted as a means of building skills, character, self-esteem, sense of commitment, achievement, and integration into the community, the latest research suggests that too much time on the job can negatively impact school success. The research concluded that "Teens should work no more than 10 to 20 hours a week, if at all and some jobs are far better or worse than others" (McNamee, 1997, p. 19). In general, the research revealed that the more hours teens worked, the lower their grades, the less homework they do, the less attentive they are in class, the less involved in extracurricular activities, and the more likely they are to be absent from school. Beyond the negative impact on academics, the research further revealed that the more hours teens work the more likely they are to use drugs, alcohol, and to experience elevated levels of stress, tension, and fatigue (p. 19).

States vary in regard to age limitations for working teens. The State of Washington, for example, is the only state that prohibits sixteen- and seventeen-year-olds from working more than twenty hours a week, while the State of Illinois imposes no such limitations on this age group but requires a work permit for fourteen- or fifteen-year olds and restricts their work hours to no more than twenty-four hours per week (McNamee, 1997, p. 19).

Sociologist Ralph McNeal of the University of Connecticut carries the debate on working teens to another level, contending that not only do increased work hours negatively impact academic performance, so too does the type of work teens do. According to McNeal, teens who work in the service sector (fast food jobs) are more likely than their counterparts who work in other sectors to drop out of school as they increase their work hours (McNamee, 1997, p. 19). Students who work in the service or manufacturing sector thirty or more hours a week have a dropout rate of 12 percent, while those in retail and farming who work these hours have a 5 percent dropout rate. However, the national average is a 4 percent dropout rate for teens who are employed part time (McNamee, 1997, p. 19). McNeal's findings remain firm even after considering such variables as the student's economic status, previous grades and test scores, and family situation. Students who work extended hours in service jobs were, unequivocally, more likely to drop out of school.

In addition to cutting into study time, increased work hours tend to decrease the number of hours of sleep. Not getting enough sleep, in general, negatively affects academic performance. Students who keep late hours or work long hours do not get the amount of sleep necessary to sustain a level of mental concentration and alertness necessary for academic success. Research has found that while high school students sleep on average 7.5 hours per night, one in four get only 6.5 hours of sleep, with 9.2 hours suggested for peak performance in school. Mary Carskadon, a Brown University sleep specialist, found a positive correlation between amount of sleep and academic performance. She found that students who earned As and Bs, generally, went to bed earlier than those who earned Ds and Fs (McNamee, 1997, p. 19).

Sleepers are the bane of every teacher's existence because most teachers take it personally. The message seems to be clear; "you are boring." However, things aren't always as they appear. For example, most schools probably have a Rhonda. Rhonda sleeps in all of her classes. Before the tardy bell has finished ringing Rhonda's head is on her desk, and she is entering deep sleep. Prodding from the teacher doesn't help her stay awake and keep her head off of her desk. Exasperated, the teacher sends her from the class with a referral to the dean's office for insubordination—failing to follow a directive. Rhonda is fortunate because she is sent to Mrs. Thomas, an experienced dean who senses that Rhonda's sleeping is only the "tip of the iceberg." She speaks with the social worker about Rhonda, and Rhonda is later called to the social worker's office. After a few sessions, Rhonda feels she can trust the social worker and confides that her mother passed away recently leaving behind Rhonda and four younger siblings. Rhonda's dad works long hours, and Rhonda has had to assume the responsibilities of her mom. Also, Rhonda has not relinquished her dream of going to college. In addition to cooking, cleaning, washing, getting the younger children off to school, and her own studies, Rhonda has a job that she needs if she is to fulfill her dream of going to college after she graduates. This case provides strong affirmation of the importance of teachers building relationships with their students, and establishing a rapport that encourages trust and sharing.

The challenge for parents and educators alike is to encourage delayed gratification, to get students to understand that education is an investment in their future that has the potential to reap significant rewards. The battle cry is always the same, stay in school.

Organic Causes

As discussed in Chapter 1, there is an interesting phenomenon that occurs in children who in the early stages of life do not receive adequate human contact and stimulation in the form of touch, cuddling, or being spoken to. Research has shown that those seemingly innocuous scenes of parents holding, cuddling, playing with, rocking, and talking to infants are essential to the development of attention, language, memory, perception, kinesthetics, and, in general, human emotion. Particularly noted among children raised in overcrowded orphanages, this phenomenon has attracted renewed interest as a result of large-scale adoptions, starting in 1991, of babies from Romania and former states of the Soviet Union by American couples. Many of these families found themselves baffled by children who exhibited such antisocial behaviors as screaming, slapping, biting, stiffening when being held. Many of these children grow up not wanting to be touched.

Overcrowded or understaffed orphanages deprive children of the human contact they need if bonding is to take place and their emotional needs met. These are children that grow up not being able to give what they have never received. The longer these children remain in institutions, the greater the developmental delay. Centers in the brain that control the senses and emotions fail to function because of a lack of stimulation.

Children caught in the web of foster care may face similar consequences, particularly those who are placed in the system at a very early age and remain in the system until they come of age (Coleman, 1996). In my own practice, I have found many of these children to be distant, sometimes defensive and sullen. Many do not know what it is like to be loved. After all, they are cared for by strangers, one after another in whose homes they will live. Even foster parents who provide loving care are not always able to bridge the gap. For these children to become emotionally attached can only create heartbreak when the system moves the child to a new home. Therefore, for their own survival, they may construct emotional facades that keep others at bay.

What are the implications for educators? Many of the "deficits" we see in these children may be organically based. Getting to know the background of problem students is essential to getting to the source of the problem and developing a strategy to assist them in better managing their behavior and our response. Sometimes, parents will openly share information, in other instances the dean, nurse, counselor, or social worker can provide some insight. Many veteran teachers have encountered students who seem to rebuff all attempts to establish a friendship. They resist an arm around the shoulder or attempts to use humor to get a smile or to create a relaxed atmosphere for dialogue. Behavior that may be defined as defiant may in actuality be a defense mechanism. It takes caring and patience to slowly chip away the facade.

Affiliation with Deviant Subculture

For many students from dysfunctional families, parents may be physically or emotionally absent. Keep in mind, however, that dysfunctional families are not synonymous with lower socioeconomic status. Humans by nature are gregarious beings. In fact, our personal identity is formed in relation to others. How we feel about ourselves in determined by others' reactions to us. Where the social dynamic necessary to form a sense of belonging or positive self-concept is lacking, there is a tendency to withdraw or to seek social situations where this fundamental need can be met. For adolescents from dysfunctional families, the peer group often fulfills this need.

At the extreme, students may gravitate toward deviant subcultures or gangs. The gang replaces the family in fulfilling their emotional needs. Membership is solidified by identification with various symbols, loyalty oaths, and code of secrecy. Gang membership also gives youth a sense of power or being in control. For gang members, there is an emotional high in evoking fear in others, in having people cross the street at their presence. For young adults from environments where they often feel powerless, this sense of power elevates their sense of being in control of their environment. The danger, however, is when this sense of power creates a feeling of invincibility.

There is a positive correlation between academic failure and students who are actively involved in deviant peer subcultures. The question becomes what role the school can play in deflecting the lure of gangs. As the source of the problem extends beyond variables the school directly controls, schools can assist by seeking solutions to keeping these students in school and offering them alternatives—alternatives that may offer them a glimpse of a brighter future.

One of the ways in which schools can do this is to capitalize on the student's strengths. Sometimes, educators so narrowly focus on the negatives that the positives escape their view. For example, graffiti is a common component of gang activity. Some of this "work" is quite unique. Why not involve the gang member with artistic ability in a school project such as painting a mural on the walls instead of gang graffiti? Some of these students are very charismatic. In what constructive ways can the school put these personal traits to use? Why not form intramural teams and use these students as captains? Sports have been credited with keeping many male students out of trouble (Coleman, 1996). "Athletic events provide a healthy release for the frustrations that often plague adolescents" (Chiles, 1986, p. 30). Unfortunately, such activity has traditionally been more available to boys than girls.

Take the student with good organizational skills and make him/her a group leader in class. What about the student who is good at poetry? You say these kids can't construct a coherent sentence? What about rap? While unpalatable to many, it does attest to the ability of these students to write poetry. To reach these students, educators must allow them to learn in ways that reflect their interest and culture. This is not to say that as educators we are to abandon rules of decency or academic standards, but recognizing their strengths gives us a place to start.

Educators can expect some resistance. Students don't always relish being held up as exemplars. The challenge for the educator is to find ways to get students to appreciate having their skills, talents and abilities respected and recognized. As one teacher said, "I haven't met a student yet who really doesn't want to be praised."

Failure to Master Basic Concepts

Students often fail to achieve out of frustration borne of years of being passed along to the next grade level without having mastered the basic concepts of the core curriculum. The lack of emphasis on mastery learning can doom children to failure and culminate in an aversion to academic pursuits. Who wants to go to a place, daily, that symbolizes nothing but frustration, anger and failure. When students feel academically prepared, fears and uncertainties become less debilitating. There is a certain confidence that comes with feeling one is equipped to handle what lies beyond the horizon. The more successful educators are in preparing students for the future, the more confident students will be. Many students who have failed to master basic concepts and are simply passed on from grade to grade are motivated to remain because of their age since school attendance is a legal requirement, or because with nothing else to do, school provides a social outlet.

Social promotion—the practice of passing to the next grade level students who have not mastered basic cognitive concepts by a certain age—is being reevaluated by many school systems. At the forefront of this new movement is the Chicago public school system, the nation's third largest, whose school reform program has been lauded as a possible national model (Cassell, 1997b). The new initiative requires students who have not met academic standards to attend summer school or, if they fail to do so, be retained. The ladder solution, as an effort to stop the cycle of academic failure by ensuring that students are academically prepared for the next grade level, is not without its critics.

Representing an opposing view, Shepard and Smith (1989) contend that current research supports the position that the detrimental effects of retention outweigh it benefits. They call attention to the fact that initial gains observed when students are retained are ephemeral. The more deleterious effect of retention is grounded in the stigma attached to being retained, culminating in increased dropout rates. They further observed that minorities, males and students from lower social economic status backgrounds, are disproportionately represented among students who are retained. Consequently, retention is not viewed as a viable solution to the problem of academic failure. The probability of a student who is retained just once dropping out of school increase by 21 to 27 percent (Malone & Bowser, 1998, p. 43).

What then is the solution? According to Shepard and Smith (1989), the solution lies in placing greater emphasis on addressing the individual needs of students. This implies a more individualized and diagnostic assessment of student academic failure and the initiation of a remediation program tailored to the student's needs. In effect, there is a need to take a more proactive stance in dealing with the problem. This calls for providing students with more support at the initial signs of trouble. Typically, retention simply means the student is exposed to the same material all over again, the implication being that repetition will solve the problem. It treats the symptom not the cause. It fails to ascertain and respond to why these students are experiencing difficulty in mastering learning. Consequently, retention in the absence of an individualized diagnosis of the student's learning difficulty and the development of strategies to correct the problem is counterproductive. Shepard and Smith contend that in the process of assisting students for whom academic success tends to be an illusive ideal, we as educators must be willing to seek creative solutions that engage the learner while addressing his/her special needs.

Conversely, those who advocate retention contend that retention is necessary to address and remedy the problem in its initial stages. Malone holds that "kids get an essential educational foundation in kindergarten, first and second grade. If they don't have a grasp of the basics at this age, they shouldn't be permitted to move on" (Malone & Bowser, 1998, p. 43). She further contends that the system should be flexible enough to transition students into their appropriate grade level at any given time when they have caught up. In educational circles, we tend to pass students along before they have mastered the fundamentals and then attempt to address the problem at each grade level. This is akin to trying to keep pace with a speeding locomotive on foot. You can never catch up. Consequently, mastery of the fundamentals is essential to building a strong foundation upon which subsequent learning can take place.

Familial Values

When parents feel education has failed to elevate their status, education loses its purposefulness and this attitude can be passed along to children. Families in which few members have completed high school and who live in neighborhoods or communities where this is the norm are often devoid of appropriate role models necessary to project a picture of a brighter future. Consequently, attitudes may be formed and standards set that are the very antithesis of the middle-class-oriented educational settings. Incongruent rules of social conduct, study habits, time management, etc., —all of the things essential to academic success,—often create a dissonance in the interpersonal relationships between middle-class teachers and these students. When this occurs, classroom management often evolves as an issue, with teachers spending more and more time dealing with disciplinary problems.

Incongruency Between Teaching Methodology and Student Learning Styles

Children do their best learning before entering school. According to Holt (1967), schools ironically stifle learning by forcing children to think in ways that do not work well for them. This has the negative consequence of making them feel humiliated, frightened, and discouraged. The school's objective should be driven by the quest to "better understand the ways, conditions and spirit in which children do their best learning" (vii). Once this has been accomplished we can structure educational environments that encourage and enhance varied student learning styles. Holt contends that this is the key to preventing academic failure in our schools. When students are allowed to learn in ways that complement their learning style, the quality and amount of learning that takes place increases measurably, for this freedom gives birth to curiosity, courage, confidence, independence, resourcefulness, resilience, patience, competence, and understanding.

The message to educators is clear. We must focus our efforts as much on exploring ways in which children learn best as we do in determining what they should learn. In fact, curriculum issues become secondary if we have failed to first identify how children learn best, how to get them to make the cognitive connection.

Unfortunately, teachers inadvertently reinforce negative attitudes toward school in a number of ways. There is in education a need for a paradigm shift. For too long, we have persisted in our attempts to fit a square peg into a round hole even though we have met with repeated failure. We, for example, require students to perform classroom activities within a specific time frame, failing to take into consideration that not all students learn at the same pace or in the same way. What is most tragic is the fact that students who are not able to complete the task within the specified period of time are often made to feel incompetent. If students internalize these feelings, further attempts to motivate them may be futile. All too often, teachers expect students to respond in the very traditional ways defined by the dominant culture. This robs students of their individuality by not allowing them to express themselves in ways that reflect and reinforce their culture and to respond in ways characteristic of their learning style. Ladson-Billings (1994) makes a strong case for culture-relevant teaching and student motivation and achievement. The issue of varied student learning styles warrants further discussion.

Academic failure, in many instances, may be inappropriately applied to some students. Instead what we may be looking at is the failure of our educational system to explore and acknowledge ways of knowing, ways in which students learn and express themselves best, particularly if those ways contradict our conventional perceptions of learning. Many educators, in spite of newly developed learning theories, are still very much constrained in their perception of what constitutes intelligence. Consequently, we come to value only those components of intelligence that have traditionally been sanctioned in academia such as analytical, organizational, verbal and written communication, logic, and mathematical skill. (Gardner, 1983; Chapman, 1993; Tobias, 1994).

Howard Gardner of Harvard University has conducted research with the potential to free educators from their microcosmic perceptions of learning and ways of knowing and provide a more comprehensive definition of intelligence. Old habits are hard to break, but if as educators we are to fulfill our mission in assisting students to discover, analyze, process, and synthesize information, we must be equally committed to discovering and acknowledging the ways in which they know and learn. Professor Gardner has brought us to the precipice, and we must take the leap of faith to allow students to learn and express themselves in ways that expand our conventional perceptions of learning and intelligence.

Professor Gardner's research acknowledges the existence of multiple intelligences, the MI theory. He found that there are a number of ways of being smart. He has identified seven kinds of intelligences located in different parts of the brain. He further contends that each of us has the potential to develop all seven intelligences, but two or three of them will be predominant and characterize our way of knowing. The most striking revelation of his research contends that when we are born, our intelligence is not fixed. With increased opportunities and the passage of time, our intelligence develops, changes, and expands (Tobias, 1994). The operative word here is opportunity. It calls into question how much of the perceived lack of intelligence on the part of some children is innate and how much can be attributed to a lack of opportunity to develop and cultivate those areas of intelligence in which the child shows a particular propensity. Gardner has identified seven and feels that are other yet undiscovered intelligences. The ones he has identified are linguistic, spatial, interpersonal, intrapersonal, logical-mathematical, musical, and bodily-kinesthetic (Tobias, 1994).

Linguistic/verbal. Individuals who are proficient in reading, writing, and verbal expression possess linguistic intelligence. Among them are Frederick Douglass, Maya Angelou, Martin Luther King, Plato, Aristotle, Socrates, and Hemingway—great writers and orators of our past and present. These are individuals who are adept at using language to convey meaning beyond the mere visual and auditory stimuli. The manner in which they are able to manipulate the spoken word through gesticulation, and voice inflection and the written word with descriptive clarity intensifies meaning and our emotional response. One has only to recall the Orson Wells saga, the radio broadcast depiction of a Martian invasion so realistic that it was believed to be factual and caused widespread panic. How many students in our classrooms possess this ability? Some students may not be adept at written expression but possess a masterful command of verbal expression. Conversely, others may lack the ability to verbally articulate their thoughts but can do so with ease when committed to paper.

Too often in the classroom setting, educators insist on having information being presented in a particular form—for example, a written paper as opposed to an oral report. If the goal is to test for writing skills, require a written paper. If the goal is to test for knowledge, why not allow students to demonstrate knowledge using a medium most comfortable for them? The key is discovering each child's primary intelligences and providing the flexibility to further cultivate them.

I can recall a teachable moment in which a group of boys in the back of the classroom in which I was subbing were off task and singing rap songs. I challenged them to compose a rap song about the event in history they were studying in a specified period of time during the class period and perform it for the class. It worked! They did a great job. Imagine the thinking about history that had to go into putting their presentation together. They also seemed to take great pleasure in rising to the challenge.

Visual/spatial. This intelligence is the ability to formulate, transform, and manipulate mental images. Individuals who possess this type of intelligence not only have the ability to view things as they are but also as they could be. These are individuals who do well on that portion of the IQ test that requires you to determine what an unfolded object would look like if folded, for example. They are individuals who perceive more than just lines and dimensions on a sheet of paper. Have you ever experienced reading something in a book or newspaper and later, if the need arises to find the article again, are able to form a mental image of where in the paper or book the article is located? Individuals with spatial intelligence are adept in this regard. They are able to formulate or recall mental images with great acuity. They are able to visualize the final product based on diagrams, blueprints etc. These are draftsmen, architects, artists, designers, sailors, engineers, surgeons, sculptors, and cartographers (Chapman, 1993; Tobias, 1994).

Interpersonal. Some individuals are what we would call people persons. They just seem to fit in and interact very naturally and effortlessly with others in any situation. They are very intuitive in defining the tenor of social situations. As Gardner puts it, they are particularly adept at sensing the "moods, temperaments, motivations and intentions" of others (Gardner, 1983, p. 239). They sense when something is wrong and are very empathetic, possessing the ability to understand and appreciate the positions of others. These are the individuals who often choose professions such as social work, counseling, civil rights advocates, and the ministry. Individuals are drawn to them because they are willing to listen and are easy to talk to. It is easy to see how students who are gifted in this type of intelligence may find themselves at odds with teachers whose classrooms are very structured and teacher centered rather than student centered. These students enjoy interacting with others. They easily evolve as the leaders when students are assigned to work in groups. Individuals with interpersonal intelligence are heavily represented in such positions as religious leaders, politicians, parents, teachers, therapists, and counselors (Chapman, 1993; Tobias, 1994).

Intrapersonal. Does "To thine own self be true" sound familiar? Of the seven intelligences Professor Gardner has to date identified, this is perhaps the most difficult for many to perceive as a form of intelligence. Intrapersonal intelligence is our ability to get in touch with our inner selves. These individuals are very introspective. They understand who they are and consequently do not allow others to define their being. One author describes them as individuals who "instinctively comprehend their own range of emotions, can label them, and can draw on them as a means of directing their own behavior (Chapman, 1993, p. 4). They generally possess very positive self-concepts and view solitude as an opportunity for reflection to ponder issues, concerns, situations, or the state of their being. In the classroom, these individuals may be negatively labelled shy or withdrawn when in fact they possess an inner strength, independence, and resolve that enables them to experience the world in which we live more intensely. Therapists, psychologists, wise elders, and introspective novelists possess strong intrapersonal capabilities (Chapman, 1993; Tobias, 1994).

Logical/mathematical. This intelligence which governs the ability to manipulate patterns, and numbers and to engage in inductive and deductive reasoning, incorporates mathematical as well as scientific abilities. It also involves abstract rather than concrete thinking. For many students, it is this distinction that forms the mental block to comprehending math or science.

They experience the world as a series of connected concrete realities. They see what they see. They don't see or think of objects in terms of their molecular structure and when asked to do so find it quite baffling to comprehend. Because this isn't the way in which they experience the world, it is often difficult for some students to develop the mind-set to view the world in ways foreign to them. It just doesn't click. This isn't to say that as educators we give up. We find ways to help them make the connection, ways that make sense to them. We can do this with the use of models, experimentation, framing concepts within the context of everyday experiences whenever possible, etc. Individuals with enhanced logical/mathematical intelligence are represented among mathematicians, engineers, physicists, astronomers, computer programmers, and researchers (Chapman, 1993; Tobias, 1994).

Musical/rhythmic. Those with musical/rhythmic intelligence are able to pick up on natural rhythms and melodies. They connect with music, sensing every beat and rhythm. Music imbues in them emotions, and the truly gifted are able to give their emotions musical embodiment. Music helps them to express themselves. Music is a very powerful influence in manipulating the emotions. Consider what it would be like to sit through any movie without the music. Have you ever noticed how in an action-packed thriller you find yourself sitting on the edge of your seat? Consider your reaction without the musical score. Consider how much of your reaction is driven not by what is visible on the screen but the musical accompaniment. Consider how the music heightens your response to the visual stimuli. Composers, instrumentalists, singers, conductors, and those with an above average appreciation and understanding of music possess highly developed music/rhythmic intelligence (Chapman, 1993; Tobias, 1994).

Bodily/kinesthetic. There is much poetic beauty to be found in the mundane. Take for example bodily movement and physical activity. Falling under the rubric of bodily-kinesthetic intelligence, these individuals are adept at using their hands and bodies. Through bodily movement and physical activity, they create art or bring it to life. They are surgeons, mechanics, carpenters, athletes, dancers, artists, actors, actresses, etc. They possess a high degree of manual and physical dexterity that enables them to experience physical activity at it most intricate level (Chapman, 1993; Tobias, 1994).

The problem with the educational system is that, traditionally, we have not recognized music, bodily/kinesthetic, and intrapersonal and interpersonal ability as legitimate forms of intelligence. Consequently, students who are adept in these ways of knowing and expressing themselves may be labelled talented but not necessarily intelligent. On the other hand, students who excel in math, science and/or writing are held in high esteem and lauded for their ability, for being smart. We have such examples as Michael Jordan (super athlete), Mozart (musical genius), Picasso (gifted artist), and Luciano Pavarotti (opera singer), but somehow we still tend to interpret their achievements as grounded in a skill or particular knack for doing something rather than in their being smart or intelligent. Yet, these individuals have left an indelible mark on our society and culture. What is needed in education is a paradigm, as we redefine what being "smart" means.

As educators we must ask ourselves what some of the ways are in which we can incorporate the concept of multiple intelligences into our pedagogy. This doesn't mean discarding all learning materials or activities. But it does require educators to be innovative, to look at new ways of presenting old material and to develop new materials. For example, while teaching *The Scarlet Letter* in what other ways than reading and discussing the book can teachers teach about moral character or generate enthusiasm for the assignment? Teachers can make the assignment more student-centered by asking students to draw parallels between the characters in the book and modern-day situations. They can ask students to assume the persona of one of the characters in the book and do a psychological profile. They can ask students to put the moral dilemma in historical perspective and predict the outcome. They can divide class members into groups and ask them to stage a production based on the book, with some students writing the script, others designing scenery, others writing music for the production, still others directing and attending to the details of putting the production together. Perhaps students may choose to present it as a musical. In this one example, think of the number of intelligences called into play but, most important, the opportunity for students to shine in ways that best reflect their primary intelligence.

The educational advantage of recognizing multiple intelligences is that it enables teachers to reach students who learn in different ways. While schools generally focus on the verbal, linguistic intelligence that relates to reading and writing or the logical, mathematical intelligence, educators are increasingly giving credence to others ways in which students know—through music, movement, performing, analyzing, visualizing, and the spoken word (Yednak, 1997).

It is ironic that in the early stages of learning, in preschool and kindergarten, movement and music are an integral part of learning. Most children this age can sing the ABC song or nursery rhymes or are engaged in various games that require movement. However, by the time students reach junior high, these methods are no longer considered as a means of transferring knowledge. Many educators at the junior high and high school level are becoming increasingly aware of the positive impact of multiple intelligences on student performance outcomes. Those who have come to recognize multiple intelligence theory as a supplement to their instructional strategies rather than a replacement have found acceptance of the theory more palatable. Two distinct advances of multiple intelligence theory is that it adds excitement to learning by encouraging teachers to vary the manner in which they teach a lesson, and it enhances the comprehension of students who need to see a concept presented in a number ways in order to grasp it (Yednak, 1997).

The more flexible and comfortable teachers are in acknowledging various ways of knowing and providing opportunities and giving students permission to learn and express themselves in ways that best reflect their learning style, the more students will become interested in the subject matter and academically successful. Teachers are very human. There is a natural sense of security in familiarity; consequently, there may be some resistance or reluctance to trying out new ideas. However, if as educators we are to fulfill our mission not to just teach facts but to teach students how to learn, we must be willing to step outside of our box and survey and explore the surrounding landscape to discover new teaching strategies and methodologies. Likewise, parents must provide their children with opportunities to discover their "gifts."

According to Professor Gardner, standard IQ tests measure conformity to the values of the traditional education system and may predict how well a student may do in school but such tests do not adequately predict how well students will fare in the real world (Tobias, 1994). Also, many contend that the extent to which the system and these tests fail to acknowledge and reflect cultural diversity may account for why some minority students do not fare well on these tests. Similarly, certain intelligences seem to predominate among various ethnic groups—for example, the disproportionate number of African Americans who have found success in the field of sports and music. However, caution is advised in attributing such success to purely innate ability, for the question arises as to the impact the interaction between cultural values predicated on sociopolitical license has had on this phenomenon. That is, is it genetic or just a reflection of the fact that these are areas in which society gives African Americans permission to access? Consequently, these intelligences become valued by the African American subculture.

While pleased with the overwhelming interest and response to multiple intelligences theory by the education community, Gardner, twelve years after the theory's inception, ventures into the very core of the tenets of MI theory. He addresses the evolution of seven myths gleamed from the practices of various educational institutions as they have attempted to implement it. These myths penetrate the very foundation upon which the multiple intelligence theory was constructed, thereby compromising its original intent, appropriate implementation, and ultimate impact on instruction and learning outcomes (Gardner, 1995).

Myth #1. There is a need to create seven tests, each of which can be numerically measured. In reality, MI theory is antithetical to psychometrics. According to Gardner, "It becomes crucial that intelligences be assessed in ways that are 'intelligent-fair' in ways that examine the intelligence directly rather than through the lens of linguistic or logical intelligence as ordinary paper and pencil tests do" (p. 202).

Myth #2. Intelligence, domain, and discipline are the same. Gardner clearly defines intelligence as biological and psychological relating to potential or capacity. Conversely, domain and discipline relate to organized activities such as gardening, chess, rap music. The major distinguishing characteristic is that domain can be realized using any number of the intelligences.

Myth #3. Intelligence, "learning style," "cognitive style," or "working style" are the same. MI theory is not a learning style. Style is a general approach applicable to the gamut of content. Conversely, intelligence references "a capacity with its component processes, that is geared to a specific content in the world such as musical sounds or spatial patterns" (p. 202).

Myth #4. The multiple intelligence theory is not empirical. Gardner responds by noting that he derived the theory after reviewing hundreds of empirical studies. Through this intense review process, he was able to isolate and identify seven intelligences. In effect, the construct for MI theory was clearly built on a solid foundation of empiricism. Gardner does not stop here. He carries the discourse even further, contending that MI theory's evolution from empirically based research imbues it with characteristics amenable to critical evaluation and discussion.

Myth #5. Multiple intelligence theory is incompatible with general intelligence and theories of the role of heredity versus environment as factors in intelligence. Gardener explains that while MI theory does not question the existence of general intelligence, it does challenge the "province and explanatory" power of general intelligence (p. 203). He continues by pointing out that the evaluating of general intelligence is centered on scholastic intelligence and establishing a correlation between test scores and intellectual capacity. Gardner's theory of multiple intelligences looks beyond the narrowly defined parameters of general intelligence to identify other intelligences. While he does concede a genetic base in intelligence, he stops short of an unequivocal acceptance of the "inherited versus learned" dichotomy. He elevates to a higher level of significance the *interaction* between genetic factors at conception and environmental factors in general intelligence.

Myth #6. Multiple intelligence theory expands the scope of the notion of intelligence, resulting in the inclusion of all psychological constructs, thereby shrouding the connotation of the term in ambiguity. In addressing this myth, Gardner turns his attention to the very narrowly defined definition of general intelligence that constricts the range of intellectual ability to that which is amenable to psychometric assessment. According to Gardner "what we call 'intelligence' in the vernacular is simply a certain set of 'talents' in the linguistic and/or logical-mathematical spheres" (p. 206).

Myth #7. There are additional intelligences. Gardner concedes the existence of additional intelligences and has embarked on an investigation in an attempt to identify them. This quest thus far has brought him to subject to closer scrutiny the notion of the exceptional ability of some individuals to distinguish between similar phenomenon in the natural world. He refers to it as "intelligence of the naturalists." These individuals are able to recognize flora and fauna and other distinctions in the natural world. He cites as an example children who are able to discriminate among cars, sneakers, hairstyles, etc. (p. 206). In the adult world, these are the art dealers, antique dealers, architectural historians. In effect, individuals who are able to not only visually identify and categorize items that comprise their field of expertise but to assess authenticity and ferret out subtle differences and imperfections. They possess a discerning eye for detail (pp. 200-206).

There are many variables that impact academic achievement. Education practitioners cannot successfully fulfill their mission without carefully scrutinizing how these variables affect their practice and adopt proactive strategies to ameliorate the problem.

STUDENT ACHIEVEMENT AND ACADEMIC STANDARDS

In comparison to other industrialized nations, American students have scored poorly in the areas of math and science. Additionally, there is national concern over low reading scores.

According to the Third International Mathematics and Science Study, based on scores on a general knowledge math and science test administered to students from twenty-one countries near the end of 1994–95, American seniors scored below the international average. There is elevated reason for concern given that even for those taking more rigorous courses such as physics and advanced math, American students still scored below their international peers. Only students from Cyprus and South Africa scored below the American students ("Math, science exam," 1998, p. A-1).

At the national level, to remedy the problem, President Clinton has called for the recruitment of more teachers, smaller class sizes, and greater emphasis on aid to poor city schools. Secretary of Education Richard Riley attributes the problem to minimal graduation requirements, a deficit of teachers with college minors or majors in math and science, late exposure to the fundamentals of advanced math and science concepts, and the fact that American high school students take fewer years of math and science. About half of American college-bound seniors have not taken four years of science ("Math, science exam," 1998).

Research has revealed long-term benefits of smaller class size. With funding from the National Education Association and the American Federation of Teachers, Dr. Helen Pate-Bain conducted the Student/Teacher Ratio (STAR)

Project (1985–89). The target population consisted of 3,000 K–3 students from rural, suburban, urban, and inner-city Tennessee. Students were randomly selected and placed in classes labelled small with thirteen to seventeen students; regular with twenty-two to twenty-five students and regular classes with a full-time teacher aide. The study revealed that high school students who were placed in small classes in the early grades were less likely to be retained in a grade, received better grades, had fewer suspensions, and higher attendance rates and were more likely to take foreign language and advanced classes. This research provides strong evidence that smaller classes have long-term academic benefits ("Small classes," 1998, p. 17).

The Third International Mathematics and Science Study also found that among American eighth-graders, poor and minority students did poorly in math compared to children in Japan and China. The study's director, William Schmidt, attributed this to the limited exposure of these students to math. This performance deficit was also noted when this population of students was compared to their American peers. In particular, Hispanics, African Americans, and low-income students were found "twice as likely as other American students not to be exposed to the critical subject of algebra." The study further revealed that while 20 percent of all American eighth graders take algebra, only 10 percent of Hispanic, African American, and low-income students do so. This discrepancy held, even among students in higher income areas (Rossi, 1997a, p. 8).

Schmidt found that Hispanic, African American, and low-income students in general are twice as likely to be deprived of basic math instruction. In his final analysis, he concluded that the achievement deficit can be attributed to lack of equity in education. According to Schmidt, "The system has lower standards for poor kids. This is something that has crept into our philosophy of curriculum. We think some children can do it and some children can't" (Rossi, 1997a, p. 8).

Other researchers have also taken a more global perspective, focusing on the learning gap between American students in general and their peers in other parts of the world. Stevenson and Stigler (1992) examined the learning gap between American first and fifth graders and their Japanese and Chinese counterparts. On standard measures of academic achievement, Asian students out-performed their American peers. In their effort to identify the determining variables, the researchers examined the structure, belief, and value system of each culture that clustered around the institution of education, with the following results:

ASIAN	AMERICAN
Focus is on the group	Focus is on individualism
Teachers are held in high esteem	Teachers are not held in high esteem
Failure is attributed to lack of opportunity	Failure is attributed to lack of ability

Differences are minimized and cohesiveness is encouraged	Preoccupation with group differences stifles cohesiveness
Effort if emphasized	End result is emphasized
Homework is valued	Value of homework is considered questionable
Discipline and order are imposed by external forces	Discipline and order are imposed by students on each other
The purpose of education is clearly defined	The purpose of education is not clearly defined
Grades are posted for public scrutiny	Grades are considered private and confidential
Students identify with the school and their peers	Students do not have a strong sense of identification with school and peers
There is a national curriculum	There is no national curriculum
School year consists of 240 days	School year consists of 180 days
Teaching loads are reduced to create more time to perfect skills	Teachers do not have time to help students perfect skills
More time is spent on task with teacher involvement	Less time is spent on task with teacher involvement

The results of this cross-cultural study provide a point of reference from which to reassess our philosophy of education, what we teach, how we teach, and how our value and belief system impact the efficacy of our practice.

For American students who live in one of the richest, most powerful nations in the world, to give such a comparatively lackluster performance, casts a pall on the state of our educational system. If we are to maintain our standing as a leader in the world community, we must thoroughly scrutinize the manner in which we educate our children and take steps to improve student performance.

Concerns regarding the state of American education gained national attention in 1981 when then Secretary of Education T. H. Bell formed the National Commission on Excellence in Education. The commission's findings were reported in a 1983 document entitled *A Nation At Risk: The Imperative for Educational Reform*. The commission was given the charge to concentrate their efforts on the following key concerns:

- Conduct a comparative analysis of American institutions of learning with those in other advanced nations
- Identify educational programs that contribute to success in college
- Ascertain the degree to which student achievement has been impacted by major social and educational changes over the past twenty-five years
- Assess the quality of teaching and learning outcomes in public and private schools and colleges and universities
- Examine the relationship between college entrance requirements and level of student achievement in high school

The commission's findings were based on an analysis of historical data evincing trends in education over the past quarter century, review of the extant literature and testimony from education practitioners. The commission found deficiencies in the American educational system to cluster around four areas—teaching, expectations, time, and content. Based on their findings, the following recommendations were made:

AREA OF DEFICIENCY	RECOMMENDATION
Teaching	Improve teacher preparation and performance
Content	Review curriculum content, what students should be taught and know
Time	Increase student time on task in the classroom; examine the length of the school day and school year
Expectations	Impose more stringent and measurable standards for student performance and promotion

This document formed the springboard for the extant school reform movement ("A nation as risk," 1983). Its recommendations are clearly evident in state academic standards.

The Illinois State Board of Education in July of 1997 adopted the first statewide academic standards for elementary and high school students (Deerin, 1997). The academic standards form the conceptual framework for school curriculum. Referred to as the Illinois Learning Standards, it identifies what students should know and by when in the primary subject areas of English, math, science, social science, physical education, fine arts, and foreign language. The Learning Standards consist of thirty broad learning goals that "set guidelines for student progress" (p. 1). In their preliminary draft, the Illinois State Board of Education clearly set forth their vision of the nature of the learning standards. The standards were that the curriculum should:

- Be clear and understandable
- Focus on knowledge *and* skills
- Set challenging expectations for all students
- Be measurable at the state and/or local school level
- Provide sufficient direction as to what students should learn, but be flexible enough to allow for different approaches to curriculum, instruction, and local testing of students
- Reflect current research and best practices in teaching and learning, including the use of technology, and emphasize knowledge and skills that prepare students for the workplace

The standards were not only designed to positively impact learning and performance outcomes for students but to guide school reform at the state level by establishing new teaching standards and providing funding to support teaching and learning. School districts are also expected to benefit from the learning standards initiative. The standards will foster greater uniformity in terms of what is taught and when, while giving school districts the flexibility to adopt approaches to curriculum, instruction, and assessment that best meet their needs (Deerin, 1997).

Academic standards, however, have not won universal support. Some critics fear that as much as 50 to 75 percent of students might fail to meet the standards. However, Joe Clark, the executive director of the Illinois Family Institute noted that in all but two of the fourteen states that have adopted academic standards this prediction has not been borne out. In fact, students in twelve of the fourteen states showed improvement when tested against the standards. Other critics contend that predictions of low test results on the standards simply indicate an orchestrated effort to secure additional state and federal funding, a mandated state and federal curriculum, year-round school, more testing, increased bureaucracy, and decreased local control of schools (Byrne, 1997).

Advocates, however, would contend that academic standards of this scope give form and definition to otherwise amorphous state-sanctioned programs of study. It also ensures that if students move anywhere in the state, they can expect a curriculum with a basic structure that closely approximates that to which they were previously exposed. As the issue of school reform has been thrust into the national spotlight, we can expect greater uniformity of expectations in regards to what students should know and by when. This is a major step in the direction of producing students with the necessary knowledge and skills to compete in a global economy.

THE IMPACT OF TECHNOLOGY ON INSTRUCTION AND LEARNING

The relationship between technology and achievement is a variable that requires some consideration. Slide rules, encyclopedias, and filmstrips—once standard instructional tools at the disposal of teachers—are fast becoming anachronisms. The approach of the twenty first century has ushered in technological advances that have impacted what we teach, how we teach, and the role of the teacher in the classroom. Consequently, the role of the teacher continues to undergo a metamorphosis from one whose primary function is to impart knowledge to the more idealistic facilitator (Rozek, 1997).

Teachers must familiarize themselves with the new technology. Computers, camcorders, and laser discs that enable history teachers to bring history to life by showing actual footage of historical events; videocassette recorders; digital or video cameras that take pictures that can be scanned into the computer and incorporated into research projects; the ability for teachers seated at a control station to manipulate individual student computer stations; special calculators with ancillary equipment that allows the computations to be projected on a large screen, etc., are all becoming standard issue. Predictions are that computers that offer students virtual reality that will enable students to take field trips replete with lifelike sensory and auditory stimuli are not more than five to seven years away. Students will be able to experience what they are studying. At the other end of the spectrum, computers as a tool for remediation have enhanced the classroom teacher's ability to provide more individualized instruction for students who are deficient in some areas. With available software programs that have the capability to assess the level of achievement in a specific area and then develop a remediation program based on that assessment, teachers have come closer than ever before to meeting the needs of individual students. Computers do not tire with the need for constant repetition (Rozek, 1997; Wagner, 1996).

Papert (1993) also recognized the benefits of computers as learning tools amenable to effort to provide remediatioh. He carries the discourse further, citing the use of the computer language LOGO that gives students the capability to explore and learn at their own pace, separately from their peers. He contends that it is a rewarding departure from the traditional pedagogy that moves all students along together in lockstep fashion. Computers, as learning tools, are also amenable to efforts to provide remediation for students experiencing learning difficulties.

Teachers, however, will now have to reassess how they teach, as well as learn how to teach students to use computers as learning tools. Furthermore, the accelerated rate at which technology changes will necessitate an ongoing staff development initiative.

Despite these technological innovations, Papert (1993) contends that education lags behind other professions in taking advantage of the full potential of technology to advance their agenda. To compete in the today's workplace, students must leave secondary schools computer literate. The school's success in meeting this challenge is predicated on its teacher training and its financial buoyancy. Obviously, financially strapped school systems will be at a disadvantage. This, of necessity, will impose a more aggressive initiative to secure funding to create an educational infrastructure that will take students into the twenty first century. Such universal curricular requirements such as writing a research paper, for example, puts those students at an advantage who have access to an Internet system. Similarly, Internet access makes the world a laboratory for learning. It enables students to travel anywhere in the world without leaving the classroom. It broadens the pool of resources and data. It provides opportunities to engage in personal dialogues with professionals and experts in various fields.

There are those, however, who project a downside to the unbridled use of technology, citing its potential to stifle the development of critical and creative thinking skills. Silberman (1970) asserts, "The approach to instructional technology that most researchers are following is likely to compound what is most wrong with American education—its failure to develop sensitive, autonomous, thinking, humane individuals" (p. 196). The debate rages as educators discuss, among other things, the use of calculators in math classes, and in English the use of spell checks and grammar-check software programs. Others have expressed concern that interpersonal communication skills will diminish as students interact more with computers than other people.

For others, the issue is one of cost and educational priorities. The Clinton administration has begun an initiative to bring the Internet into every American classroom within the next three years. At a cost of $50 billion, and in the midst of grappling with many more pressing, fundamental, and unresolved issues in education, some critics question this national priority (McNichol, 1997). They ask whether, as many schools struggle to operate on dwindling resources, and cope with overcrowding and other issues that directly impact the quality of education at such a fundamental level, funds should be diverted from more urgent needs a large expenditure for educational software and hardware (McNichol, 1997).

Some critics question the value of computers as a learning tool. Others like Clifford Stoll, an acknowledged computer guru, hold that "computers solve a problem that doesn't exist. The one thing they do well is bring more information into the classroom. But, I've never heard teachers complain about a lack of information. The real problems are class size, shrinking attention spans, a lack of discipline, drugs and guns" (McNichol, p. 10). Still others focus less on the presence of computers in the classroom and more on the extent of the use of computers for instructional purposes. They contend that a fundamental knowledge of wordprocessing and spreadsheet computer applications should define the role of computers in the classroom. Use of computers beyond this level of application, according to these critics, tends to teach data collection at the expense of critical thinking and "substitutes virtual contact for real relationships with teachers and peers" (McNichol, p. 12). However, proponents of computers as a learning tool outnumber the critics, pointing to its effectiveness in enhancing learning skills.

As we enter the next century, computer technology in the classroom is not likely to go away. As the emphasis is placed on teaching students to use computers to produce and access data, concern has risen over stifling the development of creative and critical thinking skills, independent thought, and the interpersonal communications skills necessary for success in the workplace.

Therefore, our success in preparing students for the future is directly impacted by our success in balancing the use of technology and cultivating these skills and thought processes. In the final analysis, computer literacy and the use of other new technologies will have a definitive impact on student success in school, the workplace, and the rigors of everyday life.

Chapter 3

Student Motivation

SOURCES OF MOTIVATION

There is intrinsic motivation that comes from within and extrinsic motivation that comes from without. When students have the desire to succeed within them, and others encourage their effort, the journey along the pathway to success is not as heavy laden.

Some students strive to do well to please a significant other, while others strive to do well to escape negative criticism or maintain a family standard. For still others, it is a means of gaining recognition or material rewards. Conversely, some are motivated by negative factors such as fear of punishment or rejection. There are those who are motivated to fail as an act of rebellion against authoritarianism. Fordham and Ozbu (1986) attributed this phenomenon in black and Hispanic students to a fear of losing their social identity and espousing the ways of the dominant culture. These students may accuse their peers of "acting white." "Acting white" then becomes a social indictment resulting in alienation from one's own culture. Ironically, in this way, students actually feel they are in control in their lives.

Educators must also deal with another baffling phenomenon, and that is the reluctance of many adolescents to accept recognition for their accomplishments. My first real experience with this phenomenon occurred in my role as the administrator of a motivational program for students. Students were selected for the program based on having all passing grades, good attendance, and discipline. Depending upon their level of success in each of these areas, they were issued various colored cards. Students issued gold cards received the most privileges and incentives, those with silver cards receive fewer—bronze, white, and so on. During assemblies many of these students refused to step forward to receive the various prizes offered. Instead, they would come to my office afterward to claim their prize. This, however, tended not to be the case when the only students in attendance at the assembly were students who qualified for the program.

In another instance, all students in the program were given a free lunch. When their names were called only one or two of the students actually came forth. Therefore, I decided to try a different approach. Prior to the lunch period, I gave each student a free lunch coupon. There were many more takers. The bottom line is, students don't like to be singled out. Sometimes, their friends make fun of them. The desire to belong or feel as one with the peer group is obviously very strong for many young adults. So strong that many think to do well is not cool, and others who continue to do well are reluctant to publicly accept recognition for their effort. This scenario suggests the need for educators to develop ways to motivate students that do not alienate them from their peers and cultivate the development of a sense of community among students grounded in common values. Within this social context, the seeds of mutual support and encouragement can take root and grow. This certainly puts a new wrinkle in the issue of student motivation.

THE ROLE OF THE PARENT, TEACHER, STUDENT, AND COMMUNITY IN MOTIVATION

How does one motivate a student to achieve academically? Too often the tendency has been to blame a lack of motivation on the teacher, student, or parent. In so doing, we forget that education is a partnership between home, school, and community. We are the innkeepers of the future. We must provide a place of comfort for children where they can receive the necessary sustenance to invigorate them to continue their journey of academic success to its final destination. Consequently, there is much that home, school, and community can do to promote student motivation. Based on my twenty-eight years of experience in the field, I have found the more synchronized they are in this mission, the more efficacious the effort. Let's briefly examine how each of these can promote positive attitudes toward academic achievement:

TEACHERS

Exude Enthusiasm

It is difficult to inspire others to greatness when our own flame grows dim. *Enthusiasm* is contagious. It is indeed difficult to motivate students when everything in the teacher's behavior is lackluster. A characteristic of highly effective teachers is an enthusiasm for the subject taught. These teachers not only project an enthusiasm for their subject matter but also in sharing their knowledge with students (Campbell, 1972).

Somehow their enthusiasm makes the student feel that mastering concepts is achievable. In a word, they make it seem easy and enjoyable. Their enthusiasm reduces any perceived obstacle to conquerable proportions.

Create a Student-Centered Learning Environment

Another way teachers can motivate students is to create a *learning environment* in which students can learn at their own pace. This does not mean allowing the student to spend an unlimited amount of time struggling to comprehend a concept. What it does mean is creating an environment in which students are not afraid to take academic risks to say "I don't understand" for as long as it takes for the "ah ha" experience to kick in. It means creating a learning environment in which the instructional time line is dictated by student needs rather than a prescribed timetable for meeting curriculum learning objectives. When students don't fear embarrassment, they will continue to seek answers to questions with which they struggle.

Create a Sense of Community in the Classroom

Where teachers have been successful in *creating a sense of community* in their classrooms, student motivation is enhanced. In such classrooms, there is a sense that students have a responsibility to assist each other in achieving academic success. Laughing at classmates, and verbal put-downs are strongly discouraged. Oftentimes, this sense of community is built by assigning students to groups. Cooperative learning is based on the concept of team effort and encourages all students to work together for the good of the group (Ladson-Billings, 1994).

Discover Each Student's "Gift"

Another way in which teachers can motivate students is to *discover each students gift*. Everybody does something well. Yes, even the student whose vacant seat is a virtual guarantee of a good day. In fact, discovering the "gift" of these students could be the force to remove the stumbling block to academic achievement. Particularly, when a student has a history of behavioral problems, it is difficult for others to see their strong suits. Aberrant behavior is often an effective mask of creativity. It is human nature to enjoy having one's talents recognized. Adherence to traditional pedagogical methods prevents educators from discovering the hidden "gifts" of many of these students. The master teacher, however, is driven by the need to see their students succeed. When a student fails, they feel they have failed. Consequently, they are often more flexible. They allow students to learn in ways that reflect their interests and talents. The class talker is allowed to give an oral report. The musician is allowed to weave the tale of *The Scarlet Letter* using rap as his medium. The artist is allowed to render visual images of slavery to explain this blot on our country's past. The history teacher allows his students to learn about history by way of collecting oral histories from their families. For the creative teacher, the list is endless.

Project a Caring Attitude

The teacher who is *affective* has a distinct edge in motivating students. Most students don't like to disappoint teachers they feel care about them. These are the teachers who take the time to build relationships with their students. They sense their moods. They know when something is troubling them, and most important, they open a dialogue.

Set High Expectations

Teachers who *set high expectations* for their students and send their students all manner of verbal and nonverbal clues that say "You are capable" enhance student motivation. What these teachers give their students is a challenge, a goal to work toward. However, before setting them on their journey, these teachers equip them with the mental attitude to navigate the obstacles along the way. Often all it takes to succeed is the firm belief that you can do it. The probability of success is enhanced when others believe in you. There are many examples in history of men and women, some extraordinary who have gained fame and some others ordinary, who attest to the ability of individuals to overcome seemingly insurmountable odds to achieve success. Abraham Lincoln rose from abject poverty to become president of the United States; Einstein, who was discovered to have been dyslexic, developed the theory of relativity that shook the scientific world; Helen Keller, blind, deaf, and mute, became an effective communicator; Stevie Wonder, and Ray Charles who were unable to see the beauty of the universe in which they lived yet used their musical ability to stir our emotions, fashioned their own beauty from the depths of the soul, and changed the face of American music. Then there are the George Washington Carvers, Madame C. J. Walkers, and John Johnsons who on the springboard of faith, strong will, and determination surmounted the wall of racial discrimination to grasp their piece of the American Dream and, in the process, impact the American economy.

I am reminded of my first day of teaching African American history. The students were all African-American, sophomores, juniors, and seniors. When they were given the syllabus, there was mass indignation over the requirement to read one novel each semester in addition to weekly journal reports from major African American publications. The general response was that this was not an honors level class; therefore, my expectations were too high. It occurred to me that these students were indeed sincere in their protestations, as few of their teachers had set such high expectations for "below average and average" students.

Indeed, it was their belief that they were not capable of meeting my demands. I also realized the challenge that lay before me. My first goal was to get these students to believe in their own ability. My first question to the class was, What makes you think you can't do this? Since they were unable to give me a reasonable answer, I set about detailing how we were going to accomplish our goal.

I found that many of my students were not in the habit of reading, and others had reading problems. I started first by selecting novels that complemented the curriculum and dealt with issues of concern and interest to students. The purpose of using novels was to stimulate discussion, critical thinking skills, and independent thought. Students were given daily reading assignments from the novel. At the end of each week, they formed a circle to do oral reading from the assigned chapters. I asked students to volunteer who felt they could read the parts dramatically and could make us believe the character. Others were asked to provide sound effects or read the narrative portions of the text. To my delight, the students came to look forward to this weekly activity. This activity provided recognition for those students with special skills and talents, while assisting those students with reading problems by having the material read aloud. For the latter group, with good listening skills they could successfully pass the unit on the novel. The dramatization also tended to enhance their memory of sequence of events and content in general. In fact, many students shared with me that their parents were reading the novel along with them.

PARENTS

Provide a Nurturing Environment

There is much that parents can do to motivate students to achieve academic success. T. D. Jakes (1994) proclaimed the process begins with parents, and the foundation must be laid early in the child's life. According to Jakes, "Nurturing is the investment necessary to stimulate the potential that we possess" (p. 39). He ventures into the very core of this basic concept, contending, that "There is a difference in the emotional make-up of a child who has had a substantial deposit of affection and affirmation. Great affirmation occurs when someone invests in our personhood" (p. 40). Ironically, the process can be virtually effortless. At its most fundamental level, it begins with parents modelling the behaviors necessary for success, clearly articulating their expectations and providing students with the requisite encouragement, guidance, and support to set and achieve goals. Parents instill in their children a sense of self-worth, and students who feel good about themselves and have their self-worth validated are primed for success. Nurturing parents also assist their children in setting realistic goals. Goals are the pathway to the future. We can allow the nuances of life to distract us, or we can keep our goals in full view and be as a moth instinctively drawn to the light.

Encourage Children to Explore to Discover Their "Gift"

In the previous section I discussed "gifts." We each have a special talent, skill, or gift. Parents are the first resource for assisting children in discovering their "gift." One of the ways in which parents can do this is to provide the child with numerous opportunities to explore varied activities—trips to the museum; travel; participation in scouting, athletic, music, dance, art, and drama programs. Many park districts and community colleges offer weekend programs for children in activities ranging from the cultural and martial arts to computers. All of these activities provide opportunities for assisting children in finding their niche. Students become self-motivated when presented with tasks they enjoy and have a strong interest in.

Provide Positive Reinforcement

Another way in which parents can motivate students is to offer praise. Watch the expression on a child's face upon receiving recognition for a job well done. Any behavior that brings pleasure is most likely to be repeated, as is most behavior that is positively reinforced.

Provide Support

Students are motivated to achieve when they feel secure that their parents are behind them. Parents must encourage exploration, but at the same time they must make themselves available as a safety net. Taking risks is not as ominous when the children feel that if they do not succeed they are not risking the loss of love or approval of their parents.

Model Behavior Conducive to Success

Perhaps the most effective way in which parents can motivate children to succeed is to hold themselves up as exemplars of the types of behaviors that sets one squarely on the path to success. Research has shown a correlation between academic success and the amount of literary materials in the home. Children who are read to at an early age acquire an appreciation for the written word. Clearly, students who see parents reading on a daily basis will not come to view reading as aberrant behavior (Shields, 1996). Similarly, parents who set goals, organize their time, demonstrate delayed gratification, perseverance, and commitment with each act teach their children valuable lessons for garnering success.

Take an Active Interest in the Child's Activities

Parents can do much to motivate students to succeed by becoming active participants in the activities they enjoy. In so doing, parents validate the worth and importance of the activity and strengthen the bond between parent and child. Most educators would concur that there is a positive correlation between students who are successful in school and the level of involvement of parents in their education. These are the parents who serve as room mothers, volunteer to serve on various school committees, raise funds, chaperone field trips, and attend various school activities and programs.

Clearly Articulate Expectations

Parents can also motivate students to succeed by clearly articulating their expectations in regard to academic performance. As parents and educators, we set the ceiling for academic success. Taking into consideration their optimal ability, students will perform up to our level of expectation. If the ceiling is low, so will be the level of performance. If the ceiling is high, so will be the level of performance. Students tend to gauge their assessments of their ability on our expectations and where we set the ceiling.

MOTIVATING THE UNMOTIVATED PARENT

In varying degrees, schools must tackle the issue of multiple failures, that is, students who fail more than one course. What is most discouraging is the number of parents who do not contact the school seeking answers. Failure of parents to consult with school officials regarding such issues can send conflicting messages to the students—among them are parental apathy and a low priority for education, both of which can erode the student's sense of commitment, self-worth, and motivation.

Schools must seek ways to figure parents into the equation for academic success. Many, however, are frustrated in their efforts to do so. In some communities, parental involvement remains problematic. Among the solutions are sponsoring workshops for parents of students with multiple failures consisting of helping parents to identify the signs of impending trouble; noting available resources within the school and community that they may consult for assistance; providing information on study skills; assisting parents in developing the necessary skills to help students academically and emotionally. The "draw" may be offering students some type of incentive if they bring a parent to a workshop or structuring experiences where parents can learn while learning how to assist their children. The underlying philosophy of Dr. Ruth Sun's book, *The Family Math Companion* (1996), is that students most often fail mathematics because of lack of mastery of the fundamental concepts. As they are passed from grade to grade, they fall further and further behind. It is her contention that one way to stop the cycle of failure is to involve parents by providing them with the skills necessary to work with their child to achieve academic success. Dr. Sun, through church and community contacts, has organized study groups in churches or at homes in the community where she teaches these skills. Other innovative programs, particularly at the elementary school level, encourage parents to attend school with their children. In the process, they can assist with more individualized instruction and learn skills that carry over outside of the classroom to assist their children in meeting learning objectives.

STUDENTS

I have often told my students no one has greater control over you than you. You may not always be able to control the forces that impact your life, but you can control how you choose to respond. To paraphrase an African proverb, it is not what you are called but what you answer to that matters. Students must be sensitized to the power within to fashion their own success. Coming to this realization is greatly enhanced by the support of some significant and caring other.

Student motivation is predicated on the existence of the following conditions:

Students Must Possess a Clear Sense of Purpose

In order for students to be motivated, they must possess a clear sense of purpose. In other words, they must have a clearly defined goal. Achieving the goal must satisfy an emotional, spiritual, or physical need.

Students will be motivated to learn if they feel that achieving the goal will bring about a desired end. Too often, in communities where few role models exist to attest to the value of education in improving one's lifestyle or life chances, students fail to see the value of education and are therefore not motivated to strive for academic success. They must be able to see the horizon. Submission and apathy evolve in the absence of hope. All, however, is not lost for children who have inherited social conditions that shroud their view of the future. Sometimes the bridge between "I can't" and "I can" is someone in the middle extending a helping hand.

Students Must Feel That They Are Capable of Reaching the Goal

Behavior is purposeful. We act for a reason. It is also important to note that no action is action. It sends a message of apathy, emotional or physical inability, or some other variable that is blocking involvement in an activity. Rational beings do not persistent in activity for which they cannot envision success or after repeated efforts fail to achieve success.

Most educators will concur that successful students in general have a parent, parents, mentor, or some significant other who provides them with emotional support. These individuals serve as a safety net of sorts that enables students to take risks, test the unchartered waters of intellectual curiosity or physical prowess, experiment, and explore their interests.

Educators must again weigh their expectations of students against the extant reality. How many of us would diligently work toward a goal that we felt we had little or no chance of achieving? This is precisely what happens when educators fail to attune themselves to the affective side of teaching. In this vein it is imperative that teachers know their students well. Particularly for the student who is burdened with flagging self-confidence, encouragement is necessary to make that student feel that he/she is capable of achieving goals. Similarly, for the student who has historically had limited success in the classroom, building self-esteem is an essential prerequisite to academic success. I am reminded of a motivational poster that states, "It is not your aptitude but your attitude that determines your altitude." The bottom line is clear: Attitude is half the battle in achieving success. The right attitude can elevate an individual to unimaginable heights. Support and encouragement can change attitudes. Teachers can accomplish this in a number of ways. They can allow students to showcase their talents or strengths; they can foster a sense of community in the classroom; they can structure learning activities in ways that ensure success. The important thing is to focus on students' strengths and interests to build positive attitudes relative to their ability.

Students Must Perceive the Goal as Beneficial and Feel a Connection with the Teacher

William Glasser (1990) makes the point that when we say we want to motivate someone to do something, what we really mean is we want to try to get them to do something that we want them to do. He further contends that motivation comes from within, that is, it is intrinsic. Ultimately, unless the action has meaning for or is perceived as beneficial to the student, attempts by others to get that student to respond in certain ways will be ineffective.

Glasser identified two types of managers—boss-managers and lead-managers. Boss-managers operate on the premise that individuals can be motivated from the outside. When teacher boss-managers lament that students lack motivation, what they are actually saying is they don't know how to get students to work. According to Glasser, the boss-manager's lack of success and continued failure is driven by his/her adherence to management strategies grounded in stimulus-response theory. Stimulus-response theory holds that when subjects are rewarded for responding in the desired manner over a number of trials, they will repeat the behavior. Conversely, punishment for responding with undesired behavior should eradicate the behavior. Glasser, however, rejects this position. To support his stance, he refers to the high rate of recidivism among prisoners, for example. Within the context of education, a teacher's threat of punishment does not always result in conformity.

Glasser's control theory offers another perspective on student motivation. His theory is that individuals will do as they are asked only when they believe the request will benefit them and they care about the individual making the request. For example, a teacher asks students to stop talking and they continue. The teacher threatens to give after-school detentions, and some students still continue to talk. Conversely, if the teacher tells the students, for example, that he/she would like to start a discussion of sample questions for the exam required of all seniors before they can graduate, students immediately settle down. Glasser points out that it is not the reward per se but the value the student or individual attaches to the reward.

Control theory asserts that coercion is ineffective in motivating individuals to do what we want them to do. According to Glasser, "Boss-managers can count on coercion to achieve only the simplest tasks. Resentful workers will not do anything well that is the least bit complicated." He continues, asserting that "Effective lead-managers never use coercive messages. Instead, they try to give the worker the kind of information that will persuade them to do as they are directed because it is as much or more to their benefit as it is to the manager" (pp. 41-42). He observed that when the worker feels a connection with or cares about the manager, motivation is less problematic. We all tend to want to please or cooperate with the people we care about.

In my own practice, there was the issue of finding an alternative to out-of-school suspensions for certain rule infractions. We found that less stringent forms of punishment such as after-school detentions worked for a while but soon showed signs of being ineffective. Some thought was given to considering those things that teenagers valued most and using them as leverage in getting students to follow the rules. Many students with chronic behavior problems welcome being suspended. With parents most likely away at work, this was an opportunity to sleep in, watch TV and perhaps have friends over. We came to the conclusion that the one thing teens valued most about school was the opportunity to socialize with their peers. Consequently, in-school suspensions evolved. These students came to school but had to report to a room where they remained for the day and had to complete assignments given by their classroom teachers. For most students, this was a very effective deterrent. Similarly, in trying to encourage students to carry their student I.D.'s, we once again found that for many students, after-school detentions were ineffective. Once again, we looked at the kinds of things students valued around the school and required an I.D. to access that which was valued. For example, students without an I.D. were served lunch last, and an I.D. was required to go to the library during study-hall, to use the computer for recreational purposes, to ride the school bus, etc.

In the classroom setting, educators are challenged to make students feel learning is beneficial. This may be accomplished by the use of various instructional strategies that promote and satisfy curiosity, the need for enjoyment, freedom to make choices, opportunity for students to express themselves in ways that reflect their talents, and opportunity to share in decision-making. The list is endless. It is within this context that what we know about multiple intelligences, learning styles, and the use of technology in the classroom acquires significance.

Students Must Have a Clear Sense of Being Supported in Their Efforts

The feeling of being supported validates ones sense of purpose. It encourages exploration without fear of failure and enhances perseverance. Encouragement is the driving force that enables us to stay the course when negative forces threaten to distract or obscure our goal. Sometimes, before we can believe in ourselves, we must feel others believe in us.

Student Must Conquer Their Fear of Failure

There is a proverb that states the journey of a thousand miles begins with the first step. Fear is a great inhibitor. Its vestiges can be seen in the very early stages of life when one observes the hesitancy of an infants as they take that first step. Instinctively, they cling to or venture not far from the security of some object to catch their fall. However, they too learn that success is built on a foundation of failed attempts and repeated trials. Ironically, the positive face of failure is reflected in the mirror of lessons learned. It is through our failures that we learn what not to do, what doesn't work. It is through this process of elimination that we discover our own truths, skills, and talents. The greatest challenge for the educator is to assist students in conquering their fears and set them squarely upon the path to academic achievement.

I am reminded of a student with an outstanding academic record who decided against enrolling in medical school. The student's parents felt that it was her fear of not being able to maintain her stellar academic record given the rigors of medical school that prompted her decision to change career paths.

The Student Must Conquer Their Fear of the Unknown

Few individuals are born gamblers. Most of us find ultimate emotional comfort in being able to predict with reasonable assurance the outcome of our actions or circumstance. Ironically, some students fear success (Tresemer, 1977). This may be attributed in part to concern about how it will impact their position among their peers. For adolescents, a sense of belonging to the peer group is a very strong emotional need. Fear of losing one's status or place within the group, anxiety over how change will impact the way their peers perceive them, or even how they perceive themselves can stifle positive change and motivation. The challenge for the educator is to assist students in formulating a view of the future. They must help students understand that there can be no progress without change. Change often involves venturing into new territory. In order to grow, we must leave the place where we are.

This precept may account for a phenomenon that in my experiences and those of many of my colleagues who are counselors have observed among a significant number of seniors. The anxiety level of many high school seniors is elevated as graduation approaches. There may be some trepidation about leaving the safe and familiar environs of home and school. This is a life transition that dictates increased independence. The safety net of parents who bear the burden of decision making and the school whose structure enables us to accurately predict what will happen next provide a comfort zone, the value of which suddenly comes into clear focus as we stand on the cusp of this life transition.

Student Must Accept That Rewards in Life for Their Effort Are Not   Always Immediate

We live in a heuristic society. Not only do we seek that which brings physical or emotional pleasure, we seek immediate gratification.   The impetuousness of youth seemingly predisposes them to pursue with a vengeance those activities that bring immediate gratification. Unfortunately, the rewards of education are often longterm. The characteristic features of its many possibilities do not come into sharp focus until we reach the climax of our education. The master teacher consistently holds the future in clear view for students to serve as a point of reference along the path to academic success. In doing so, they keep the purpose of education in focus.

Teachers today have a formidable challenge before them, as they seek to maintain the interest of students nourished by a steady diet of Sesame Street and MTV. Consequently, many students enter academia expecting to be entertained. Master teachers successfully meet the challenge by embarking on a steady and persistent search for innovative techniques to spark and maintain student interest in learning. They accomplish this by networking with their colleagues, attending workshops, and giving students a greater role in determining what and how material is delivered. These teachers cast themselves in the role as facilitators and not dictators of learning (Campbell, 1972). While the skeptic may scoff at allowing students a greater role in determining what and how material is taught, the realist understands the odds they struggle against and develop techniques that will enable them to meet educational objectives while giving students a greater voice. They are able to take traditional goals and objectives and wrap them in a more appealing package. By manipulating the variables to discover answers to questions, they allow students to learn by doing. Experience is the best teacher. The constructivist approach, with an emphasis on information learned by doing, leaves a deeper intellectual and longer lasting impression (McBrien & Brandt, 1997).

Students Must Accept That the Pavement on the Road to Success Is Not Always Smooth

The road and surrounding landscape may be scattered with obstacles that obstruct our view, slow our progress, or in general temporarily place the goal just beyond our reach. Such disappointments or frustrations sometimes form the cornerstones of life, providing experiences conducive to personal growth. Such experiences may inspire introspection or, at the very least, cause us to pause and take stock of our circumstance and reflect on a course of action. It is at this point that encouragement from teachers, parents or significant others in the lives of students becomes the pivotal point, setting students on the course to success or failure. Those who impact the lives of students should not underestimate the power of a word of encouragement, pep talk, or arm around the shoulder. Sometimes the difference between "I can't" and "I can" is a positive attitude girded by another's belief in us. We are as we believe. Educators must recognize that preparing students for the future extends beyond traditional pedagogy. It also encompasses teaching lessons about life grounded in the interpersonal relationships between teacher and student.

Students Must Be Provided an Environment in Which They Are Not Afraid to Take Academic Risks

Students must be made to feel that their attempts to reach learning goals and objectives will not be met with humiliation or ridicule by the teacher or their classmates. The message must be conveyed that failure is sometimes part of the learning experience. It is only when we get an answer marked incorrect on a test that we know it is incorrect and search for the correct answer. Otherwise, we would continue down the wrong path. In this regard, immediate feedback is an important tool in learning. It limits frustration and promotes continued effort.

In classrooms where teachers have been successful in establishing a sense of community, where students are encouraged to work together cooperatively and support each other's efforts, the fear of taking academic risks is attenuated. Teachers must engender the attitude that one person's lack of success reflects upon the entire group and that efforts to assist the individual better the group. Students are more motivated to learn when they are assured of support not only from the teacher but their peers.

Students Must Be Able to Relate Present Effort to Future Goals

Educators sometimes fail to examine the reasonableness of their expectations of students. In the adult world, we have come to realize that certain things must be done irrespective of our desire or personal preference. We must work to make a living for ourselves. We must accept responsibility for our children, parents, and property. We take additional courses to increase our marketability or to move up on the pay scale. As adults, while we might dread the additional demands on our financial resources and the time required to meet these objectives, we nevertheless can envision what lies beyond the horizon. It is this view of the future that motivates us to stay on course.

Conversely, the vision of youth is often shortsighted. Students often operate emotionally and intellectually in the here and now. The challenge for the educator is to continually connect the present to the future. Students must be able to relate to the long-term benefits of learning objectives. The new brand of textbooks is meeting this need. Math textbooks, for example, are now placing more emphasis on word problems relative to actual experiences. Math problems are contextualized to reflect real-life usage. In this manner, students come to understand the purpose of studying math and to practice how to incorporate it into their own lives.

COMMUNITY

An African adage tells us that, it takes a village to raise a child. The veracity of this adage has withstood the test of time and transcends cultural distinctions. Unequivocally, children benefit from a unified support network. Consequently, let's direct the discourse to an exploration of the role of the community in motivating students to achieve. Driven by a sense of social obligation, commitment, and realization that to invest in children is to invest in our own future, there are a number of ways in which the larger community can impact student success. Among them:

Sponsoring Mentoring Programs

Particularly for students in geographical areas where there tends to be a deficit of positive role models to emulate, mentors can provide a glimpse of the possibilities. Within this social context, mentors who hail from backgrounds similar to most of the students with whom they are working acquire greater credibility, for they serve as living proof that it is possible to elevate oneself above extant circumstances. Most important, through relating personal experiences with which students can identify, they are in the unique position of being able to provide students with concrete measures they can take to change the course of their lives. True mentoring entails establishing a relationship with students, promoting trust, guidance, direction, and exposure to the possibilities.

Providing Work Opportunities for Students

Providing opportunities for students to apply what is learned in school to the world of work strengthens the cognitive connection between the purpose of education and future goals. Businesses that are able to closely match student skills and knowledge to their function greatly enhance this connection. Students who are afforded opportunities to experience firsthand the usefulness of what is learned in school are motivated to continue to achieve, as the work experience validates learning. Furthermore, the work experience enables students to assess their knowledge and skill level in relation to the demands of the job. The outcome can influence their decision to continue along a career path, change paths, or enhance their skills and knowledge. Many schools have formalized work-study programs whose purpose is to bridge the gap between learning and the world or work.

Sharing Knowledge

Much of the learning that takes place in school is detached from practical application. Consequently, students aren't motivated because they cannot make a connection between what is being learned and its usefulness. One way to bridge the gap is to invite professionals into the classroom. For example, teachers can invite a physical therapist as a guest lecturer in a physical anatomy class or an ophthalmologist or optometrist to a biology class to discuss the human eye. This can be accomplished in any discipline. The underlying principle is to bring practitioners into the classroom who can relate personal experiences to demonstrate the application of knowledge.

Providing Incentives

Some communities with a strong economic base anchored by industry or major retailers have initiated partnerships with local schools. They frequently take the form of Adopt-A-School. Such programs may consist of providing incentives for students for academic achievement, attendance, behavior, etc. They may provide discount coupons, free stereo systems, bikes, movie tickets, etc. In other instances, they may donate needed equipment or lend employees for special projects. In general, they provide additional resources for rewarding students for exemplary behavior and accomplishments.

Supporting Existing Programs

Some schools form intergovernmental agreements with local park districts. Such agreements culminate in a win-win situation for both parties. Park districts that are strapped for space, in exchange for use of school facilities, offer the school certain services such as maintaining the baseball field, purchasing equipment, etc. Many park district programs cater to students from the local school as well as the larger community. In effect, they expand opportunities for participation for students who are not a part of organized school programs, for whatever reason. Some park districts hire older high school students to staff their after-school programs as well.

Establishing Youth Councils

Many communities have established youth councils. The purpose is to give adolescents a forum from which to express their concerns about a wide range of issues that impact them directly. They may discuss such issues as gang violence, the need for recreational programs, or curfew. In effect, they give students a sense of empowerment at the community level. Student involvement will increase if students feel their opinions matter and their voices are being heard. In the process, they learn much about governmental processes, negotiating ones position, organization, planning, and clearly articulating ideas. The list is virtually endless.

Most successful individuals have had the good fortune to have the support and encouragement of significant others who believed in who they are, validated their self-worth, and cultivated their "gifts." Few achieve success without having walked in the shadow of others who either paved the way for them by their example or labored to build bridges to the future for them. All who touch the lives of children have a responsibility to provide the necessary emotional, social, and intellectual environments in which their potential can take root and grow. To do less than this is to turn our backs on the future.

Chapter 4

Teacher Attitude

Teaching is a profession in which so much emphasis is placed on the acquisition of technical and cognitive skills required for certification that we sometimes underestimate the affective aspect of human behavior and the role it plays in the efficacy of our practice.

If teachers believe that students are incapable of learning, this often becomes a self-fulfilling prophecy. The danger of this type of thinking is that teachers may cease to attempt to challenge students, and students, sensing the teacher's attitude, internalize the negative assessment (Rosenthal & Jacobson, 1968). Additionally, teachers may not aggressively seek ways to meet the needs of students by investigating new teaching strategies, resource materials, or other innovative methods. Once again, the tendency is to blame the student.

When students fail to achieve, the teacher's need for success is not met. This breeds frustration that may in ways explicit or implicit impact students, and the vicious cycle continues. Consequently, some student behavior problems and lack of achievement may be a manifestation of both the student's and the teacher's frustration.

The more effectively teachers can connect with their students, the greater their impact on learning. To teach students one has to be able to reach them first. The successful veteran teacher is cognizant of the importance of building a strong foundation of trust, mutual respect, and sense of community as a prerequisite to learning and effective classroom management. Particularly in schools with large minority populations, staffed by teachers from the dominant culture, the time and effort expended in creating this kind of environment can greatly impact the degree of learning that takes place (Denbo, 1986).

BUILDING BLOCKS TO SUCCESS IN THE CLASSROOM

For teachers to be successful in the classroom, in addition to attitudinal variables, it is necessary to structure a classroom environment in which students feel comfortable emotionally, physically, and intellectually. This sets the stage for learning on a daily basis. Some of the things teachers can do in establishing this kind of environment are:

Build Relationships

Students are more receptive to learning when there is the feeling of personal investment in them. Relationships enhance interpersonal communications. They give us a knowledge base that defines the nature of our interactions with each other. They create a level of comfort that breaks down barriers to sharing information. When teachers build relationships with their students, they build trust.

An indication of a teacher's efforts to build relationships with his or her students is manifested in any number of seemingly innocuous behaviors such as physical proximity, active listening, patience, cognizance of changes in behavior, offering assistance, advocacy, engaging in appropriate social as well as professional interactions with students, and setting limits. Veteran administrators look for these traits in assessing teacher effectiveness, realizing its importance in the educational process.

Teachers who are in touch with their students do not place social or physical distance between themselves and their students. Upon entering their classroom, one would have to look around the room to find the teacher, as they generally move about the room and rarely spend long periods of time at the front of the room lecturing or at their desk. When dealing with students regarding more personal issues, these teachers will place an arm around the shoulder as a gesture of concern or empathy. They allow students to express themselves without interruption and then paraphrase to establish the accuracy of their interpretation of what was said and proceed from there. Teachers who are in touch with their students are very cognizant of changes in student behavior and will pull the student aside to talk and offer assistance or make the appropriate referral to support staff if necessary. They take time just to talk with students about nonacademic matters such as their interests, etc.

One is not to assume that building relationships blurs the boundaries that separate the roles of teacher and student. In fact, some educators may feel that this is exactly what may happen. However, veteran teachers understand the need to set limits and where to establish the boundary of interpersonal relationships with students so as not to compromise the integrity of their role as teachers.

Establish a Sense of Community in the Classroom

When students are encouraged to work for the common good, the substance of conflictual situations is greatly dissipated. When they come to understand that their actions affect the well-being of the group, they will typically respond and react in ways that contribute to the success of the group, or if they fail to reach such an understanding, group pressure evolves as an effective means of encouraging consensus or cooperation (Stevenson & Stigler, 1992; Ladson-Billings, 1994). A sense of community is conducive to cooperation and the development of genuine concern for others members of the group. It encourages the perception of the individual as being only a part of a whole that in and of itself cannot function to achieve a common goal. All the parts must work together to achieve success.

Teachers can begin to establish this sense of community by teaching self-respect and respect for the rights and opinions of others. For example, in such classrooms, students are not allowed to make negative statements about each other; they are encouraged to accentuate the positive in all of their and the group's endeavors; they are taught to be accountable and to evaluate their own performance; they are taught the difference between criticism and objective evaluation and most important, they are taught to be supportive of each individual's effort and to offer assistance when shortcomings are noted. Where there is a true sense of community in the classroom, students feel that the failure of the individual is commensurate to the failure of the group—that is, when one fails, we all have failed.

Building a sense of community in the classroom is not an easy task, for it represents the very antithesis of the ideology that drives the dynamic of what normally occurs in U.S. classrooms. In American classrooms, students are typically taught to work independently, and we use competition to encourage excellence. In so doing, we pit students against each other. To build a sense of community requires a mental paradigm shift for teachers and students, where less emphasis is placed on competition and more on cooperative effort to reach goals and achieve excellence. In effect, competitive individualism and a sense of community are diametrically opposed ideologies. There can be no true sense of community in social systems where competition is encouraged and the battle cry, to the victor belong the spoils. This is not the case in some non-Western cultures where the concept of self holds a totally different meaning. Ladson-Billings (1994) explains that in such cultures, "Self comes into being as a consequence of the group's being. The African world view suggests that I am because we are and because we are, I am" (p. 69). The logic of this position affirms no real distinction between the self and the group. "One's self identity is therefore always a people identity, or what could be called an extended self." (p.69) In these cultures, self comes to be as a consequence of the group's being.

In my own practice, during a teacher observation I had occasion to observe firsthand a classroom activity that exemplified building a sense of community among students. Students were assigned to work in groups. The class was studying biomes. Each group was to prepare a presentation on a specific biome. The assignment actually consisted of three parts: a group presentation, the creation of a brochure about their biome, and a poster illustrating the biome. Every member of the group had to participate in the oral presentation. This activity held merit for a number of reasons. It allowed students to present in ways that best fit their primary intelligences (Gardner, 1983), and it encouraged cooperation as each student could make a contribution by doing what he or she did best. The fact that everyone had to contribute to the oral presentation made each student accountable to the group (Johnson & Johnson, 1993). Another unique aspect of this assignment was that each student in class was provided an evaluation sheet that indicated the evaluation criterion. The group presenting was issued the same evaluation form but in a different color. Using the criterion, students were asked to evaluate each group presentation, and the presenting group was asked to evaluate themselves. By giving the students a grading criterion, the teacher was able to assist students in making the distinction between negative criticism and personal judgments and objective evaluation. This provides each student with valuable input to improve rather than tear each other down. Support came in other ways as well, such as applause, a show of enthusiasm, and active participation of the class. Students were specifically asked to comment on the things they liked best about each presentation and what each group did particularly well. After completing the evaluation forms, students discussed the rationale behind their assessment. The criterion was structured so that students would probably do extremely well on some part of the activity. Having the criterion in advance allowed group members to check each person's contribution to ensure that all of the criteria were met.

This activity was obviously highly motivating. It gave students ownership by allowing them to make choices about what biomes to study and how they could present it. Everyone had the opportunity to succeed because they were allowed to express themselves in ways that best fit their learning style and primary intelligence, while giving expression to their ideas. Clearly, this was an assignment where one individual could not carry the load and the group achieve its goal. The range of formats students used to make their presentations was impressive. This is just one example of how teachers can use classroom activities to encourage a sense of community.

Set High Expectations

For the most part, students will perform up to the level of expectation teachers set for them. The teacher determines the ceiling for learning. This was clearly illustrated in the Rosenthal study on the self-fulfilling prophecy (Rosenthal & Jacobson, 1968; Rosenthal, 1973). A self-fulfilling prophecy is a prediction that influences the course of events toward fulfilling the prediction.

One hundred U.S. Air Force Academy Preparatory School airmen were randomly assigned to five math classes. When teachers were told the students assigned to their class were high achievers, they treated them accordingly, and student performance was commensurate with the expectation. Conversely, when teachers were told the students assigned to their class were low achievers, they treated them as such and once again, student performance was commensurate with the level of expectation set (Rosenthal, 1973).

This replication of an earlier study suggests that teachers send subliminal messages to students via tone of voice, body language, and the offering of encouragement or criticism that affect student performance. The Rosenthal study clearly illustrates the power of perception. High ability students performed at a lower level when teachers were told they were low ability students and vice versa (Rosenthal, 1973).

This study has significant implications for the variety of interactions that take place in the average classroom. For example, a student who has been labelled a disciplinary problem in one teacher's classroom may be perceived as such by other teachers who have had no prior personal experience with the student. A student whose reputation precedes him/her may find themselves assigned a front row seat, have his/her actions misinterpreted or questioned. Teachers may be unconsciously less tolerant and patient in dealing with students that have been so labelled. Sometimes, such students live up to their reputation, because they feel it is expected. In other instances, because they sense the teacher is less tolerant, patient, or in general vary drastically in their affective response to them, these students may act out as a personal vendetta or as a result of their frustration and resentment of being singled out.

We can carry this discourse a bit further when it is placed in the context of race relations. Teachers must consciously guard against internalizing stereotypical perceptions of various ethnic groups. Such thinking can likewise direct the nature of interaction and expectations the teacher holds for certain ethnic groups (Kuykendall, 1992). Some examples of these stereotypes might be, accepting such ethnic stereotypes as Asian students are good in math and science and are quiet and obedient; African American students do not perform well in math and science and are hyperactive; or American Indian students are not very competitive. In fact, for all ethnic groups there is a range of behaviors and abilities, and very often in comparing groups environmental variables are not factored in.

Good (1981) found that teachers convey their expectations of students they perceive as underachievers in the following ways:

Offering praise that is not genuine
Providing less feedback
Expecting less effort
Interrupting them more often

Creating greater physical distance between student and teacher
Providing less personal attention

Capitalize on Student Strengths

Master teachers operate from a position in which they accentuate the positive and capitalize on each student's strengths. In doing so, they increase opportunities for students to achieve success. Such teachers tend to correct mistakes, behavioral or academic, without compromising the student's self-esteem. Once the teacher accepts that every student has the potential to excel in something, is successful in discovering what that something is, and provides opportunities for them to use their individual "gifts," the stage is set for meaningful and active learning. The student who shows artistic talent can be asked to design a monthly bulletin that reflects a teaching unit or design and work on a hall mural after school; students who possess a strong command of the language can be asked to read the announcements over the PA system or to serve as mistress/master of ceremony at a school assembly. The list is endless of the various ways in which schools can capitalize on the strengths of students in the classroom and the larger school setting. These opportunities make students feel good about themselves, and when they feel good about themselves their interactions with others will be more positive. Similarly, such activities give students a sense of ownership in the school and their education. This sense of ownership can have some surprising consequences.

In one school, a fairly isolated area of the building was the frequent target for graffiti. To solve the problem, a display case with plexiglass was designed and student artwork was displayed. Needless to say, this solved the problem. This measure personalized the problem. It involved that which belonged to students or their friends.

Make Learning Relevant

Not only is the intellectual comfort level enhanced but also the enthusiasm for learning, when learning is relevant to students' lives and experiences. Relevancy gives purpose and direction to learning. Learning acquires more intense meaning when students can envision its applicability. It answers the perennial question, Why do I have to know this? It generates more intense interest as it provides a foundation of familiarity upon which to build. It is a starting or reference point from which students can begin to formulate and engage in more complex thinking. Teachers who conscientiously strive to make learning relevant for their students bring the unknown or the unexplored into the realm of possibility.

Other researchers have affirmed the significance of making learning culturally relevant. Cheyney, Fine & Ravitch (1987) found that for students in schools where they were not exposed to or taught a knowledge of their history, prospects for realizing their full potential were greatly diminished.

Teacher as a Facilitator

Many students are turned off to learning because traditional educational philosophy and learning environments support teacher-centered instruction. Consequently, students are cast in the role of bystanders to their own learning. They stand on the outside looking in rather than on the inside looking out. Teacher-centered learning environments stifle creativity and critical thinking, as students are told what to think or given information rather than engaging in inquiry and discovery. Lessons that are learned from experience or from the opportunity to physically or intellectually manipulate data is more easily synthesized and results in long-term retention. In some institutions of learning more emphasis is being placed on developing student-centered learning environments in which students are required to take more responsibility for their learning, and the role of the teacher is to assist them in the process. For many veteran teachers, this role reversal is difficult. Breaking with tradition, and the mind-set that drives it, is a challenge for teachers and administrators. Consequently, staff development is needed to help change perceptions and clear the path for exploring new teaching methodologies in addition to teaching teachers the necessary skills to be effective facilitators for student learning and to feel comfortable in this new role.

Engaging Activities

Learning occurs when there is student interest. The challenge for teachers is to find activities that pique student interest. These are the types of activities that keep them focused and involved in their own learning. Finding the right activities may be a matter of trial and error or simply networking with colleagues. Students tend to be very amenable to activities that mimic the format of their own interests such as computer games, game shows like Jeopardy, and Wheel of Fortune or table games such as Monopoly or Bingo. Students enjoy interactive activities that allow them to engage in exchanges with their classmates. This format holds the added merit of allowing students to adapt the game to the discipline or subject matter—that is, to formulate the questions to be asked and to select players (contestants), moderator, scorekeeper, announcer etc. Popular game show formats are particularly applicable to such subjects as science, social studies, English, foreign language, and math. In some disciplines, labs generate the same type of interest and enthusiasm. The most popular science teachers are those who are adept at illustrating scientific principles through experimentation and showing how they relate to everyday lives.

Discipline, Set Limits

As much as students may decry the imposition of rules and consequences, there is an underlying desire for structure and boundaries. All students deserve the right to learn in an orderly environment. Errant students do not have the right to deprive those who want to learn from doing so. The challenge for the teacher is to establish equilibrium between structure and flexibility, establishing boundaries that allow room for students to express themselves without sacrificing order and stability. This requires skill. The novice teacher sometimes lose control of the class because of a lack of skill in this area, setting boundaries that are so expansive that he or she is unable to effectively manage and monitor behavior and learning.

Too much structure can adversely affect social interaction and stifle both creativity and intellectual curiosity. The key is to strike a balance. However, structure gives students a sense of comfort in knowing what to expect and assists them in developing self-discipline. As self-discipline increases, the boundaries can be expanded. Students can be given the privilege to opt to go to the library to do research rather than remain in class to review material they have already mastered or to work in groups to discuss issues, etc. An orderly environment is an essential element in student learning and achievement. Little learning takes place in classrooms where more time and energy is expended in maintaining order than in instruction.

Teacher Attitude

You reap what you sow is an old adage whose relevancy has remained current for centuries. Teachers are not exempt. The nature of the dynamic of social interaction in the classroom is driven by the attitude of the teacher. Teachers set the tone for what transpires in the classroom. If teachers lack enthusiasm, students will be equally unenthusiastic. If teachers are sarcastic students will respond in kind. In general, teachers who are enthusiastic about teaching, personable, and caring will, by their example, encourage the same traits in their students. Teachers with positive attitudes make a concerted effort to create a positive learning environment for their students. This attitude is reflected in many seemingly innocuous ways such as displaying work, motivational posters, and seasonal bulletin boards; using bright cheery colors; playing music as students enter or leave the room (quantum learning strategies); assigning students special tasks to perform on a rotating basis (encouraging ownership). Additionally, the way the teacher dresses says something to students about how the teacher feels about them. Teachers who come to class well-groomed and appropriately dressed send the subliminal message to students: you matter and I care about the impression you have of me (Kukenydall, 1992).

Cultural Sensitivity

There is often a hidden dynamic played out in the interaction between minority students and teachers that represents the dominant culture. Minority students' perceptions are often based on the experiences of their ethnic group within the larger culture. To the degree that their ethnic group feels alienated or marginalized in the dominant culture, this may be carried over into the classroom. These are issues teachers must acknowledge and deal with to effectively teach. These students are often very affective. Kuykendall (1992) points out that black youth are particularly proficient in nonverbal communication with a heightened sensitivity to perceived teacher bias. Others have also noted the powerful impact of nonverbal communication in defining interpersonal interaction and relationships. Weinberg and Catero (1971) conducted an intensive study of communication and found that communication takes in everything about the person. It is total person to total person. They further observed that 7 percent of communication is through words, and 38 percent nonverbal, conveyed through such behaviors as eye contact, body language, and posture.

Minority students glean as much from the attitude of teachers as from what they actually say or do in the classroom. They are sensitive to any perceived social distance the teacher places between them. They tend to be able to sense if the teacher has set low expectations for them based on stereotypes (Coleman, 1996). I am reminded in my own practice of an incident in which a colleague expressed being uncomfortable working with a group of low-level minority students. He was to be commended for openly admitting feelings which many others may harbor yet not express for fear of being labelled racist. His motive, however, was driven by a desire to meet the needs of all of his students. He maintained that he usually taught from the front of the room and rarely intermingled with the students. To increase his level of comfort, it was suggested that as, this was a small class, he should have the students sit in a circle of which he was a part.

Further support for teachers being in touch with their students, acquiring a knowledge of and respect for their culture, involved a student who was referred to the dean for wearing a hat that was part of a traditional outfit worn in his father's homeland for special occasions. While the teacher was aware of the week being one in which students were allowed to wear items that reflected their cultural heritage, because school policy forbade the wearing of hats in the building (turning the visor of a hat to one side or the other was a show of gang affiliation), the teacher insisted (in front of the class that the student remove the hat, which did not have a visor).

Although the student appealed to the teacher that the hat was part of the traditional outfit, the teacher held firm to the rule and sent the student to the dean with a discipline referral. The teacher expressed his indignation when the dean did not impose the usual penalty for wearing a hat. In fact, the dean, who fully understood the student's position, impressed upon the teacher the need for some flexibility, given the circumstances. As the class was composed of minority students from the same culture, the message sent though perhaps not intended, was construed as a lack of respect for their culture. There are those who would argue that, rules are rules and there should be no exceptions. Then there are those who would argue that, under the circumstances, some flexibility was in order for the sake of acknowledging and respecting cultural differences.

On a similar note, teachers must understand the necessity of stepping outside of their box and viewing the educational experience from the perspective of the student. In education, as in many other fields, there tends to be an aversion to admitting that one does not know all the answers or has made an error in judgment. Perhaps there is a fear that such admissions may be considered a sign of incompetence, lessening one's status as the "reigning expert" or authority figure and thus diminishing one's credibility. However, in my own practice, I have found that when a teacher admits to not knowing an answer, it has just the opposite effect. It casts the teacher in the light of being human, as well as showing students that the quest for knowledge is an ongoing pursuit. It also further establishes the teacher's commitment to seeking knowledge and to answering unanswered questions. Students learn that it is, initially, OK not to know all the answers to all the questions, but it is not OK to cease to seek answers to those questions.

As the face of the American population has taken on more ethnic characteristics with a spectrum of complexions ranging from pale white to ebony, issues of cultural diversity in the boardroom and classroom have acquired added significance. By the year 2000, 42 percent of students in public schools will be black or Hispanic (Kuykendall, 1992, p xi). The year 2020 will usher in a demographic shift in which 30 percent of the U.S. population will be black and Hispanic.   In several states, minorities will make up the majority population. These changes will impact the composition of public schools. The effective educator must be sensitized to the impact of culture on the way one perceives the world.

Deciphering the Cultural Code

A rudimentary knowledge of the culture of students is imperative to establishing positive interpersonal relationships and creating greater understanding and appreciation of diverse cultural groups. Such knowledge is necessary to decipher or accurately interpret the culture code. For example, a teacher from the dominant culture calling an African American male student "boy," is certain to spark conflict. However, teachers who know the history of African Americans would understand the error of using this terminology based on the African American experience in U.S. history. Similarly, Kochman (1983) alludes to variations in the manner in which blacks and whites communicate. These differences are not confined to African Americans. In some other cultures, an entourage of family members may appear for a parent conference, or students may not look an adult in the eye when being spoken too as in their culture it is a sign of insubordination. In still other cultures, the family bears the disgrace of any indiscretions of its members. In some cultures, competition is encouraged while in others it is discouraged. All of these cultural idiosyncrasies make up the culture code, which if not understood and accurately deciphered can led to misunderstanding and seriously compromise classroom management and/or learning, as well as parent-teacher communication. A knowledge of the culture of the students whom we teach carries over into our interactions with their parents and the larger community.

"The importance of cultural awareness often lies in subtleties and details" (Coon, 1992, p. 666). For example, the increasing presence of Korean immigrant merchants in many large cities has been the source of racial conflict. Some Korean American merchants have been criticized for being cold and hostile to their customers. A lack of cultural awareness was the spark that ignited an African American boycott of Korean grocers in New York City in 1991. The source of contention was the Korean's refusal to place change directly in customers' hands. Given the African American experience with racism, the assumption was obviously made that this was a racist gesture. In this country "thank you" and "excuse me," smiling, and certain touch are gestures of courtesy and politeness. However, in the Confucian-steeped Korean culture, a smile is reserved for those with whom we have more intimate bonds. In this culture to smile without reason is considered silly, and one simply doesn't smile if he or she feels there is no reason. These are actions that are in no way connected with opinions of the person with whom they are interacting at the moment. There's a Korean saying: "If you smile a lot, you are silly." Likewise, saying "thank you" or "excuse me" are not characteristic in this culture, and strangers rarely touch each other, not even to return change in a business transaction. Consequently, the true source of the conflict was a lack of cultural awareness and not feelings of racial superiority (Coon, 1992). Other cultural taboos in Asian countries are "Never touch the sole of your shoe. Never touch a child's head. Do not write a living person's name in red because red is used for the dead" (Ahern, 1998, p. 56).

In another instance, an African American woman, as a gesture to ease racial tensions between herself and her neighbors, who were Orthodox Jews, baked a pie and delivered it to the neighbor's house. When her neighbor answered the door, the woman extended her hand (the traditional American greeting) but the gesture was not reciprocated. Upon entering the kitchen, the neighbor picked up a knife to cut the pie. The good Samaritan did not know that Orthodox Jews don't shake hands on the Sabbath and as the couple were kosher, they use different knives for different foods. The good Samaritan felt all of her efforts to bridge the racial gap were being rebuffed and an argument ensued. Once again, the lack of cultural awareness of each other's cultures fueled the conflict (Coon, 1992).

Clearly, a knowledge of the idiosyncrasies of the culture of the ethnic groups represented in the student population is imperative to interpersonal communication. Being able to accurately decipher the cultural code reduces misunderstanding and forms the basis for a more accurate assessment of the behavior of others. Teachers can actively seek to acquire a knowledge of the culture of their students by attending community events, reading about the culture, or dialoguing with colleagues who are members of or have had extensive contact with the ethnic group. This clearly sends a message of interest in and respect for their culture. Teachers will ultimately find that such knowledge helps them to teach more effectively. Contact with cultures different from one's own dispels myths and stereotypes and creates greater understanding and personal growth.

Interaction Equity

Many researchers have acknowledged that a teacher's attitude affects the manner in which he or she interacts with students. Consequently, student academic success can in part be attributed to how teachers feel about the students they teach. As minority students, in particular, are very affective, they glean much from their perception of teacher attitude. In an 1982 study of dropouts from a culturally diverse high school, these students were found to perceive teachers as unhappy with their jobs, disgruntled, bored, boring, unfair, and sometimes humiliating (Olsen & More, 1982). In a similar study, teacher attitude was found to be pivotal in the academic success of urban students. Negative teacher attitudes were found to undermine students' self-concept. This frequently leads to avoidance behaviors such as cutting classes or other measures that limit contact with teachers who students feel compromise their level of comfort and dignity (Fine, 1986). Teachers who view their students negatively are less likely to seek teaching strategies or other innovative measures to increase student academic performance and motivation (Cooper, 1979).

Negative stereotypes are detrimental because they tend to drive our expectations and the nature of our interactions with those who are the source of the stereotypes. In the classroom, this can have serious consequences for student learning.

EFFECT OF STUDENT CHARACTERISTICS ON TEACHER ATTITUDE

Kuykendall (1992) identified eight student characteristics that adversely impact teacher attitude. They are gender, race, physical attractiveness, language skills, prior student placement, prior student behavior, prior student treatment, and socioeconomic status (pp. 4-11). Individuals may not always be cognizant of how their stereotypical images of others or their attitudes are manifested in their behavior or perceived by others. Consequently, educators would be well advised to give serious conscious consideration to how the characteristics listed below impact their expectations and interactions with students. How would you answer these questions?

Gender. Is there a tendency to call on boys more than girls? Are there discrepancies in the wait time allowed for girls and boys to answer questions? The fact that gender bias is a distinct reality in academia is embodied in Title IX of the Elementary and Secondary Education Act of 1965, which calls for gender equity (Kuykendall, 1992).

Race. Is the amount of time spent in interacting with minority students equitable to time spent interacting with students who represent the dominant culture? How often are the self-worth and academic contributions of minority students acknowledged with encouragement, praise, and special attention? One study showed that teachers held lower expectations for black and Hispanic students as evinced from giving them less positive feedback in the form of praise, encouragement, attention, etc. (Denbo, 1986).

Physical attractiveness. Are students who are more attractive called on more than less attractive students? Is there disparity between the closeness and time spent with attractive and unattractive students? Unfortunately, ours is a society with an inordinate preoccupation with youth and physical attractiveness. Gender distinctions also acquire relevancy here (Huard, 1997). Evidence tends to suggest that men choose partners based on physical attractiveness, while women choose partners based on economic considerations such as the ability to provide financial security. This cultural preoccupation with physical attributes is carried over into the classroom. Clifford (1973) found that the teacher's perception of parental interest in education, the student's popularity among peers, and his/her projected success, tended toward a negative assessment of these variables for unattractive students. In other words, they held lower expectations for unattractive students, assumed a lack of parental interest in their education, and held low expectations of their future success and integration into the peer group.

Language skills. For some educators, the greater the cultural and/or social economic difference between the student and teacher, the greater the propensity to project negative attitudes toward students. This is borne out even in consideration of something as mundane as language skills. Smith and Denton (1980) found that teachers held lower expectations for students who spoke with dialects, as opposed to those who spoke standard English.

Prior student placement. Tracking has long been advocated as a means of leveling the academic playing field in an attempt to afford students the opportunity to learn at their own pace and to limit the potential for frustration that evolves as students attempt to compete with students of higher intellectual ability. While it has had its share of critics, one fact remains constant, and that is ability grouping or tracking often results in labelling students. According to Howard Becker (1963), labelling theory focuses on society's reaction to a behavior and not the behavior itself. There are social-psychological consequences to labelling. Most often, the individual who is labelled comes to internalize the label and act accordingly. This was borne out in the Rosenthal and Jacobson studies where teacher behavior was greatly influenced by information given to them about students and this in turn impacted student performance. Irrespective of actual intellectual ability, teachers responded less favorably to students who they were told had low intellectual ability and vice versa. Not surprisingly, student performance rose or fell accordingly (Rosenthal & Jacobson, 1968; Rosenthal, 1973).

Some research suggests that tracking students based on intellectual ability can have long-term consequences. Herrnstein and Murray (1994) noted that prior to 1900, individuals with higher intellectual ability were represented across the spectrum of occupational groups. However, 1900 ushered in progressive changes in this pattern that would continue through the century. Increasingly, a pattern was developing (that continues today) of individuals of higher intellectual ability gravitating toward occupations that require higher level cognitive thought, while those of lower intellectual ability gravitated to occupations that did not require more complex thought processes. Higher level occupations came with certain amenities that would significantly impact life style and life chances such as power, prestige, and financial reward.

Herrnstein and Murray further observed a pattern of discrimination in educational institutions against individuals with less advanced cognitive skills. They contend that starting in the 1950s, the practice has been to place greater emphasis on educating the brightest. Consequently, students were sorted based on intellectual ability to more effectively carry out this agenda. Many would agree with these authors that this practice creates and perpetuates an underclass, because once students are intellectually compartmentalized, a label is attached and it is extremely difficult to break out of the compartment and shed the label.

Prior student behavior. Are students judged on the basis of information received from other staff members? Do we allow this information to color our perception of students and predetermine our relationship with them? In some instances what is labelled errant behavior may in fact represent cultural differences in patterns of social interaction. Kuykendall (1992) makes the point that many black children are enthusiastic and assertive in school when they are required to be passive and nonexpressive. Some teachers are likely to react to this enthusiasm by limiting the mobility, action, exuberance, and motivation of children who thrive on movement and excitement. Such labels as "hyperactive" or "behavioral disorder" often are given to these students, even though their in-school behavior merely reflects their out-of-school socialization.

Prior student achievement. Many educators use a cookie-cutter approach to education, expecting that one pattern can be used to meet the needs of all students. These educators hold to a standard expectation for all students. When students fail to meet their expectation, there is often the tendency to respond to them negatively. Educators must be cognizant of the fact that not all students learn at the same pace or in the same way and must therefore develop strategies that meet the varied needs of their students and give them license to learn in ways amenable to their learning style and cultural preference.

Socioeconomic status. Research in the '70s affirmed the relationship between socioeconomic status and teacher attitude and expectations. The socioeconomic status of students impacted teachers' perception of student ability, potential, and performance (Cooper et al., 1975)

THE MAKING OF A MASTER TEACHER

The first ingredient in the making of a master teacher is desire. Desire drives our commitment to perfect our skills, expand our knowledge base, and connect with students. Prof. John Campbell (1972) developed a comprehensive list of the characteristics of a master teacher. That these characteristics transcend a historical perspective attests to the universality of their impact on the field. These characteristics remain as current today as when Campbell developed his list and are borne out in contemporary research findings. The master teachers, those who possess these characteristics, serve as a template for the rest of us to emulate. For those who are sincere in their effort to continue to seek ways to improve the efficacy of their practice, and those who are contemplating entering the field, the degree to which they master each of these characteristics will serve as a measure of their success in meeting the social, psychological, and academic needs of students. The making of a master teacher is a long laborious process of perpetual evolution; the reason for which is clearly evident as one reviews the characteristics identified by Professor Campbell. It is not a pursuit for those who are reluctant to engage in some introspection and are not open to change. These are the characteristics of a master teacher: (pp. 130-157)

Is an exemplar	Is honest and truthful	Possesses profound knowledge of teaching skills
Has broad interests	Is humorous	Possesses profound understanding of subject matter
Challenges students	Influences students	Has a professional attitude
Is considerate	Initiates improvement	Is progressive
Is cooperative	Is interested in students	Is resourceful
Is dedicated	Is interested in subject	Is respected
Is demanding	Is not jealous	Seeks the good will of students
Enjoys teaching	Shows leadership	Is self-confident
Is enthusiastic	learns continually	Sets a good example

Is friendly	Is loyal	Is sincere
Has good judgment	motivates and challenges students	Puts students ahead of self
Is a hard worker	Is patient	Is tolerant
Hits the strike zone	Is personable	Is understanding

The following checklist is based on Campbell's characteristics of the master teacher, as well as findings from current research. It will, hopefully, assist the reader in contextualizing the characteristics and providing clarity for his or her own practice. Although the focus of the checklist is teacher attitude, I think many of the characteristics he has identified are applicable to parents and others who work with children. Read through the checklist and discover if you possess the characteristics of a master teacher. This is not a test you can fail, for any item(s) you are unable to check off can be viewed as yet another opportunity to excel. Keep in mind that master teachers are always evolving, always looking for ways to improve upon their best performance. This is the source of their eternal flame.

The master teacher:

- Focuses not only on the acquisition of knowledge but on teaching students how to think
- Understands that students learn at different rates and in different ways and is cognizant of the difficulties students may encounter in understanding concepts and provides assistance in bridging the gap to understanding
- Sets high goals for him/herself and conscientiously works to attain them
- Is not afraid to raise the curtain to allow students a glimpse of his/her personal side to bridge the gap to understanding
- Seeks to make learning relevant by showing the connection between principles and concepts and the life experiences of students
- Refrains from using sarcasm when the target of criticism
- Takes an interdisciplinary approach to instruction, focusing on showing the ways in which what is learned impacts many aspects of our lives
- Is a lifelong learner and reads extensively to keep abreast of current events, trends, and issues in his/her field
- Facilitates learning by encouraging students to express their opinions and is genuinely interested in what they have to say
- Challenges students to perform at their highest level
- Provides opportunities for students to share in decisionmaking, for example, selecting topics for discussion, formats for presenting reports, due dates for assignments
- Respects the opinions of others even when diametrically opposed to his/her own
- Works well with colleagues, both subordinates and superiors

- Is a role model who projects a strong commitment to teaching and inspires others to strive for excellence
- Is self-motivating
- Operates by the same standards he/she expects of students, does not impose a "Do as I say, not as I do" double standard
- Genuiunely enjoys teaching and working with students
- Disciplines with dignity; is able to allow students to save face; corrects behavior without humiliating or denigrating the student
- Projects infectious enthusiasm, is energetic
- Establishes a warm rapport with students, is friendly
- Builds relationships with students, gets to know them on a personal level—their likes, dislikes, issues, and concerns
- Is flexible, able to discard that which does not work and use new methods
- Works until the job is done, not until the clock marks the end of the workday
- Reacts to the errant behavior not the students; makes it clear to the student that it is his/her behavior the teacher dislikes not the student
- Presents materials at a level students can understand and refrains from trying to impress students with polysyllabic terminology
- Is not afraid to admit to not knowing an answer to a question but seeks an answer and reports back to the class
- Possesses a sense of humor and uses it appropriately
- Is not above apologizing to a student if he/she has judged a student wrongly or responded inappropriately to a student
- Is always cognizant of the fact that his/her behavior (questionable or unquestionable) will effect students
- Critically evaluates his/her teaching and seeks feedback from others
- Takes proactive measures to ensure a classroom environment that is conducive to learning
- Is concerned when students do not understand the concepts being taught and seeks new approaches to guide students to understanding
- Devotes time outside of class to students who need additional help
- Consciously strives to create a learning environment in which students are not afraid to take academic risks, that is, to continue to ask questions if they do not understand a concept
- Strives to establish a sense of community in the classroom
- Does not cultivate professional jealousies; his/her actions are guided by the desire to be an effective and productive teacher
- Possesses good classroom management skills
- Shows school spirit and pride
- Actively seeks ways to motivate students to learn and do their best
- Is patient and caring
- Has a strong command of the subject matter and is able to reach students intellectually

- Is willing to try out new ideas and techniques
- Is innovative, seeking new ways to teach old principles and concepts
- Is respected by students and colleagues
- Makes students feel he/she has their best interest in mind
- Projects confidence in self and his/her ability
- Is a role model and conducts himself/herself accordingly
- Projects sincerity and is trustworthy
- Is tolerant, doesn't expect all students to fit the same mold
- Allows students to learn in ways that fit their learning style
- Is understanding, looks beneath the surface to discover the cause; is empathetic
- When things go wrong in the classroom, is willing to examine how his/her behavior may have contributed to the problem; refrains from immediately placing blame on the students

Master teachers possess a clear vision of their purpose. They are student oriented and gauge their success by the success of their students. Master teachers are firmly committed to the belief that the teacher plays the pivotal role in creating an environment conducive to learning. They are cognizant of the importance of the affective side of teaching and understand the need to educate the whole child.

The words of Ralph Waldo Emerson and Charles F. Kettering capture the essence of what it means to be a master teacher. Emerson said, "No great achievement was ever accomplished without enthusiasm" (Campbell, 1972, p. 135). We cannot hope to inspire greatness in others when our own flame has grown dim. Kettering reminds us that, "where there is an open mind, there will always be a frontier" (p. 150). The master teacher is in a perpetual state of evolution. He or she perceives every obstacle, not as a stumbling block, but an opportunity to excel. The master teacher is not a pessimist with a proclivity to concede defeat before the battle is waged. The master teacher is an optimist who is flexible enough to stray from the well-trodden path when students' needs are not being met. Master teachers are not afraid to explore new territory or carve out new paths to lead their students to academic success. Master teachers are committed professionals who clearly understand the importance of their role in shaping the future. As Henry Adams so eloquently stated, "A teacher affects eternity; he can never tell where his influence stops" (p. 132).

TYPES OF TEACHERS

There is a characteristic style that reflects a teacher's attitude, philosophy of education, and role perception. Most educators can probably recall situations that thrust them into categories atypical of themselves. However, much akin to the concept of personality that focuses on individual uniqueness, consistency of behavior patterns, and psychological characteristics, teacher types reference modal types of behaviors and attitudes—that is, things that appear with such frequency and regularity as to be predictable and characterize the teacher. Some teachers may fall into two or three categories, and the categories are by no means finite. I am sure the reader or others who have had ongoing contact with educators can think of additional categories. The purpose is to get teachers to think about their style, how others perceive them, and most important how their style impacts their practice. Veterans educators would probably concur that the types discussed below represent a cross section of most educational settings.

Professorial

This teacher is the lecturer. Possessing an immense interest and strong command of the subject matter, the professorial teacher tends to focus on the presentation of material. The lecture format complements these teachers' immense interest in the subject matter, affording them an opportunity to talk about and share their passion for it. The Professorial teachers, however, sometimes assume the interest of their students in the subject matter is commensurate with their own. Similarly, they may use vocabulary beyond the academic level of students to fully comprehend. One study of achievement found that American students lag behind students from countries in Europe and Asia. A contributing factor was that in the American system, we tend to cover a wide range of material. In the European and Asia system, greater emphasis is placed on determining what students need to know and narrowing the curriculum to concentrate on those areas ("The learning lag," 1996).

The professorial teacher tends to be preoccupied with covering a wide range of material. Consequently, the lecture format tends to be more amenable in meeting this objective. Many of the newer innovative teaching strategies may be viewed as timeconsuming and limit the amount of material that may be covered. The question becomes, Is more better? Is it better to cover a wide range of materials, much of which may be forgotten in a short period of time, or cover less material in ways that will enhance retention? Retention is enhanced when students are afforded an opportunity to learn by doing. This constructivist approach to teaching holds that each "individual 'constructs' knowledge rather than receiving it from others and students learn best when they gain knowledge through exploration" (McBrien & Brandt, 1997, p. 24). To accomplish this, textbooks are replaced with hands-on materials; memorization and recitation are replaced with an emphasis on thinking and metacognition (McBrien & Brandt). This is not to suggest that the lecture method is an anachronism. However, it is a method that at the secondary level, at least, should be used in conjunction with other teaching strategies.

Professorial teachers are sometimes so focused on the delivery of information that they may not realize when they no longer have the students' attention or have lost them cognitively. Teachers who are in touch with students are very cognizant of the nonverbal clues that suggest they have lost the students. Heads on the desk, doodling, daydreaming, poor sitting posture, and dozing are all signs that may suggest students are not being intellectually stimulated. Teaching and learning is not a cause and effect relationship. Because teaching occurs does not mean learning takes place. How we teach is as important in learning as what we teach. Consequently, while the professorial teacher may share a wealth of knowledge with his/her students, if it is not executed in a manner to capture and maintain the interest of students, it is akin to pouring water into a bucket with a hole in the bottom. While students, generally, will acknowledge the professorial teacher's strong command of the subject matter, many will also express sentiments of being bored in class.

Humanist

The humanistic teacher is very affective. In conflictual situations, these teachers consistently send a message to students that it is the behavior, not the student that they find unacceptable. The humanistic teacher's underlying philosophy tends to be that kids are not innately "bad." They view defiant behavior as a manifestation of deeper emotional issues with which the student is struggling. They perceive their role as teacher as more expansive, not narrowly focused on the dissemination of subject matter. Humanistic teachers understand the need to educate the whole child, providing them with opportunities that will expand the boundaries of their world. This is the teacher who is very sensitive to changes in student attitude and behavior and, most important, will take the time to talk to the student and offer assistance.

Humanistic teachers may go so far as to establish ongoing contact with the families of students (Coleman, 1996). A respected dean (for discipline) in one high school made house calls, the purpose of which was to focus on the strengths of at-risk students to get them back on track. His underlying philosophy was that if you can get these students to focus on and direct their energy into those things at which they show potential or excel, the negative behavior will dissipate. It also sent a message of caring to the student, causing both parent and student to redefine the role of dean of students as something other than punitive.

Other humanistic teachers, having observed special skills or talents of students, have gone to the forefront to provide avenues for them to cultivate their special gifts. Still others assume the role of mentors for students with potential who seemingly lack the necessary support or encouragement from an adult. The humanistic teacher makes a point of telling a student who was absent that he/she was missed. These are teachers who accentuate the positive and encourage a sense of community in their classroom. Through word, deed, and action the message to their students is clear: you are somebody, and I value you as a person.

Students with problems view the humanistic teacher as someone they can trust and confide. in. Oftentimes, this individual is the first line of defense for students experiencing personal problems. It is oftentimes difficult for these students to seek assistance from support staff with whom they may have had limited contact. The humanistic teacher may intercede, with the student's permission, talking to support staff and arranging for the student to meet with these persons. Students feel comfortable with humanistic teachers, as they sense they will not pass judgment and will honor any requests for confidentiality. The humanistic teacher, however, may find him/herself in a catch-22 situation, if the student's request for confidentiality would repress knowledge of criminal activity or in some other way bring harm to the student.

Innovator

The innovative teacher's classroom is a laboratory. This teacher is always looking for new and exciting ways to pique the student's interest in learning. This is the teacher who is unafraid to take risks; who consistently evaluates the efficacy of his/her practice. The innovator is flexible, willing to change or modify teaching strategies to positively impact learning. While emphasis is placed on mastery of learning objectives, the innovative teacher is as much preoccupied with how learning takes place as with mastery. In fact, this teacher's preoccupation with the how of learning is designed to increase mastery.

Upon stepping into the classroom of the innovative teacher, one's senses are immediately bombarded with visual stimuli. Students' work is displayed about the room, colorful bulletin boards and mobiles seem natural to the classroom environment, interesting projects catch the eye, motivational posters serve as silent cheerleading sections; computers, video recorders, and cassette players (tools of the trade) are readily accessible. The classroom exudes an energy with the teacher at its nucleus. Even when students are working at their desks, there is a sense of excitement or focus on the task at hand. Students in these classrooms come to expect that something interesting will happen before the class period ends. Indeed, the innovative teacher strives to fulfill that expectation on a daily basis. It could be something as innocuous or serendipitous as turning the discovery of a caterpillar crawling across the classroom floor into a science lesson. At the secondary level, a comment about an event in history may be turned into a discussion on ethics or values.

The innovative teacher may sometimes feel constrained working in systems that require strict adherence to curriculum timelines. This limits opportunities to take advantage of teachable moments as they occur. Innovative teachers may opt for nontraditional seating patterns. When such is the choice, it is usually to accommodate their teaching style. Some may prefer to arrange student desks in a circle, others a U-shape. Innovative teachers prefer to blend in with rather than set themselves apart from their students. They are mobile, moving about the room, as they share information or monitor students' work.

They reject the traditional role of teacher as one who deposits information, feeling more comfortable in the role of facilitator. They acknowledge that all students have opinions that are to be respected and afford them an opportunity to do so in group discussions. In the innovative teacher's classroom, students are given a voice in making decisions about how learning will take place. They acknowledge the varied learning styles of students and allow each student to learn in ways that best fit their learning style. For example, the student with a strong interest in rap music, who may feel somewhat intimidated by having to present a written report on *The Scarlet Letter*, may be totally at ease if given the opportunity to put it in the form of a rap song and perform it for the class. The innovative teacher recognizes that the student's level of comfort and confidence in performing a task may be tied to his/her preferred learning style. Similarly, the innovative teacher acknowledges the concept of multiple intelligences and is therefore less reticent in accepting nontraditional ways of assessing student achievement or performance.

Eight to Three and Out

These teachers view teaching as a job. There may be little personal investment in their interactions with students and colleagues. Beyond fulfilling their required responsibilities, their contribution to the total school environment is limited. They arrive on time, perform their prescribed duties and responsibilities, and leave at the appointed time. The Eight to Three and Out teachers are not actively involved with students outside of the classroom setting. They are not likely to accept coaching positions or volunteer their services to assist with activities beyond the normal school day. The Eight to Three and Out teachers do not get involved in school politics. They are not likely to express strong feelings about school-related matters unless such matters have a direct bearing on them. When asked, they may be willing to make a contribution if the activity takes place within the confines of the school day.

These teachers have narrowly defined their role as teacher. They perceive it as relegated to the dissemination of information, assessment of student performance, recordkeeping, and attending mandatory faculty meetings. Because of this narrow focus on fulfilling responsibilities, the Eight to Three and Out teacher may project an air of indifference and aloofness. The Eight to Three and Out teacher may appear not to be as committed to establishing relationships with students and networking with colleagues. Sometimes, the focus on getting the job done may be so intense that the teacher loses sight of the more affective variables affect learning.

The elements take a natural toll in gradually wearing out the soil, if proper measures are not taken. To preserve the soil, it may be necessary to rotate the crop or add additional soil or simply allow it to rest and naturally replenish itself.

Before massive cutbacks in educational funding, many school districts offered teachers sabbaticals or unpaid leaves of absence for graduate school or career exploration. Additionally, the structure of educational institutions is such that there are not many opportunities for promotion or change. The number of positions are finite, limited to classroom teacher and three or four administrative positions. Consequently, most teachers remain in the position of teacher for their entire career. Change in position is typically lateral and comes as a result of transfer between schools within a school district. Familiarity can breed boredom unless measures are taken to infuse vitality into the extant condition. Schools can do this by providing conference and staff development opportunities for teachers so they can get out of the building occasionally to pursue training that will assist them in becoming better teachers. Such activities expose teachers to ways in which they can revitalize their own practice with new teaching strategies and techniques. Education has undergone significant change over the past decade, forcing it to become more global in its mission. Many students come to school heavily laden with personal issues that negatively impact learning. There is a need for veterans teachers and those contemplating entering the field to receive training to learn how to deal with such students and in so doing prevent the emotional erosion that takes its toll on classroom teachers trying to deal with the symptoms of the pain and frustration felt by these students, symptoms that are often manifested in disruptive behavior in the classroom.

Burned out teachers are well intentioned but suffer symptoms similar to those of battle fatigue, which places tremendous emotional strain on them to carry out their duties. They do not look forward to the start of each school day with great anticipation and enthusiasm. Some, finding the pressures too overwhelming, may opt for early retirement while others may become more lackadaisical in carrying out their duties. At the extreme, others will leave the field. Teacher burnout is an issue that requires serious administrative consideration as it shakes the very core of education, that is, effectively educating students. When teacher investment is minimal, so will be the educational returns for our children.

In conclusion, teacher attitude is an important variable in the dynamics that drive the nature of student/teacher interaction and academic success. It calls to the forefront the need for educators to be more introspective and to examine their own underlying assumptions about the students they teach. Master teachers understand that fear of vulnerability stifles the blossoming of that innermost part of ourselves capable of empathy. As the institution of education has become more global in response to social change, teachers too must become more global in their perception of their role.

Chapter 5

Discipline

Student discipline is a growing concern among classroom teachers and administrators in the '90s (McWhinnie, 1998). The traditional problems of yesteryear such as playing hooky or sneaking a smoke in restroom have given way to the more serious infractions of gang violence and intimidation; the use, sale, and possession of a wide range of drugs; weapons possession, assault of staff, hate crimes, theft, vandalism, and gross disrespect for adult authority. While this list may read like a litany of the ills of inner-city schools, the veteran practitioner knows that such problems are not relegated solely to the confines of the inner city.

The tentacles of this behemoth stretch wide and far, high and low. They do not discriminate on the basis of race, creed, color, religious affiliation, social economic status, or geographical location. In fact, holding to the fallacy that these problems are confined to the downtrodden of our society prevents us from openly confronting the problem among students in more affluent areas. There are those who would contend that the problem of drugs in schools may be as pervasive in the more affluent areas as in economically depressed areas because money for the purchase of drugs is more accessible. Then there are those who believe that money builds a facade shielding the outside world from a view of the harsh realities of life at the top. It is sometimes very difficult to associate many of the ills of our society with individuals in positions of wealth or power. Forward (1989) points out that alcoholism, drug use, emotional, physical, and sexual abuse damage the psyche of its victims and does not bow out in deference to the weight of one's bank account, the color of one's skin, or an address in an upscale neighborhood. Many of these victims get caught up in a web of rebellious or destructive behaviors that negatively impact their interpersonal relationships. In the final analysis, no matter what side of town you live on, the underlying causes, self-destructive behavior and its consequences, strike the same nerve.

The reasons for poor student behavior in school are varied and complexed. Consequently, the traditionally held belief that the problem would take care of itself if only teachers were well prepared for class and were giving students enough meaningful work to do, no longer holds true. Certainly, this can ameliorate the problem but in and of itself, it is no longer the panacea. In some schools in large cities, hopelessness and frustration attributed to long-term neglect in confronting issues that impact student learning on the part of both students and staff, have created school environments where the daily goal is to simply get through each day physically unscathed (Jones, 1972). In more and more schools, city and suburb, security guards are as natural to the setting as teachers, secretaries, and custodians. In some inner-city schools across the nation, students must pass through metal detectors before entering the building to ensure that they are not carrying weapons. This is not to suggest that chaos reigns in American schools, as most students obey the rules and respect their teachers, but it does attest to the growing number of students who fail to do so. Veteran teachers are well aware of the negative impact of just one unruly or uncooperative student on classroom atmosphere.

Establishing an academic environment conducive to learning does not stand squarely on the shoulders of school administrators alone. Creating a safe, orderly environment for learning requires the input and support of students, teachers, parents, and the community. Later, we will discuss how each of these groups can make a difference. But first, let's identify the problem and examine some of the causes.

COMMON BEHAVIOR PROBLEMS

Among the most common behavioral problems confronting educators in the '90s are substance and alcohol abuse, fighting, disrespect for adult authority, theft, belligerence, vandalism, verbal confrontations, gang violence, and truancy. Many therapists would concur that for many students these behaviors are symptomatic of deeper unresolved social or psychological issues. Through the use of oral histories and case studies, both Coleman (1996) and Forward (1989), provide a clear picture of the evolution of psychological traits of physically, emotionally or sexually abused children that left untreated or without some kind of intervention shape their personalities and carry over into adulthood.

WHY ADOLESCENTS REBEL

Human behavior is very complex. Consequently, identifying the reasons for misbehavior does not evolve as a simple exercise in deductive reasoning that in the final analysis can be explained away as the growing pains of youth. There are many variables that give root to behavior problems and in this section, we will explore some of them.

Values Transformation

In some schools, educators rank discipline as the number one problem, complaining of having to spend an inordinate amount of time trying to establish and maintain order before instruction can begin. However, the problem tends to reflect the more global issue of child and adolescent behavior and changing values and attitudes.

In a 1997 study commissioned by Ronald McDonald House charities and the Advertising Council and released by Public Agenda (a nonpartisan group which examines public policy issues) most Americans surveyed characterized today's youth as unfriendly, undisciplined, and disrespectful. Even more startling was that they attributed the problem to bad parenting. With two working parents, the amount of time parents spend with their children has diminished. The typical working mother was found to spend, on the average, less than an hour a day with her children and for fathers the figure was a dismal seventeen minutes. This pessimistic view of our children was far reaching. Of those surveyed, only 37 percent felt that today's youth would have a positive impact as adults, making the country a better place. When respondents were asked to state the first word that comes to mind when describing teenagers, 67 percent used negative words such as "rude," "irresponsible," and "wild." The picture darkens. Only 12 percent of the respondents felt it a common occurrence for children to treat people respectfully. The study defined children as between the ages of five and twelve (Cassell, 1997a, p. 14).

The tenor of this perception is consistent with a growing concern among educators. More and more teachers have to contend with such disciplinary problems as theft, fighting, attention deficit, disobedience, talking back, verbal abuse, physical assault, and intimidation. Such problems, once confined to high schools, have now filtered down to the primary level.

Others would contend that deviant behavior is exacerbated by a decline in religious instruction and training at home (Lerman, 1998). For individuals with a strong commitment to religious precepts, there tends to be a higher level of consciousness regarding distinguishing between right and wrong and governing one's behavior accordingly. There is a decrease in moral conscience evinced by the lack of remorse on the part of many who commit crimes or other wrongs.

In 1997, a high school student in Paducah, Kentucky entered the school and opened fire on a group of students that had formed a prayer group, killing some and injuring several others. Two months later in Pearl, Mississippi, a sixteen-year-old killed his mother and then proceeded to the school he attended where he opened fire, injuring seven students and killing two more. On December 15, 1997, a fourteen-year-old hid in the woods outside a school in Stamps, Arkansas, and aimed, wounding two students. Tuesday, March 25, 1998, an eleven-and thirteen-year-old lured classmates outside of the building by setting off the fire alarm. Wearing camouflage clothing, they opened fire on the students wounding eleven and killing one teacher and four students (Rotzoll, 1998, p. 2).

These incidents and other similar ones received national television coverage. Child psychologists agree that these troubled kids are products of a troubled society. The violence that erupts at their hand does not just happen. These adolescents give many warning signals that are frequently overlooked by adults or attributed to the growing pains of youth. The experts advise parents and other adults who interact with adolescents to take seriously such behaviors as a sudden drop in grades, isolation from peers, uncontrollable anger, bullying other students, insomnia, and nightmares. These are often warning signals for serious and troubling emotional issues. According to Dr. Mark Smaller of the Chicago Institute for Psychoanalysis, "When children behave violently, it really comes from some severity of problems going on at home. The problem is that when children are in trouble emotionally, they're often not aware of what's causing it" (Rotzoll & Dodge, 1998, p. 6). Dr. Smaller points out that because these children are unable to verbalize the emotional pain or troubling issue, they express their feelings in actions or other symptoms such as poor grades.

In most cases, the teen perpetrator was described as a loner who was rejected by his peers and, in some cases, mocked to the breaking point. Many showed no remorse for their actions. As innocuous as it may seem, students who taunt their peers also have issues that need to be addressed. Such behavior has consequences for the perpetrator as well as the victim. An act of simple cruelty, it evinces a lack of respect for others.

Frustration Due to an Inability to Compete Academically

Mastery learning is essential to academic success. Students who fail to adequately comprehend the rudiments of the subject matter can expect to fall further and further behind. All too often, students are passed from one grade level to the next without a firm grasp of the subject matter. In many systems, the practice has been to employ what is commonly known as a "social pass" for those students, who upon reaching age fifteen, have failed to meet the requirements to enter high school. As these students, physically and emotionally, grow out of the junior high school cohort, concerns are raised about their impact on younger students, as well as their often flagging self-esteem. Many school systems are taking a closer look at the practice (Malone & Bowser, 1998).

The Chicago public school system, after many years of employing social passes, is now taking a tougher stance, not just on this issue, but promotions without evidence of mastery in general. If students in specified grades fail to pass a standardized test evincing mastery of the subject matter, they are required to attend summer school. Those who fail to do so are detained at that grade level (Cassell, 1997b). There is the realization that the best interest of the student, overall, is not being served when he/she is promoted without being equipped with the academic skills to succeed at the next level. We are condemning these students to failure.

High schools who receive "social passes" are equally frustrated. These students often enter with poor self-concepts and attitudes about school based on their lack of success. We can stop the cycle of failure by insisting on mastery at each grade level. This can be accomplished by providing diagnostic testing of students who are struggling academically to determine the cause and then provide them with the necessary support to close the gap—remedial classes, tutoring, or special education placement. In other instances, frustration may evolve from incongruency between instructional methodology and learning styles. In the final analysis, frustration that evolves from inability to master learning, regardless of the source, is often manifested in either passive or overt errant behavior.

Attention Getting

Some students who have for whatever reason failed to get attention through positive means, have found that negative behavior is just as effective in calling attention to one's self. Other students simply may not know how to garner positive attention or recognition from others. Then there are those who have learned, through personal experience, that only negative behavior is rewarded with attention. In either case, negative behavior becomes self-reinforcing. This is a concept that teachers sometimes fail to understand.

Therefore, teachers need to scrutinize more closely a student's motive, particularly if the student persists in exhibiting negative behaviors despite receiving consequences for his/her actions. The most logical question that is rarely asked becomes, Why would anyone persist in behavior that results in negative consequences or punishment? Can we assume that such individuals are innately masochistic? I think not. For these students, the reward, that is, the attention gained, outweighs the punishment. In other words, the punishment is worth it, if it gets the student the attention he/she desires.

This dynamic is not only carried out in the classroom but on the home front as well and in fact may have been learned as children interact with their parents. For example, if the only meaningful communication a parent has with a child is when they are scolding or criticizing the child, the child soon learns that to behave in negative ways will at least get a parent's attention. For the classroom teacher, the solution may be to somehow acknowledge in a positive way that student whose absence is a virtual guarantee of a good day. Allow this student to pass out papers, or erase the board, compliment his/her appearance, his/her unique answer to a question, or anything positive the student does that the teacher can capitalize on. Sometimes ignoring students who crave attention may only exacerbate the problem. The more they are ignored, the harder they may work at getting attention by engaging in negative behavior.

Show of Independence and Control over Their Lives

Unlike many primitive cultures, ours does not have a prescribed rite of passage that validates one's attainment of adult status. Instead, what we have is this ambiguous period called adolescence in which many adolescents engage in a tug-of-war with authority figures to assert their independence. This may be manifested in blatant disregard for rules—challenging conventional values, language, hairstyles, or dress. All of these tend to serve to establish a separate identity for adolescents from other age groups. Their own language, dress, hairstyles, etc., form the psychological infrastructure of a world all their own—a world in which they make the rules and set the standard, a world so unique that any attempt by the older generation to cross into its boundaries would be viewed as ludicrous. Imagine the typical response to a fifty-year-old who follows the latest fad in teenage attire, hairstyle, or speech. It is this reaction that serves to protects their world from "outside intruders."

Children want their parents to be parents not pals. They need someone to look up to, someone who recognizes their need for increased independence; yet knows that it is more judicious to gradually extend the boundaries of permission. The assumption is sometimes made that as children reach the teen years, the need for parental involvement decreases. In fact, because the teen years are perhaps the most turbulent, parental support and involvement take on a new dimension. As teens wrestle with issues of peer pressure, physical image, and in general feeling comfortable with themselves, parental support, understanding, and guidance are imperative in stabilizing the turbulence ("Parents Remain," 1997).

Frustration over Perceived Inadequacies

Adolescence is not only a period in which children embark on a seemingly endless journey of self-discovery, it is also a period in which they struggle to resolve the self-doubt about the mundane as well as germane issues that make up their life experiences (Rhule & Soriano, 1998). In the classroom setting, students who feel, for whatever reason, that they are incapable of competing with their peers may manifest their frustration in socially inappropriate ways. Here is yet another instance in which teachers can be so focused on the inappropriate behavior that they fail to decipher the underlying message. The tendency is to remove the disruptive students and deal with the behavior without asking the most important question and that is why the student misbehaves. Socially inappropriate behavior is likely to continue until the all-important why question is answered.

Adults often take too much for granted in their expectations of adolescents. We expect that they know how to verbalize their frustrations. Obviously, this is not the case. Consequently, there is a growing need for educators to be more affective in their interactions with students in an effort to get at the root of the problem. All too often, the school yard bully is nothing but a very frightened and insecure child who feels invisible and attempts to make his/her presence known and acquire a sense of power or being in control through brute force and intimidation (Hazler, Hoover, Oliver, 1993).

Deep-rooted Emotional Scars

Some students come to school carting the problems of a lifetime, problems that negatively impact their interpersonal relationships with staff and peers. Some bear physical scars, evidence of abuse. Others enter school psychologically battle fatigued and wounded. They are consumed by emotional turmoil that tugs at them like a strong current and against which they must struggle to prevent being carried away by the undertow. These children confront their circumstance in a variety of ways. Forward (1989) gives a clear and succinct presentation of the dynamic that drives the development of the personality of children of toxic parents. She defines toxic parents as those who inflict ongoing trauma, abuse, and denigration on their children and, in most cases, continue to do so even after their children are grown. Strongly asserting that toxic parents transgress all racial, ethnic, social, and religious boundaries, she divides them into these six categories:

The inadequate parent. This parent is so consumed by his/her own problems that the child is forced to become a "mini-adult" to care for the parent.

The controllers. They control their children's lives through the use of manipulation, guilt, and over-helpnessness.

The alcoholic. Consumed by their alcoholism and accompanying mood swings and denial, these parents are incapable of fulfilling their parental responsibilities.

The verbal abuser. These parents destroy the self-esteem and self-confidence of their children with hurtful words, sarcasm, or put-downs.

The physical abuser. The epitome of displaced aggression, these parents are incapable of controlling their own deep-seated rage. They transfer blame to the child and find release through exhibiting physically aggressive behavior toward the child.

The sexual abuser. These parents destroy the very core of childhood by robbing children of their innocence through flagrant or covert sexual exploitation.

To reach these wounded students, teachers must be sensitized to reading the hidden messages. The child who seems to never smile or resists a comforting arm around the shoulder or takes the belongings of others or who has a low threshold for frustration and explodes into physical or verbal aggression against others may be struggling with deep unresolved issues. Unfortunately, teachers who are responsible for at least thirty students in the classroom cannot always provide the immediate care and attention these students require. Consequently, schools have had to rely more heavily on the support services of school psychologists, social workers, nurses, and substance abuse counselors to help these students take the first step toward confronting their past and present. Indeed, many of these students, depending upon the extent of trauma, may require long-term therapy beyond the capability of educational institutions to provide.

Fetal Alcohol/Drug Syndrome Babies

In a society where alcohol and substance abuse have reached alarming proportions, many children are born mentally and/or physically challenged. Fetal alcohol syndrome is characteristic of babies born to alcoholic mothers. Research has shown that heavy drinking during pregnancy results in infants being born with a number of maladies—typically, low birth weight, mental retardation and facial malformations (Matarazzo, 1984).

The first three months of pregnancy are crucial as other researchers have shown that even the consumption of small amounts of alcohol during this period of fetal development may significantly lower the child's intelligence (Streissguth, Barr, Sampson & Darby, 1989). Smoking has been shown to have a similar effect. Children born to women who smoked during pregnancy produced lower scores on general tests of intelligence and language development (Fried & Watkinson, 1990). Despite a massive government effort to communicate to the public the perils of alcohol and substance abuse, the message, for many, has gone unheeded. Consequently, those in positions of authority have had to reevaluate their strategy, concluding that the campaign to educate the public must begin in the early grades. Indeed network television repeatedly broadcasts infomercials specifically directed at this age group.

Expectant mothers are cautioned against smoking and the use of drugs during pregnancy. The problems of children born of mothers who do not heed these warnings impact all of us. Taxpayers pay for medical costs, as many of these children are born into poverty and will experience numerous medical problems.

As these children reach school age, many will require special education services. Hyperactivity, attention deficit disorder, learning disabilities, etc., are among the problems many of these children will bring to the classroom. Their success in school is contingent upon the extent of special education services, resources, and trained staff available. Ironically, wealthier school districts with the financial resources to provide the very best services for these students typically have fewer of these students in their population. Conversely, the least wealthy school districts have a larger proportion of these students in their population. This dilemma raises the issue of equity in educational funding to another level.

Consequently, behavior that may be interpreted by teachers as conscientiously rebellious may stem from organic causes that are beyond the free volition of the child to modify. The challenge to the classroom teacher is clear: how to maintain discipline and create a learning environment conducive to learning and simultaneously meet the special needs of these students. Some would contend that segregating these students into self-contained special education classrooms is the solution. Others contend that this only reinforces the behavior by depriving these children of the opportunity to interact with "normal" children, to experience appropriate behavior firsthand.

Attempts to mainstream these children have not always been successful. Oftentimes, the regular classroom teacher has not received sufficient staff development training to acquire an understanding of not only the special needs of these children but of how best to meet those needs. In a heterogeneous classroom setting with larger numbers of students, the question looms as to the ability of the classroom teacher to provide special needs students with the individualized attention necessary for academic success. Without an adequate and consistent support system, these students are destined to be labelled behavior problems, routinely suspended for disruptive behavior and/or placed in alternative schools.

Parental Permissiveness

Increasing numbers of students are allowed by parents to engage in behaviors that are clearly illegal or morally questionable (Dodge, 1997). This is not a lower-class phenomenon, for many of these students hail from middle-class environments. These are students who are allowed by parents to host parties at which alcohol is served, and marijuana smoked, to keep late hours and/or to smoke in the home. Cities are now strictly imposing curfew laws. Others have adopted ordinances that hold parents financially responsible for their teens and can take them to court for their children's truancy, vandalism, curfew violations, etc. These actions attest to the severity of the problem.

A new trend is coed sleepovers. At its extreme, parents allow boys and girls to share sleeping bags (Dodge, 1997). Consider the parent who attempted to enroll the teenage father of her daughter's child, explaining that the young man was now living with their family. Also, it is not uncommon for parents to request that they not be called by the school regarding their eighteen-year-old seniors on issues of absences, tardies, or disciplinary referrals. At the risk of passing judgment, such scenarios attest to more relaxed morals, and values in the way some parents define their role. Environments where adolescents are given permission by parents and guardians to engage in adult or illegal behavior exceed the boundaries of traditional acceptable, age-appropriate behavior.and create a mind-set of permissiveness that is diametrically opposed to the values and attitudes espoused by educational institutions. Consequently, conflict is a likely outcome when students who are allowed such freedom enter into the school setting where there are clearly defined rules and expectations for behavior and interpersonal relationships with staff. Such students often resent or resist being told what to do. Being afforded adult privileges, they consider themselves adults, on equal footing with staff.

Retaliation Against Authority Figures

Children often feel powerless to deal with their negative feelings toward adults, especially parents. Power is an imbalance of exchange. The position of power belongs to the individual in a relationship who possesses or controls that which is needed or desired by the other. These needs and desires may be material or nonmaterial, ranging from basic human needs such as food, shelter, and love to the less essential yet highly prized possessions such as cars, designer clothes, etc. It is needs and/or desires that drive our behavior and the principle upon which behavior modification is built. Through threat of punishment or withholding that which is needed or desired, we can create conformity. It is socially unacceptable for children to engage in physical or verbal confrontations with adult authority figures. Consequently, their frustration must be released in a less overtly defiant manner. It is not uncommon for this to take the form of deliberately engaging in behavior that the parent or authority figure would disapprove.

This dynamic may be cloaked differently in a classroom setting. As a former dean, I find it curious that some teachers tended to write an inordinate number of discipline referrals. Closer scrutiny of the situation often revealed a dynamic driven by students' attempts at retaliation against the teacher for some perceived unfair treatment or unreasonable demand. The term that best describes this dynamic is classroom guerilla warfare. Among the innumerable and subtle ways it can be played out are: not coming to class with needed materials; frequent and persistent requests for restroom, nurse, or locker passes; talking out of turn; not paying attention; tardiness; complaining; the traditional construction of paper airplanes skillfully put into flight—in general, a lack of cooperation. You can imagine the atmosphere in a classroom when all of these behaviors are in play. The measure of their success is the degree to which the teacher appears visibly frustrated or exasperated. The teacher, needless to say, may feel overwhelmed and more likely to respond by writing disciplinary referrals.

For classroom teachers, professional growth, in part, must entail the ability and willingness to objectively assess such behavior to discover the cause. In the process, they must not rule themselves out as a partial contributing factor. Everyone in the classroom impacts what takes place there, students and teacher alike. Consequently, to restore the social equilibrium of the classroom, it is necessary to examine the behavior, role, and responsibilities of both.

A CLOSER LOOK AT SUSPENSIONS

In many schools, the present system of dealing with students with behavioral problems does not benefit the teacher or the student. Teachers feel they lack the support of administration when these students are routinely suspended and returned to class. It becomes a vicious circle with no end or purpose. Clearly, the punishment is not eradicating or modifying the behavior; yet we persist in imposing the penalty. For the student, valuable time from class is lost for those who can least afford the time out. In fact, many of these students welcome the suspension. What is the solution?

Every year 1.5 million students miss school as a result of suspension or expulsion. Many of these are at-risk students most in need of academic instruction. Generally, suspensions or expulsions are imposed to ensure the health and safety of staff and students, to reinforce the authority of those responsible for maintaining an environment conducive to learning, and to conform to state laws and local school board policies (Rosen, 1997).

Against this backdrop, Rosen (1997) began an investigation to determine how schools today use suspensions. In 1996, he conducted a survey of over one hundred high school administrators responsible for discipline. The results of the survey revealed that the top ten reasons students are suspended from school are: defiance of school authority, failure to report for after-school or Saturday detentions, class disruption, truancy, fighting, use of profanity, vandalism, theft, dress code violations, and violation of closed campus policies, that is, leaving the campus.

There are those who contend that schools use suspensions and expulsions indiscriminately, taking the position that many behaviors for which suspensions are imposed can be ameliorated without removing students from school. In 1984, the National School Board Association took a closer look at suspensions and expulsions and its impact on students (Rosen, 1997). They concluded that:

1. At-risk students view suspension as a reward not a punishment.
2. Suspensions are counter-productive, as they deny access to learning to students who need it most.
3. Expulsions and suspensions encourage delinquency by placing students in unsupervised situations.
4. Expulsions and suspensions result in students being labelled "problem kids."
5. Suspensions distract teachers from developing effective classroom management strategies.
6. Suspensions are inappropriately imposed for minor rule infractions.
7. Suspensions and expulsions are disproportionately imposed on minority students.

While some of these conclusions have merit, after twenty-eight years in the field, this author finds considerable ground for debate. First and foremost, I think most veteran educators would take issue with relatively simplistic analysis of the problem by persons who have had no direct experience in dealing with errant students. The conclusions drawn by the National School Board, taken out of context of what actually transpires on a daily basis in many classrooms all over the nation, does not do justice to the extent and the complex nature of the problem and its impact on the total learning environment. It clearly attests to disparate opinions on the severity of certain student behaviors. For example, the board proposes that the only suspendable offense should be those behaviors that jeopardize the health and safety of others.

The board suggests that such behaviors as disrespect and defiance of school authority figures, for example, should not warrant an out-of-school suspension. In many schools, however, such behaviors represent the rule rather than the exception. In such environments, many staff members begin to feel fearful and intimidated. Under these circumstances, the problem acquires added dimension. I wonder how many of those who propose less drastic measures in dealing with such behaviors have been verbally threatened or cursed by a student. What are staff members to do when they tell a student to stop, and the student continues to walk away? What are staff members to do when parents take the side of students who curse them and tell them what they are not going to do? Platitudes read well on paper but acquire a totally different perspective when contextualized within the extant reality. The reality today is that many students seem to be immune to the consequences no matter how inobstrusive, and their numbers are growing. The problem is exacerbated when the student's actions or their negative behavior is defended by their parents or reinforced by virtue of their gang affiliation.

The board's position suggests that lack of respect for adult authority is a minor problem. This type of thinking represents what has brought us to this juncture: a society that, in general, shows a lack of respect for authority figures. There can be no control or order in an environment where those who are served lack respect for those responsible for their well-being. Alternatives to out-of-school suspensions, such as detention or in-school suspension seem to be effective for the non at-risk student but not for students who have a history of behavior problems.

That suspended students are labeled problem kids is not a misnomer—many are problem kids or, more appropriately troubled kids. Through no fault of their own, many are students who come to school bearing a lot of baggage. Do they have the right, however, to disrupt the learning of others? How is society going to react to these students when they leave the protective environment of the school? What about counseling for the at-risk student? Rosen (1997) alludes to current research that revealed "Successful treatment of conduct disorders is extremely difficult and requires collaboration among the numerous community agencies serving at-risk children and youth" (p. 10).

In most schools, suspensions are imposed for major rule infractions or after other interventions have failed. The issue is what constitutes a major infraction. This author takes the position that institutions of learning must guard against diluting their expectations of acceptable behavior. Some systems have taken a firm stance on this issue. The Chicago public school system has proposed to expel students not only for crimes committed on school grounds, but also for crimes away from school. Texas and Maryland already have laws that allow for the transfer of students from regular school for non-school-related offenses. Students are afforded a due process hearing that can be initiated prior to a conviction. The process can be set into motion by an arrest (Rossi, 1998, p. 11). We must give careful consideration to the conditions under which suspensions are imposed to insure that such disciplinary measures do not prevent us from seeking the source of the problem. However, such measures can prove counterproductive for society as a whole in the absence of viable alternatives characterized by appropriate interventions to meet the special needs of these students. Repetitive acts of deviant behavior signal serious underlying issues with which the student is struggling.

Similarly, serious consideration should be given to an investigation of the inordinate number of suspensions imposed on minority students. This is by no means to suggest that these students should be judged by a different standard of what constitutes acceptable behavior. It does, however, suggest that we need to find out why more minority students tend be suspended as a result of rule infractions. Could the source of the problem lay in a lack of knowledge of cultural diversity and the accompanying cultural idiosyncrasies? Could the source of the problem lay in our allowing the stereotypical images we hold of others to color our perception and interpretation of their behavior?

Consider this scenario. A Caucasian teacher who is admittedly uncomfortable teaching in a school with a predominantly Hispanic population becomes engaged in a confrontation with an Hispanic student. The bell rings and the student rushes by the teacher to get to his seat. In the process, he bumps into the teacher but makes it to his seat just under the buzzer. The teacher responds by writing a referral. The students protests, stating that he did not intentionally bump into the teacher and that he was in his seat on time. When the teacher persists in writing the referral, the student continues to argue with the teacher and proceeds to snatch the referral from his hand. During this exchange, the teacher is scratched on the hand and insists on filing assault charges against the student. Given the no physical contact rule, the student withdraws from school in lieu of expulsion. The teacher maintains that out of anger the student physically assaulted him. How would you interpret what happened here?

Consequently, as we attempt to account for the inordinate number of suspensions for minority students, there is a need for educators to consciously examine their motives (of which they may be genuinely unaware), to discern if the source of conflict stems from a lack of cultural awareness or insensitivity to understanding the very personal and emotional issues that sometimes drive students to respond inappropriately.

IMPROVING STUDENT ATTENDANCE

As mentioned previously in Chapter 2, student attendance is a significant variable in academic success and among the most frequent reasons for student suspensions. There are numerous reasons why students may develop a pattern of poor attendance. Poor school attendance may stem from frequent foster care reassignments, custody battles, or frequent changes in domicile for the families of migrant workers and military personnel (Gutloff, 1998). Of particular concern is the high dropout rate for minority students. The Hispanic dropout rate is twice that of African Americans and three times the dropout rate for Anglos. While many of the reasons students drop out of school are consistent across ethnic lines, the higher rate for Hispanics warrants a closer look. Among the most commonly cited reasons why Hispanics drop out of school are poverty, language barrier, feelings of being unwanted in the classroom by teachers, lack of respect for their culture, peer pressure and low parental expectations (Headden, 1997; Knight, 1997; Michie, 1997).

The U.S. Department of Education and various reform groups have proposed a number of measures that can be taken to reverse the trend. Among their recommendations are: expand curriculum offerings, maintain high standards and expectations, counsel the at-risk student and their family, and provide Hispanic role models and mentors. A consideration of the work schedules and child care needs of Hispanic parents would pave the way for increase parental involvement (Headden, 1997; Knight, 1997; Michie, 1997).

The challenge for the school is to develop proactive, as well as reactive measures to adequately address the problem. The type of interventions may vary depending upon the causal factor. However, there are a number of things schools can do improve school attendance:

Employ Truant Officers

Having an individual with the assigned task of establishing attendance patterns and making contact with the home is a distinct advantage for those school districts who can afford the service. It is a means of making parents accountable, identifying problems that may endanger the well-being of students, and alerting the appropriate authorities. However, for this system to work, the school district must be willing to follow the rules regarding school attendance to the letter of the law. That is, they must be willing to take to court parents who are not in compliance. The court system, similarly, must treat such cases in a manner that supports the gravity of the situation.

Daily Calls to the Home

In districts which lack funding for hiring a truant officer, assigning some staff member the task of making phone calls to the homes of students who are absent from school is a viable alternative. This system is hindered, however, in communities where a large percentage of homes may be without phone service. Where parents can be reached, phone calls home to verify the legitimacy of student absences may serve as a preventive measure for at-risk students.

In a society where, in many instances, both parents are in the work force and may leave for work before students leave for school, truancy can be an attractive alternative to going to school. Therefore, unless the school maintains contact with the parent regarding student absences, truancy may go undetected for long periods of time. Parents also have a responsibility to encourage school attendance and call the school to report absences. Serious consideration should be given to the reasons for allowing the child to miss school. Good school attendance forms the foundation for attitudes toward work.

Expand the Evening High School Concept for Students Who Must Work

Parents have a responsibility to assist their young adults in setting priorities. Students should be made to understand that their first priority is school. Work hours should be limited or eliminated, when and if it interferes with a student's academic performance (McNamee, 1997). However, for those students whose families depend upon their income for survival, balancing school and work can be problematic. It is for these students that the evening high school concept can offer a viable alternative. It removes the barrier to completing an educational program that can impact their future earning potential. Working during the day and attending school at night might present a formidable challenge, but for students who are highly motivated, it is an attainable goal.

Establish Teacher-Mentor Programs

Some schools have instituted programs where each teacher is assigned a specific but manageable number of students to counsel. Such programs are not intended to replace the school counselor. The role of the mentor teacher is to establish a relationship with students (Siegel, 1997). That is, on a one-to-one basis, the teacher monitors the student's grades, and attendance and is available to discuss with the student any other concerns he/she may have. In one school, the first step consisted of identifying a small group of academically at-risk students and assigning them to the classes of four teachers in the core curriculum (math, science, English, and social studies. Each teacher was assigned four or five of these students to track and counsel. The group of four teachers met on a weekly basis to discuss each student. The teachers shared information about the student's performance in their class. Decisions were made regarding how best to respond to the concerns raised about each student. The strength of this program was obviously the more personal contact with students and parents. Parents were notified by the teacher at the first and subsequent signs of trouble and the appropriate support staff notified, if necessary.

Perfect Attendance Incentives

While many balk at rewarding students for attending school, their argument being that education is a privilege, young adults are strongly motivated by rewards. Those who support such programs contend that if offering incentives is an effective means of modifying behavior, then it is acceptable and appropriate to use such measures. This debate will undoubtedly rage for some time.

Special Recognition for Perfect Attendance

For those who find providing material rewards objectionable, providing students with good attendance special recognition at assemblies serves as a reasonable alternative. These students may be provided with a certificate for perfect attendance. Such assemblies provide opportunities for administration to expound the long-term rewards of such virtues of dedication, commitment, and self-discipline.

Establish Alternative Schools

Creating alternative schools with more flexible hours and teaching methodologies that are not subject to time constraints allows students to learn at their own speed.

ALTERNATIVES FOR THE HARD-TO-REACH STUDENT

A car slowly drives down the street. A twelve-year-old white youth is let out at the corner of an African American neighborhood in a large city. He approaches two African American males, a fourteen -and a fifteen-year-old, pulls a gun and fires, killing both youths. He did not live in the neighborhood; he did not know the youths. He was on an assignment. His assignment was to commit murder as part of his initiation into an Hispanic gang. Who was this child? There had been parent conferences, in-school suspensions, detentions, after-school mentoring, counseling, and finally suspensions (Carpenter, Rossi & Lawrence, 1998). This no doubt was a troubled youth. At the time of the murder, this twelve-year-old was on his fifth suspension.

Even though this incident occurred after school hours, it renewed the debate regarding out-of-school suspensions. The Chicago school system is considering a number of alternatives, among them, Saturday detention and short-term student placements for five to ten days (Rossi, 1998, p. 11). The proposal would call for Saturday detentions, in lieu of ten day suspensions or expulsions and temporary placements that would be housed at churches or social service centers. There are, however, those who would take issue with equating an offense that would traditionally warrant an expulsion with one that typically results in a five-or ten-day suspension.

In some systems where the number of disruptive students have reached such proportions as to negatively impact the learning environment of the entire school, there has been no choice but to remove these students and place them in alternative schools. However, to be effective, the alternative school should not be viewed as a warehouse or holding cell of sorts for disruptive students. Ideally, these schools should be staffed by well-trained, caring teachers with the necessary support staff to provide extensive counseling to help these students get in touch with the root of their problems. Both teacher and student would benefit from small class sizes with the support of a paraprofessional.

The nation's 2,604 alternative schools have become the lifeline for students who have gotten lost in overcrowded classrooms with low teacher-student ratios. Alternative schools are designed to meet the needs of students who are at risk due to attendance, behavior, academic, or motivation deficits. However, the definition of at risk may vary from state to state. In the state of Wisconsin, for example, students are considered at risk if they have dropped out of school, are two or more years behind in basic skills level or credits, are habitual truants, are parents or are adjudicated youths. In Milwaukee, which has a dropout rate of 10 percent and a graduation rate of only 46 percent, the alternative school concept has helped at-risk students find success. Their highly touted Northwest Opportunities Vocational Academy (NOVA) program found a formula that works. It formed a partnership with business and community leaders to get these kids back on track. Members of the community are enlisted to serve as mentors, and businesses create student internships in hospitals, manufacturing companies, and banks. This program gives at-risk students what they need most: structure, goals, caring adults, and the opportunity to experience firsthand the connection between education and the world of work (Wilberg, 1997).

As the number of students with special academic, emotional, and social needs increases, so will the need for schools to go beyond the capability of regular placements to meet these needs. They will be challenged to develop alternative schools for these students, schools staffed by trained professionals with a clear understanding of the needs of at-risk students and the necessary skills to effect change in their lives.

DISCIPLINING WITH DIGNITY

Oftentimes, so much emphasis is placed on the punitive aspect of discipline that not much attention is given to a study of proactive measures to ameliorate or discourage errant behavior. Additionally, educators don't often take advantage of the most accessible resources in dealing with classroom discipline—their colleagues. In a nutshell, educators don't network. That usual cadre of teachers who on a daily basis gather in the teacher's lounge to bemoan the ills of the youth of America are spending negative energy, travelling down a road to nowhere discussing how rude, disrespectful, and devious Johnny is. Virtually every classroom will have at least one Johnny.

However, where one teacher may find Johnny a virtual terrorist in the classroom, another may find Johnny a pleasure to have in class. Why is Johnny cooperative in one classroom and disruptive in another? In pinpointing the causes of discipline problems in the classroom, the teacher as a variable is usually not at the top of the list. Educators must be willing to more closely scrutinize their role in creating a classroom environment where discipline does not evolve as a primary issue. They must be willing to engage in some introspection, examining themselves and their practice to seek cause and effect relationships that impact discipline. Shaughnessy, Coughlin, and Smith (1997) conducted a research project in which they asked eighteen secondary school administrators in large urban school systems to identify the characteristics of teachers who effectively managed disruptive behavior. The results of the survey revealed that teachers who were effective in managing disruptive behavior:

- Were positive, confident, and handled disciplinary problems on their own and in a professional manner
- Were active listeners and possessed good communication skills
- Were affective, showing concern that students achieve success
- Were perceived by students as fair and equitable, earning their respect and trust
- Were firm, fair, and consistent
- Effectively used conflict resolution and behavior management strategies to quell potentially explosive situations
- Related well to students and were sensitive to their needs
- Were team players, willing to work with support staff, counselors, parents, and administrators to assist students (p. 44)

The research team then asked administrators to specifically name the teachers on their staff who exhibited these characteristics. They in turn asked these teachers to reflect and comment on why they thought they were effective in dealing with disruptive behavior. In perusing this list, it is interesting to note that all of the behaviors listed are teacher centered. These are things teachers can do to create a learning environment in which disruptive behaviors are kept to a minimum and effectively managed when they do occur:

- Build and maintain positive relationships with students
- Allow students to maintain their dignity and foster self-esteem
- Maintain a professional demeanor and remain calm
- Offer an explanation, succinctly state the lesson to be learned from the incident (i.e., teach) and be consistent in enforcing rules and consequences
- Be consistent and fair
- Seek to get to the root of the problem
- Set high standards for students
- Keep students actively engaged and on task
- Respond immediately to potentially disruptive situations
- Try to dissipate the level of anger
- Contact and involve parents
- Use active listening skills
- Use private confrontation when possible
- Use and teach students how to use problem-solving and team skills
- Avoid power struggles
- Immediately isolate disruptive students
- Use positive reinforcement to encourage desired behaviors
- Have a well-thought-out plan of action
- Defuse a threatening situation by separating students
- Model the desired behavior (p. 44)

Having clearly articulated what they do, the researchers then asked the same group of teachers to more specifically relate the techniques, procedures, and behaviors efficacious in preventing disruptive behavior. Once again, it is interesting to note that to a large extent the procedures and techniques were grounded in teacher attitudes, that is, their perception of their role as a teacher and their attitude toward students. To prevent disruptive behavior, effective teachers:

- Accentuate the positive, teach positive rules and expectations
- Respond immediately to small disruptions to prevent escalation
- Provide students with a variety of experiences and activities commensurate to their ability and interests
- Emphasize accountability, that is, teach, remind, and enforce consequences
- Create learning environments where students feel safe and secure
- Start the school year with a mission to create a positive learning environment
- Are cognizant of what is going on in the classroom at all times
- Get to know their students, taking a genuine interest in their problems, concerns, and interests

- Use seating arrangements amenable to their methodology, learning goals, and educational philosophy.
- Know when to challenge and persist and when to back off
- Allow students to maintain their dignity and save face
- Become adept at nonverbal communication
- Use a calm and firm tone of voice
- Circulate around the room and use proximity control
- Exhibit a sense of humor
- Implement organizational procedures and structure
- Give clear verbal orders to desist
- Provide a cooling-off period
- Project an upbeat, positive, enthusiastic attitude
- Make students aware that help is available from counselors, parents, administrators
- Teach and use negotiation
- Call students by their name
- Use peer mediation
- Anticipate problems
- Seek outside support for students (p. 46)

The above list represents a comprehensive list of preventive measures. However, even the most effective teacher may find that there are times when, despite one's best effort, disruptive behavior will occur. These effective teachers, however, proved to be a valuable resource for identifying measures which can be taken after the fact. They are:

- Meet with the student in private
- Remove students from scene where the problem occurred
- Involve parents
- Make the student accountable for his/her actions and stress the importance of making choices
- Provide a cooling-off period
- Try to pinpoint the flash point, what set things off
- Do not confront the student in front of the class
- React with accuracy
- Build student's self-esteem
- Avoid, if possible, dean referrals
- Use peer influence
- Provide appropriate alternative behaviors
- Get students back on track
- Call for assistance before breaking up a physical confrontation
- Review the school rules on discipline with students and follow them
- Use the disruptive behavior as a teachable moment

- Be flexible, change teacher behavior if necessary
- Ensure that discipline techniques are appropriate for students (p. 46)

The Shaughnessy research results provide a vivid blueprint for creating learning environments built on a firm foundation of discipline, respect, dignity, responsibility and caring—environments in which students can learn and feel safe and secure. It attests to the importance of the consistent application of those things that have been proven to work in regard to behavior management techniques, instructional strategies, school policy, and parental involvement.

Most important, the researchers have shown us that viable solutions to disruptive behavior can be found within the confines of each school. All it takes is networking among peers. Colleagues can be a valuable resource in answering such questions as What do you find works when a student does this? or How do you get students excited about learning? Seek out that teacher whose classes always seem to be under control. Seek out that teacher whose classroom seems to burst with energy, with students enthusiastic about learning. Use peer coaching as an opportunity to visit such colleagues' classrooms to experience firsthand the dynamics that drive their success. In turn, ask an effective teacher to observe you and make suggestions. Start out by formulating an objective, something you would like to improve in (it should be an observable and measurable behavior), and ask a colleague to observe you and in descriptive, not judgmental terms, assist you in determining your success. What did you want to do? Based on the description of your colleague, what did you actually do?

INNOVATIVE DISCIPLINARY MEASURES

At another level, many school administrators are aggressively looking for disciplinary measures with a greater emphasis on modifying behavior and less on punitive action without regard to its effectiveness. To this end, a variety of innovative approaches to behavior modification have evolved. Among the most popular are:

In-School Suspensions

The aim of in-school suspensions is to send a message to students that certain behaviors will not be tolerated. In-school or in-house suspensions are only effective if well structured. Programs that require students to do meaningful work or behavior modification activities are the most successful. At one school, prior to being assigned to an in-school suspension, students are required to take an assignment sheet to each of their teachers (this is done when they attend each class the day before). The teacher records the assignment they are to work on while in in-school suspension. The in-school suspension monitor then places the completed assignment in the teacher's mailbox at the end of the day. There are many variations of in-school suspensions. Some require students to remain in one room all day, while others send students to in-school suspension only for the class period in which the infraction occurred. Still other programs assign counselors to the in-school suspension room on a rotating basis to discuss such topics as anger management, making choices, coping skills and conflict resolution. Other in-school suspension programs require students to complete packets of information that address the kinds of issues that most frequently send them to in-school suspension. The success of in-school suspension tends to be that, without depriving students of much needed time in school, it isolates them from that which they value most—interaction with their peers.

My years of experience as a dean, however, revealed that while in-school suspensions are effective in dealing with students with moderate behavior problems, for students who are frequently referred to the dean's office by a number of teachers, such measures fall short of serving their purpose. Many of these students so dislike the thought of being confined that they deliberately behave in ways to get themselves removed and placed on out-of-school suspensions. These are the students for whom more intense and ongoing counseling is needed to modify behavior.

While in-school suspension programs can take many forms, the goal is the same. Such programs were developed in an attempt to correct errant behavior without removing students from the school setting. Many parents applauded the school's effort. As many parents work, students placed on out-of-school suspension were free to just take the day off or, worse yet, find trouble elsewhere.

Saturday Detentions

Saturday detentions are used in some schools as an alternative to assigning students multiple consecutive days of in-school suspension. In schools where it is offered to students as an alternative to multiple days of in-school suspension, it makes students accountable while giving them a voice in deciding the consequence for their actions. Saturday detention requires students to relinquish their free time. Such programs generally require that students remain quiet, reading or completing homework. Schools may also have volunteer tutors on duty to assist students with homework or other academic problems. Saturday detention programs may run for a half or a full day.

Peer Mediation

Peer mediation is the quintessential model for student ownership of conflict resolution. Peer mediators are typically students with good leadership skills, respected by their peers and possessed of a level of maturity that enables them to handle the responsibilities and demands of conflict resolution. These students undergo intensive training in conflict resolution and work under the supervision of an adult staff member, usually a counselor or social worker. Students who are in the midst of a brewing conflict can request mediation. The purpose is to settle the dispute before either party takes inappropriate action that might result in a suspension or some other consequence. The peer mediator, using skills learned in training, listens to both sides and helps each party identify and come to terms over the source of the problem. The adult staff member, while present, does not participate unless circumstances warrant his or her intervention. Peer mediation encourages students to dialogue, to think, to evaluate the problem, their perspective and that of their "adversary" as an alternative to resorting to violence. Unlike other forms of punishment, peer mediation requires students to think about what has brought them to this point and what can be done to resolve the problem. In the process, they learn to compromise.

Self-Evaluation

At one Chicago south suburban high school in Illinois, out-of-school and in-school suspensions dropped significantly with the institution of a post-fight questionnaire. Students who fight are required to complete a seven-page questionnaire that asked such questions as "Have you been angry about anything lately? How much sleep did you get last night? Do you have problems with people in school? and How are you getting along with members of your family?" (Franchine, 1998, p.4).

Special Programs

Many more schools are implementing special programs in an effort to be more proactive in their response to disciplinary problems. The students selected for these programs are typically those who have had a number of referrals to the dean's office or seem to be developing a pattern of disciplinary problems. Such programs may be staffed by counselors, deans, social workers, or a team of professionals. Programs can be conducted after school or during a study hall period with these students being assigned a common study hall. Sessions are typically one hour in length. Students are encouraged to discuss issues; to view and discuss videotapes about the types of situations, issues, and concerns that result in their making poor choices, to role-play, etc. At one high school, the program is run after school hours, students are served refreshments during the session, and special transportation is provided for them. Such programs afford students the opportunity to talk about their common experiences and brainstorm solutions. It lets them know they are not alone in many of the problems they face. Most important, they leave the program equipped with bolstered self-esteem and the necessary skills to make good choices and maneuver the challenges of the adolescent years.

Group Counseling

Group counseling is another proactive measure to assist students in steering clear of trouble and helping them and others get back on track. Where resources and personnel are limited, group sessions are a viable alternative to individualized counseling. Once again, group counseling can be utilized to reach the at-risk student and those who have already experienced multiple suspensions or other disciplinary action as a result of their behavior. While some might question whether or not students would open up and discuss their feelings and opinions in such a public venue, my experience has been that this typically is not the case, as long as there is mutual trust. As a case in point, the state police at one school sponsored lectures to high school students on conflict resolution. At one point during the lecture, the police asked students how many of them had a relative or friend killed as a result of violence, particularly gang violence. To my surprise, not only did students raise their hands but they also shared many of the private details of their lives. The officer also left a contact phone number so that students who did not feel comfortable sharing with the group could call her. It appears that when students feel there is trust and a common bond between them, they are less reticent about sharing their feelings. Group counseling sessions afford students the opportunity to get in touch with the forces that drive their behavior and to look for more appropriate responses.

Police Liaison

Many schools employ the services of a police liaison. When a police officer is assigned to a school, his responsibilities may range from monitoring the halls and school grounds to counseling students with known gang affiliations, gang wannabes, or those that have come into contact with the law in the community. The police liaison concept was developed to forge a more amicable relationship between students and police officers. Its aim is to change the perception of police officer from that of adversary to that of a person whose job is essentially to serve and protect. Police departments support the concept, as it enhances community relations and enables officers to get to know the adolescents who live in the community in a more personal way. Police officers can bring a different perspective to counseling and conflict resolution, one that enhances students' understanding of the importance of making right choices and the short- and long-term consequences of errant behavior.

Faculty Presence

The mere presence of staff members during passing periods is a very effective deterrent to errant behavior by students. Teachers standing outside their classroom doors during passing periods and as students enter the classroom send a message that says you are welcome, as well as letting students know they are expected to be in class on time. Where schools have clearly articulated expectations and consequences for student behavior, students are not as likely to break the rules in the full view of a staff member. Many times, teachers view discipline and maintaining an orderly learning environment as the responsibility of administration. The reality is that on a daily basis six or seven individuals cannot engage in hands-on student management and monitor student behavior. It takes teamwork. Twenty or two hundred staff members by their mere presence can shape school climate. For example, teachers sometimes have the tendency to assume the role of bystander when deans or other administrators are assigned along with them for cafeteria or study hall duty. There is sometimes the tendency to call upon the administrator to address problems that teachers have just as much authority to handle. This problem can be ameliorated by giving teachers clearly defined instructions regarding what is expected of them in such situations and following through to ensure that they are fulfilling their responsibilities.

Particularly at the high school level, teachers often expect to be challenged by students when the student is reprimanded. Consequently, while getting an administrator to handle the situation may eliminate the stress for the teacher, it also tends to inadvertently lessen his or her authority. A Caucasian teacher shared with me when asked why he didn't seem to experience disciplinary problems with his predominantly minority students, that he had developed a relationship with his students ,and that he wasn't afraid of them. When asked to expound on this further, he said many of the teachers acted as if they were afraid of the students. When students sense their fear, they take advantage of the situation. In general, teachers who show they care about students in a personal way, build relationships with them, are assertive (not to be confused with aggressive) in confronting them about their behavior, and are visible can significantly impact school climate, creating an orderly learning environment.

DISCIPLINE AND CLASSROOM MANAGEMENT STRATEGIES

Our discussion thus far suggests that discipline is a complex issue that can be approached from a variety of perspectives. Previously, the discourse centered around teacher attitudes and interactional styles as variables in creating learning environments where minimal class time is consumed with resolving disciplinary problems. Grossnickle and Sesko (1985) identified a number of classroom management strategies that contribute to the creation of orderly classroom environments where learning can take place uninhibited by misbehavior. The key elements in the creation of such classrooms are student involvement, cooperation, enthusiasm for learning, respect for peers, and the teacher (p. 3). These elements find definition in specific instructional methods.

There is a positive correlation between effective classroom discipline management and the effectiveness of the teacher's instructional method. A number of researchers have identified specific instructional methods or strategies that are conducive to academic success and orderly learning environments. They include:

- Clearly articulate and establish classroom procedures the first week of school
- Create a flexible classroom environment that is task oriented yet relaxed
- Establish clear and reasonable standards, expectations, and tasks
- Be consistent
- Establish consequences and rewards
- Explain the reason for rules and procedures
- Present material in good, logical sequential order connected by clear transitions
- Present activities in units small enough so as not to overwhelm students and create confusion
- Monitor behavior unobtrucively and respond immediately to off-task behavior
- Include students in as much decision making as possible
- Stress accountability
- Offer positive reinforcement, such as praise and feedback
- Provide a variety of activities
- Show a personal interest in students
- Teach to the student, not to the subject (Grossnickle & Sesko, 1985, p. 3)

What about the student who disrupts class as a result of an inability to simply sit still? These are the students who are constantly out of their seats, jumping around, talking out of turn, etc. They represent the 3 to 5 percent of all K–12 students diagnosed with some form of attention deficit disorder. Approximately two million take the prescription drug Ritalin or some other medication to help them stay focused. Effective classroom management strategies can also assist these students in staying focused ("Keeping kids in focus," 1998, p. 4).

The National Education Association conducted a poll of teachers, social workers, counselors and psychologists in an attempt to find out what works best for these students and offered ten strategies teachers can use in keeping them focused and on track for learning:

Alter the classroom environment. Seat students who are easily distracted close to the teacher, or pair them with a student who is noted for being on task, or seat them where they can move about without creating a distraction for others.

Establish routines and structure. Be consistent, clearly articulate rules, consequences, and expectations and review the rules daily.

Present with enthusiasm. Encourage as much student interaction as possible with hands-on demonstrations, role-playing, computers, calculators, tape recorders; vary the pace at which material is presented; use as many manipulatives as possible.

Change the nature of assignments. Present information in small frames, have more than one activity per class period, and allow students to present in ways that interest them or with which they feel comfortable.

Provide immediate and positive feedback. As a students with attention deficient disorders are usually being told what they are doing wrong, rewards and other incentives can be effective behavior modifiers. Students with attention deficient and impulsivity problems find it difficult to work toward long-term goals. They need immediate gratification or reinforcement. Consequently, for these students the use of stars, points, tickets, etc., which can be accumulated and redeemed in short intervals for some privilege or tangible reward, are most effective.

Don't be afraid to discipline. What works well here is determining what the students value the most and removing that privilege or reward for rule infractions. It is also recommended that consequences for rule infraction be incremental. Teachers can also be proactive by identifying the distractors and adjusting the learning environment accordingly.

Assist students with their organizational skills. Organization helps keep attention-deficit students focused. School planners in which students can record assignments, rules, consequences, and other important information provide a good start in this direction.

Communicate with parents. Russell Barkley, professor of psychiatry and neurology at the University of Massachusetts Medical Center, strongly advocates the use of the "daily school-home report card.". This consists of listing on an index card various behaviors on which the student is rated daily. This information is sent home by the student for the parent to review. The parent follows up by creating his or her own system of rewards or consequences at home. The school-home report creates continuity of expectations between the home and school.

Be tolerant. This requires education on the part of teachers. It is vitally important that teachers have a clear understanding of attention deficit disorder. Otherwise, there is the tendency to view these students as deliberately disruptive and uncooperative. Knowledge creates understanding, and with this, teachers understand the need for patience and the importance of implementing strategies that meet the needs of these students.

Hang in there. Sometimes the easiest out is simply to blame the student and remove the student from class whenever possible. However, while this may alleviate the immediate problem for the teacher, long-term it spells failure for both teacher and student. The student's needs are not being met. Instead, the student is being penalized for a condition over which he or she has no control, and teachers fall far short of meeting their ultimate purpose, which is to educate all kids (pp. 4-5).

DEALING WITH AGGRESSIVE PARENTS

Oftentimes, despite our best effort, problems will arise in our interaction with students. Sometimes, issues can be resolved by talking with the student or involving support staff. However, if the problem reaches such proportions as to require a referral for disciplinary action, parents are usually figured into the equation. Parental involvement in such matters is usually uneventful. However, for some parents, whose involvement has lain dormant, such incidents serve as the catalyst for action, and all too often, the manner in which they respond to the situation is emotionally charged.

Incidents of bad parental behavior are becoming a concern all over the country. The magnitude of the problem reached such proportions in one California town that they issued guidelines for staff spelling out what to do when parents become abusive or threatening. Parents who engage in such inappropriate behavior as cursing, shouting, or making demeaning comments to staff are "suspended". They may be barred from the school for specified periods of time. The guidelines and penalties are sanctioned by state criminal statutes and the California Education Code ("Schools vow," 1998).

Virtually every educator, at some point in his/her career, will encounter an irate parent. The looming question remains, How do you deal with an irate parent? Unfortunately, this is an area of teacher training that has been overlooked. Many veteran teachers also feel unprepared to deal with irate parents. This can be attributed to a lack of staff development to address the issue. Few would question that we live in a more stress-filled and aggressive society than our parents. Consequently, the very definition of "aggressive" acquires new meaning in the context of today's social climate. Brooks-Bonner (1997) offers these sensible, concrete measures that can be taken to ensure conferences with irate parents that are productive and safe:

Defuse the Situation

Bring the emotional level down, so as not to detract from the issue at hand. Depending upon the familiarity of the staff member with the parent, this may be accomplished in any number of ways, such as allowing the parent to vent or disarming the parent with statements that show your concern. As the irate parent tends to act first, without knowledge of all of the facts, diffusing the situation creates a climate conducive to open communication. The object is to prevent the sound of their fury from drowning out reason and civility.

Use a Strong and Assertive Voice

This projects a sense of confidence, caring, and concern. It tends to level the playing field, as timidity on the part of the school official may give the irate parent a sense of power and control over the situation. The school official should avoid raising his/her voice, as this tends to escalate the emotional level of the "confrontation." His/her object is to maintain an even temper characterized by a calm demeanor, even lowering the voice to force the listener's attention by having to concentrate to hear what is being said. This slows the pace of the dialogue and produces a calming effect.

Be Aware of Body Language

Good eye contact suggests the other individual has your attention. Being able to look your "opponent" in the eye establishes an assertive stance. A lack of eye contact may suggest a feeling of intimidation, prevarication, or defiance. Similarly, it is imperative that the staff member make the parent maintain eye contact. If the parent avoids eye contact, wait until eye contact is made. However, this may also signal an instance where increased cultural sensitivity and awareness provides an advantage in accurately deciphering the cultural code. Among Asians and Hispanics, direct eye contact is atypical of the culture.

Body language says a great deal about how we feel and how we are processing information during interpersonal communication. It also helps us understand an opponent's intent. In fact, there is a considerable amount of literature on the subject. In dealing with irate parents, paying attention to body language can translate into a matter of safety. Pay attention to what the parent does with his/her hands, sudden movement, etc. In highly charged situations, including additional staff members in the conference or having a security officer nearby would be a well-advised precaution. In conducting the conference, the school official should be cognizant of his/her body language as well. Particular attention should be paid to such behaviors as looking away or turning away from the parent, folding the arms, or showing facial expressions that project a lack of openness to listen or downplay the gravity of the situation.

Perceptions are important. The tone of the parent-teacher conference can be set based on initial perceptions. Consequently, it is important that school officials guard against behaviors that communicate the attitude that the parent is inferior or unimportant.

Allow the Parent to Vent

The irate parent tends to use verbal aggression as a means of baiting the perceived adversary into an argument. While it may be very difficult when on the receiving end of a verbal attack, it is important to not interrupt the parent's tirade. The school official must remain silent, allowing the parent the opportunity to vent. Eventually, the parent will run out of steam. This provides an opportunity for the school official to present his/her case and respond to the parent's concerns.

Prohibit the Use of Profanity

Perhaps out of the misguided notion that the use of foul language is necessary to clearly define the level of one's frustration or the inability to clearly articulate one's feelings, some irate parents might resort to the use of profanity. Clearly, the use of profanity exceeds the boundary of acceptable behavior. School officials should not tolerate it. Once engaged, they should let the parent know that they are aware of the anger but that such behavior is unacceptable. Should the parent persist in the use of profanity, the conference should be ended and the parent instructed to make another appointment.

Maintain Physical Proximity

In dealing with irate parents, the school official must not invade their physical space. Conversely, they may attempt to intimidate by invading the school official's physical space. Nose to nose confrontations have the potential to turn physical. Consequently, the school official should maintain a distance of at least three feet between themselves and an irate parent. The official must always communicate with the parent at the same physical level. For example, during the conference, the parent should not be allowed to stand while the official is seated at his/her desk. The parent should be asked to be seated. The desk also serves as a barrier to prevent each person from moving into the other's comfort zone.

A prerequisite to any classroom environment conducive to learning is the implementation of effective classroom management strategies that create order and control without stifling student intellectual curiosity and creativity. The onus of responsibility for creating safe and orderly environments in which learning can take place does not fall squarely upon the shoulders of educators alone. Home, school, and community all share a vested interest in education and can impact the learning environment. Parents can set the stage by clearly articulating their expectation in regards to respect for adult authority, proper decorum, and the establishment of education as a priority in the family value system. Educators can redirect their energy, investing more time in seeking proactive measures to minimize disciplinary problems and providing alternative placements for students who have severe behavioral problems. Such students need help in grappling with the troubling issues that drive their behavior. The community can assist by providing mentors, or tutors or by sponsoring motivational programs that encourage academic success and respect for self and others.

Chapter 6

The School and the Social Order

Each generation has had its own demons to wrestle. Certainly, some of the problems students face today are no different from those of their predecessors. However, society changes over time. Mores, norms, and values may become distorted. Certainly, many rules of social and moral behavior characteristic of yesteryear are today extinct. The moral fabric of our society is much more loosely woven than a generation ago. Some would contend that the liberalism of the '70s and the focus on individualism has caused us to reap a sparse harvest, one lacking in social responsibility and commitment to those values that sustain social stability and order. These societal changes permeate our basic social institutions. They have forced us to tenaciously seek solutions to halt the downward spiral of those values that would sustain our culture.

As the problems are complex, so are the solutions, often requiring a wide variety of institutions and agencies to join forces. However, for our purposes, let's examine those social problems that directly impact the ability of educational institutions to carry out their mandate to provide our children with an environment conducive to learning, one in which each child's needs are met and each child is prepared to assume the role of informed citizen and consumer.

NON-TRADITIONAL FAMILIES

The portrait of the traditional American nuclear family consisting of mother, father, and offspring has changed over time. Based on 1991 statistics, half of American children or 32.3 million lived in households headed by a single parent, stepparent, grandparent, relative, or nonrelative ("Half of nation's children," 1995, p. 841). The rise in single-parent households is attributed to increases in the number of out-of-wedlock births and divorces. The statistics also revealed racial differences in the family constellation with 56 percent of white children living in a traditional nuclear family compared to 26 percent for African-Americans and 38 percent for Hispanics (p. 841).

According to one report, based on Census Bureau statistics, 18.9 million children under the age of eighteen live with one parent. The data further provides an examination of the interaction between single-parent homes and other variables that impact lifestyle and life chances. It distinguishes between never-married and divorced single parents and concludes that children who live with a divorced parent fare better than children who live with a never-married parent ("Single-parent kids," 1997, p. 48). There were significant economic disparities in income between the two groups, with 45 percent of children of divorced single mothers living below the poverty line compared to 69 percent of children living with a never-married single mother. This can be attributed to the fact that 59 percent of never-married mothers were unemployed compared to only 29 percent of divorced mothers. The employment differential is tied to differences in level of education with fewer than two-thirds of never-married mothers completing high school compared to 85 percent of divorced mothers (p. 48).

Add to these statistics the impact of women on the national economy and another dynamic enters the picture. As more and more women enter the workforce, whether as a result of the dissolution of marriages, personal fulfillment, or the need to supplement the family income, the demands of balancing work and career produce stress. Having a stay-at-home mom to greet children as they return from school, for many, is an aberration of the past. Consequently, a generation of latchkey kids were born. With most students arriving home hours before their parent(s), there arises the problem of unsupervised time that has spawned such problems as loitering in the community, and shopping malls, vandalism, loneliness, and in some instances association with deviant youth subcultures.

Many school and community groups have responded to the problem by establishing after-school programs. Some programs are quite comprehensive in providing services that range from leisure activities such as art and intramural sports to homework assistance and counseling. In many communities such programs have had an ancillary effect of saving children from having to assume adult responsibilities of caring for younger siblings, preparing meals, housekeeping, etc.

In single-parent homes, homes where both parents are employed, or homes where a parent or parents are emotionally absent, children cannot always enjoy the carefree days of youth, particularly in cases where the family cannot afford the high cost of daycare. Many of these children's lives are governed by a routine of remaining indoors until parents arrive home, calling or beeping a parent to signal their safe arrival home, picking younger siblings up from school, starting dinner, etc. These are homes where working parents have provided some structure. In other instances, children are simply left to their own resources without parental guidance. They are free to come and go, wherever and with whomever they please. It is this unrestricted use of time and the lack of monitoring and supervision that result in problems for the family, school, and community.

For many parents, the rigors of work and family responsibilities can be emotionally and physically draining (Brownlee & Miller, 1997). Consequently, they may lack the emotional energy required to discipline, "debate" with children, or otherwise actively engage themselves in parenting. Some may compensate by being overly permissive or strict in regards to rules of conduct. This is not to say that all single-parent or two-working-parent families do not effectively manage the rigors of balancing work and family or that all stay-at-home moms possess good parenting skills and raise happy and well-adjusted children. We can all think of examples to the contrary. What it does attest to is the need for parents to spend quality time with their children.

Children left to their own resources often lack the emotional maturity to make informed decisions about the choices they make, hence the need for parental guidance. When parents are preoccupied with work, there may be a lack of focus on some of the mundane issues of parenting such as monitoring the child's homework, following up on other school related issues, getting to know the child's friends and their parents, maintaining discipline, attending school programs, and involving the child in special activities such as Little League, music, art, dance, computer classes, etc. Without proper parenting, children can lose their direction, and the blossoming of their innate potential can be jeopardized. For example, we often make assumptions about the lack of ability of young offenders and gang members, when in fact if one closely examine the intricate structure of this subculture and the role that each member plays within it, we often find a highly organized and efficient social system. Many of these juveniles are thinkers, firmly indoctrinated in the norms, values, and customs of their subculture. Though many may be categorized as disciplinary problems, learning disabled, or any number of other labels we attach to juveniles, the behavior may betray the reality. We often fail to see the redeeming quality in many of these kids.

Sometimes this occurs because we lack the resources to provide appropriate interventions; sometimes we are overwhelmed by the sheer number of kids in need. In other instances the problems are symptomatic of children of dysfunctional families requiring social service agencies to deal with a plethora of issues before being the child can be reached, and sometimes we fail to recognize a child's "worth" because of stereotypical images and low expectations. Within educational institutions, the structure is not always amenable to meeting such children's needs and teachers often lack training in how to meet them. The unfortunate end result is that we often categorically write these students off as losers. Some in fact may be so hardened by their experiences that their behavior has turned pathological, requiring a different type of more clinical intervention that may or may not be sufficient to modify the behavior. For many others, the solution may be as simple as some caring adult seeing their potential and providing encouragement. These are children who need a positive alternative. Peer pressure is a very powerful force, and our most effective defense against its lure is strong parental involvement and commitment or that of another caring adult.

Single parents who live in extended families or otherwise have the support of other family members may find that having assistance from others alleviates some of the stress. Then there are those single parents who exhaust themselves both physically and emotionally to provide the best for their children. They manage to find the time for their children, their work, and other interests. We have all encountered them and marvel at their tenacity and energy level.

Parenting under the best of circumstances can be, paradoxically, rewarding and challenging. However, the single parent climbs a steeper mountain.

CHILD ABUSE

Child abuse is so widespread that it can be considered the shame of the nation. Somehow, despite our advances in technology that enable us to maintain life in outer space, we have been unable to protect our children from the people who are supposed to love them, virtually, more than themselves—their families. It is estimated that 3.5 to 14 percent of children are physically abused by their parents. Even if the figure is put at 3.5 percent this translates into 1.7 million children who are victimized in this manner. The abuse is so severe in about one-third of the cases that it results in serious injury. Hundreds of children are killed by their parents each year (Browne, 1986).

The profile of an abusive parent is usually an individual under thirty years of age with low social economic status who lives under circumstances that produce a high level of stress and frustration. Stress and frustration emanate from such life conditions as loneliness, marital discord, unemployment, drug or alcohol abuse, unemployment, domestic violence, and job anxiety (Giovannoni & Becerra, 1979). The operative word in profiling the abusive parent is "usually," for child abuse crosses all socioeconomic boundaries.

Abusive parents are like runaway locomotives, cognizant of the destructive power and voracity of their rage, yet unable to contain it. Some abusive parents literally despise their children because of behaviors the child exhibits with which they are unable to cope. For others, the source of abuse is the child's inability to fulfill the parent's need for love and happiness. The abuse is the punishment for failing to meet these needs. Researchers have also found that abusive mothers, more so than nonabusive mothers, believe that the child intentionally engages in behaviors to unnerve them (Bauer & Twentyman, 1985).

Perhaps the most devastating consequence of child abuse is that it evolves as a thread of violence that will weave its way through successive generations unless there are interventions at some point in the very early years of the child's life. Approximately 30 percent of adults who were abused as children will become abusive parents (Kaufman & Zigler, 1987). Unfortunately, abused children come to accept how they were treated as the norm if they are not exposed to a different standard. Consequently, those who are able to escape the cycle of abuse in rearing their own children are those who at some point in the early years bonded with individuals who showed them love, who received therapeutic counseling, or who found an emotionally supportive relationship with a significant other (Egeland, Jacobvitz, & Stroufe, 1988)

What are the implications for education? One study observed abused one- to-three year olds as they interacted with other children to observe their reaction when another child cried or showed signs of distress. With few exceptions, the abused children responded with fear, physical assault, and threats. The conclusion drawn was that abused children will learn to respond to others in the same abusive manner as they are treated at a very early age. This translates into trouble in the classroom, as these children interact with larger numbers of their peers. They learn to respond to frustration and conflict with combative behavior. The implications of the study are compelling, for they affirm the devastating personality altering consequences of child abuse rapidly transforming the abused child to an abusive child (Main & George, 1985).

Educators must take a second look at students who develop a pattern of aggressive behavior. These students may require interventions by support staff to ascertain the cause of the problem. No longer can such behavioral problems be summarily dismissed as abject disrespect for adult authority or others in general.

SUBSTANCE ABUSE

In regard to drug and alcohol consumption, it appears as if we have taken a step back in time. Statistics show that increases in drug and alcohol consumption are at levels reminiscent of the late 1960s and 1970s. The most recent indication of a rise in substance abuse surfaced in 1992. Of even greater significance is that in 1993, drug use was up in all categories at all grade levels. Experts concur that drugs on the scene today present a greater health risk to users as they are more potent and lethal than in the '60s and '70s. Many drugs on the streets today have been chemically altered to heighten the high the user receives (Thomas, 1997, p. 1).

The initial response to the chemical effect of drug and alcohol use varies from individual to individual with some experiencing a 95 on a 100 degree pleasure scale. For these individuals, the probability of repeat use is substantial and the point at which they get caught in a web that becomes increasingly difficult from which to extricate themselves (Thomas, 1997, p. A-4). Findings also show a positive correlation between the duration of drug use and the use of alcohol. That is, the longer an individual uses drugs, the greater the likelihood he/she will begin to consume alcohol as well. According to one source, "Many people who abuse alcohol choose it as a second drug to level the effects of their drug of choice when it is wearing off" (Thomas, 1997, p. A-4).

As the substance abuser of today defies the profile of yesteryear (a middle-aged male), substance abuse counselors and others who work with this population must reevaluate their strategies. The composite picture of today's substance abuser reflects variations in age, gender, and cultures. They are adolescents, women, retirees, the mentally ill, and people of different cultures. Consequently, rubber-stamp counseling strategies and treatment programs no longer offer a universal panacea. As each group brings with it issues peculiar to their group, treatment must address their special needs (Thomas, 1997, p. A-4).

A survey commissioned by The National Center on Addiction and Substance Abuse at Columbia University in New York and conducted by Luntz Research Companies and QEV Analytics revealed that of the 1,115 adolescents aged twelve to seventeen surveyed, 41 percent of the high school students had witnessed the sale of drugs at their school compared to only 25 percent who had witnessed the sale of drugs in their neighborhood. Twenty-four percent indicated that the accessibility of marijuana was such that they could buy it in one hour or less. While alcohol is the most commonly abused drug among teens, followed by marijuana, the survey revealed that 56 percent of those surveyed knew someone who had used hard drugs. Most discouraging was that only 36 percent indicated they would report another student selling drugs ("Survey Reveals," 1997, p. 22).

As long as this code of silence prevails, parents and school officials will have to continue to be strident in getting the message across to adolescents that drugs not only negatively impact the life of the user but also those with whom he/she interacts on a regular basis. Students must understand the power they possess to make schools safe places. I am not certain that students know how to deal with situations where they have witnessed illegal activity. Schools and parents need to make a conscientious effort to explain to students how they can assist in maintaining a safe school environment. Adult authority figures must strive to cultivate relationships with adolescents that inspire trust. The strength of such relationships will provide the impetus to break the code of silence and preserve educational environments where learning can take place because students feel safe and secure.

The importance of a good relationship between parents and teenagers is often understated. This was the seminal finding of a federally funded study conducted by Dr. Michael D. Resnick of the University of Minnesota in Minneapolis. Dr. Resnick notes that parents often relinquish their influence over teens to the peer group, perhaps feeling that they need less direct guidance and support. However, the Resnick study found that teens who felt loved by their parents and comfortable in school were less likely to engage in early sexual activity, to commit suicide, to commit violent crimes, or to abuse alcohol or drugs. Parental expectations significantly influence adolescent behavior through twelfth grade, irrespective of income, race, or single-or two-parent households ("Parents Remain," 1997).

The Resnick study went a step further, challenging the commonly held belief that school size, or type of school and teacher training were pivotal factors in school success. He found of greater significance was a school environment where students felt comfortable, liked coming to school, had a sense of belonging, and perceived teachers as fair and caring ("Parents Remain," 1997, p. 23).

The extent of substance abuse in our culture has reached such proportions as to create a national call to study the issue and educate the public. There are those who contend that it wasn't until the problem began to permeate the tranquility and security afforded by middle- and upper-class status that it received national recognition and sparked an initiative to deal with the issue. When the grim reaper began to touch the lives of children of suburbia and the rich and powerful, society took note and went on the defensive. Drug addiction destroys lives—those of the addict and the addict's families. As previously mentioned, its victims come from all walks of life. They are rich, poor, young, old, male, female, professionals, laborers, and CEOs; their faces are the color of the rainbow, and they represent all creeds and religions. This causes one to question why individuals get caught in the web of drug addiction. When it was thought the problem was relegated to society's poor, the answer seemed simple enough: it was a means of escape from a world where hopelessness followed its inhabitants everywhere they went.

As the drug culture became firmly entrenched in inner cities of America, the "entrepreneurs" among the inhabitants soon discovered that while the American Dream was clearly beyond their grasp, they could capitalize on the misery of their neighbors by selling drugs and thus create their own version. It was as if they were saying, If you close the door to your world and forever hold the American Dream just beyond my grasp, I will create my own world, one in which I can define my own success. For many children of the ghetto, this sends a message that education is not the key that unlocks the door to the American Dream. There are few examples or role models represented before them as proof. In their world, who seems to be "successful"? Who seems to have money and all of the materials things that attest to success, and most important, who seems to possess power and command control of those around them? More often than not, it is the gangleader/drug lord. The children of the ghetto have great potential, too, but when you live in the shadow of hope, dreams and aspirations of a bright future are sometimes obscured by the harsh realities of everyday experiences.

Numerous studies have revealed a neglected weapon in the war against drugs and other social pathologies—religion. Religion gives structure to our lives by providing a set of values and moral beliefs that govern our actions. It is a significant factor in redirecting the course of people's lives, even those already in the throes of a personal crises (Shapiro & Wright, 1996; Lerman, 1998). For teenagers, the most reliable predictors for remaining drug free was optimism about the future and regular church attendance. Among African American youths, these variables proved to be of greater significance than family structure or income (Shapiro & Wright, 1996).

One survey cited religion as the second strongest influence in the lives of teens, superseded only by parents and edging out teachers, peers, the media, girlfriend, or boyfriend. The results of the survey were borne out by teen expert William Damon of Stanford University who observed that "religion is one of the most powerful influences on young people. There aren't a lot of positive things that predict avoiding risks—not I.Q., where you live. Religion is one of the few positive things you can add to a child's life" (Lerman, 1998, p. 12).

At the most fundamental level, these studies suggest that schools and the religious community can do much in the fight by providing adolescents with structure and a nurturing environment in which to develop positive self-esteem and formulate goals to set them on the path to a brighter future (Leland, 1998).

PEER PRESSURE

Some students feel that in order to belong, it is necessary to conform to the behavior patterns of the group to which they seek membership. For the most part, they are correct, particularly in instances where group members are engaging in illegal activities. Under such circumstances, the conformist represents the weak link that may break the chain of the code of allegiance and secrecy that governs the group.

ESCAPISM

Adolescence can be a tumultuous period. Most parents would agree that it tests their parenting skills to the limit. As adolescents struggle to define themselves, and establish their own identity, the process can be just as frustrating for the adolescent as it is for the parent. The search for a personal identity can lead adolescents through a maze of emotions and trial and error experiences. Some teens come through emotionally unscathed, while for others it is a period marked by rebelliousness and recklessness, all in an effort to establish their independence and sense of self. Where parents have been successful in providing guidance and instilling strong values, this period can be relatively uneventful. Yet, sometimes, under the best of circumstances, the physical and emotional changes that occur during this life stage can be more than some adolescents can bear.

In the absence of adequate coping skills and/or a strong support system, some adolescents may turn to drugs or even suicide. They serve as a means of escape from issues and problems perceived as too overwhelming to resolve. High schools also bear the brunt of the tumultuous teen years. A major complaint among high school teachers is a lack of respect for adult authority marked by talking back, disobedience and flagrant disregard for established rules. Schools can assist teens through these turbulent years by providing structure, clearly defined expectations and consequences, opportunities for students to discover their potential and capitalize on their strengths, recognition, open and frequent communication with parents, instruction on conflict resolution, and the development of coping skills.

Many schools have instituted peer coaching programs where peer mediators hear disputes between students and assist them in resolving the problem. This often saves students from getting involved in physical confrontations that lead to out-of-school suspensions. We make an assumption that as we mature we learn how to deal effectively with frustration and the pressures of everyday life. As youth today are confronted with many more issues and choices than their predecessors, we can no longer assume they possess coping skills commensurate to the problems. To save our youth, we must specifically teach them how to confront and effectively manipulate the pressures and curves that everyday life may throw their way. There are those who will ask, How much more responsibility can the school assume? The answer is as simple: as much as is required to ensure that the generation of kids today will be physically, emotionally, and psychologically prepared to meet the needs of the older and future generations.

GANGS

Gangs have been part of the American landscape for decades. Once considered the scourge of inner cities, over the past fifteen years they have begun to spread their influence into small town America and suburbia (Pearlman-Debelak, April 9, 1995, p. B-3). In search of new territory to ply their trade and for some to bolster their personal sense of power, small town U.S.A. and suburbia have suddenly awakened to find a stranger in their midst. There was a time when the mention of gangs conjured up stereotypical images of tough-looking Hispanic or African American boys. We have now come to realize or acknowledge a fact that has perhaps lain dormant for many years, that gang activity is not confined to the Hispanic and African American communities. White and Asians gangs are very much a part of the landscape.

An even more startling observation has been the growing active and aggressive participation of girls in the gang culture. Even though gang experts say that independent girl gangs are rare, they represent a threat because of their affiliation with male gangs. Chicago alone has in excess of 130 male-dominated gangs with female affiliations. Girl gang members basically hold cash, hide drugs, etc. However, one is not to underestimate their potential for aggressive or deviant behavior. They too engage in fighting, drinking, stealing, and tagging (defacing property with graffiti). Authorities agree however that they are rarely moved to acts of deadly violence (Smith, 1997).

Girls succumb to the lure of gangs for the same reason as boys. The gang fills the void in their lives for family, a sense of belonging, protection in a hostile environment or just being noticed. They are willing to pay the price of membership. A female Latino gang in Chicago willingly submits to the initiation rite called "on the wall." The recruit stands against a wall and is beaten by fellow gang members. Why do they submit to this? The typical response is, "You got to show you're strong." The initiation complete, girl gang members maintain a lower profile than the males. Those who are able to leave the gang admit to the lack of reason for the violence. One ex- member said, "We used to just fight. It wasn't nothing. Just like hanging together as a crowd. We all used to dress alike, carry steak knives just to be noticed. Just to get with certain guys. All kinds of stupid reasons." Without a doubt, however, active, aggressive female involvement in gang activity is forcing police departments to look more closely at the growing seriousness of the problem (Smith, 1997, p. 6).

While few cities gather statistics to verify the extent of their participation, Los Angeles, which has traditionally monitored gang activities found that girls make up 15 percent of the gang population. Federal statistics note a 25.4 percent increase in violent crimes perpetrated by female juveniles over the past decade, twice that of male juveniles (Pearlman-Debelak, 1995, p. B-1).

Irrespective of geographical location, gender, or ethnicity, gang members share a number of common characteristics. These are adolescents who often are in search of a sense of belonging, who suffer from low self-esteem, have a prior history of brushes with the law and records of substance abuse, disciplinary problems in school, poor academic performance, and a lack of participation in sports or other organized community-or school-based extracurricular activities. For many, the gang lifestyle provides respite from abuse and neglect at home. While some gangs are female only, most are composed of boys and girls. Sexual exploitation of female gang members is not uncommon, at one time used as a rite of initiation into the gang. As girls became more aggressive, they "earned" their place in the gang structure by fighting other females (Pearlman-Debelak, 1995).

Gang members are angry young people who live their lives as if to say, If others will not acknowledge my worth as an individual, I'll force them to acknowledge me by sheer force and intimidation. This in turn spawns their sense of power. Ironically, this attitude betrays their feelings of hopelessness. The violence that is so characteristic of gangs purports a disregard for life, theirs as well as others. The reckless abandon of gang members as they open fire on their perceived adversaries in public or the openness in which they engage in other illegal activities attests to a total and flagrant contempt for life. Many of these adolescents come to accept the probability of an early death as a fact of life.

When there is no hope of expanding the boundaries of your world, the purpose of life is diminished. What does the future hold for these kids that would motivate them to press forward? Many are products of a cycle of poverty that has spun for generations. In the absence of positive role models and strong support systems, they will take up the cadence of the cycle as it spins and spawn yet another generation of children who will become entangled in the web of poverty and a degenerative lifestyle destined for failure.

It is often very difficult for gang members to dissociate from the gang. The process, however, is more difficult for male than for females who often opt to leave after becoming pregnant. Gang members who try to leave the group are often harassed and they and/or their family members may be threatened or intimidated. Parents sometimes respond by sending the juvenile to live with friends or relatives in another area. Conversely, sometimes students who are noted gang members also are sent to live with relatives, as their parents desperately attempt to remove them from the influence of their gang member peers. All too often, however, these students will seek out gang members in their new environment or attempt to establish a new gang. In effect, parents attempting to save their children may inadvertently be contributing to the spread of gang activity. This is a common problem for many schools, as parents illegally cross attendance boundaries or submit other fraudulent documentation to enroll their children in schools free of gang influence.

What can the school and community do to disrupt the cycle? Leon Bing, in her book *Do Or Die* (1991), describes her experiences as she is allowed into the inner circle of gangs in South Central Los Angeles. Noting the gang members' average life expectancy of nineteen years, she concluded that "Where we have failed, the collective 'we', society, government, is that we have not provided enough meaningful options and opportunities for young people in too many of these communities where gangs flourish" (p. 271). As Ms. Bing points out, to repel the lure of gangs is more than just a matter of providing something for them to do. We must provide them with those things they get from gang affiliation. Ironically, as materialistic as our society is, it is not the material things that gangs can provide that they covet. What they tend to value most is the sense of power, control, security, protection, opportunity, and belonging that the gang provides.

For those whose indoctrination into the gang culture has not yet been solidified, the solution can be as simple as getting these kids into school or community-organized programs such as basketball or boxing or by introducing them to activities unique to their experiences such as aviation, fencing, etc. The very positive impact of such programs has been consistently noted in personal accounts of adolescents who have overcome adversity (Coleman, 1996). Such programs give students an opportunity to feel good about themselves, expend energy in a socially constructive manner and belong to something with positive consequences. These programs bring them into contact with caring adults. Our target group should be those kids who are pre-gang, pre-drug. Sadly this means focusing on children under the age of nine or ten (Bing, 1991). We must ensure that gangs are not an option for our children.

Parents, too, can be proactive in their efforts to shield their children from gang influences. They can monitor their children's activities, get to know their friends and their friends' parents; question changes in behavior; volunteer at school; attend school programs, encourage participation in organized sports, church or other programs; and most important spend time with them.

VIOLENCE

The violence and rage that is so characteristic of gang members is another issue that commands priority attention. To save lives, we must dissipate the rage. "Aggressive adolescents often are the products of angry, violent households" (Callahan, 1997, p. 38). Callahan writes about a number of programs in California aimed at helping adolescents deal with their aggressive behavior. So intense and deep-rooted is this rage in some that it can be precipitated by something as innocuous as a look or touch. Many educators can identify with the following scenarios:

Two students end up in the dean's office after a physical confrontation in the halls during a passing period. The dean listens to both sides only to surmise that one of the combatants didn't like the way the other was looking at him/her. The "look" is called "mad-dogging," that is, attempting to make eye contact or giving someone a dirty look (Callahan, 1997, p. 38). Another common complaint that frequently evolves into physical confrontations is "he said, she said." This is a common problem that frequently brings girls into the dean's office. Girls tend to deal with rumor by aggressively confronting the alleged source. Callahan reported an incident where a girl responded by hitting another in the head with a brick. Most remarkable was her response that she felt her actions were appropriate because when her stepdad physically assaulted her mother, the mother did nothing. As difficult as this is to phantom, this is the logic of many kids. The actions of parents become the standard against which they evaluate their own behavior.

Here is another scene that is played out in schools much too frequently: A principal, teacher, monitor, or any adult in authority asks a student to do something (take your cap off, pick up paper she/he threw on the floor, stop running, etc.) and the student refuses, ignores the staff member, continues to walk away. In confronting the student, the staff member touches the student's arm to get his attention. The typical response is, "Get your hands off of me, don't touch me." This sets the stage for the incident to escalate. It is not uncommon for a simple request to escalate, culminating in anything ranging from a suspension to an assault on a staff member and the student's being carted off to jail. This is a reality in many schools across America, including elementary schools.

Schools must be more proactive in their response to student aggression. Part of teacher training should include teaching prospective teachers how to deal with aggressive students and defuse potentially volatile situations. Additionally, schools must teach students how to manage their anger.

Nineteen eighty-seven to 1994 showed a steady increase in violent crimes committed by juveniles. According to United States Attorney General Janet Reno, however, the latest statistics suggest the tide is turning. Data gathered by the Federal Bureau of Investigation showed that teenagers arrested for murder dropped 10.7 percent in 1996 reflecting a three-year decline. In 1996 there were 464.7 arrests for violent crimes per 100,000 juveniles age ten to seventeen, down from 511.9 in 1995 and 527.4 in the peak year of 1994. Despite the decline, these figures should be viewed with cautious optimism, as the nature of violent crimes, in general, is reason for concern, irrespective of numbers. The numbers are still much too high to ease our social conscience. The battle has just begun, the war is yet to be won ("Teen Crime", 1997, p. 10).

The alarm for violent crimes committed by juveniles was first sounded in 1987 registering 311.3 arrests per 100,000. The problem was attributed to the nationwide proliferation of gangs who traffic in drugs, recruit teenagers as couriers, and arm them for the task. This had a domino effect. The lure of quick, easy money made recruiting their peers and bringing them into the fold an effortless task ("Teen Crime," 1997, p. 10).

The decline in violent crimes committed by juveniles can be attributed to a number of programs. However, their effectiveness is grounded in the political initiative sparked by Attorney General Reno who has sounded the clarion call for proactive measures to curb juvenile crimes. Prof. Alfred Blumstein of Carnegie Mellon University credits the decline in juvenile violent crimes to such innovative police tactics as voluntary and involuntary searches and gun bounties. Attorney General Reno cites President Clinton's crime plan which funnelled more money to cities to fight crime and the institution of more stringent laws. Additionally, at the local level, police departments, community mentoring programs, prosecutors, and juveniles themselves have committed to providing juveniles with choices that do not lead down a wayward path. In some cities businesses have offered various incentives for those who turn in guns ("Teen Crime," 1997).

The war against violent crimes committed by juveniles is being waged on two fronts—one proactive, the other reactive. Older adults who use juveniles to commit illegal acts, noting a more lenient disposition of cases involving juveniles, and juveniles who feel that their age will give them impunity have been put on notice with more states trying juveniles as adults for violent crimes and imposing prison sentences. At the other end of the spectrum is the institution of such deterrents as special programs for at-risk students, providing after-school programs and summer jobs ("Teen Crime," 1997).

A study based on FBI figures for the states of Alabama, Colorado, Iowa, Idaho, Illinois, North Dakota, South Dakota, and Utah and conducted by James Alan Fox, dean of the College of Criminal Justice at Northeastern University, revealed that half of all violent crimes committed by juveniles occur between the hours of 2 p.m. and 8 p.m. on school days, and two-thirds of such crimes occur between 2 p.m. and 11 p.m., while only 21.5 percent occur between 11 p.m. and 7 a.m. These statistics suggest the need for constructive activities to occupy students between the time they are dismissed from school and parents arrive home from work, as well as the effectiveness of community juvenile curfew ordinances. Clearly, schools, communities, and parents must each work to establish and maintain constructive after-school programs for children as a buffer against negative peer group influences. Innovative measures must be taken to compensate for changing lifestyles, as work responsibilities of single- and dual-parent families consume more of their time. Children cannot be left to their own resources to fill the gap ("Study Reveals," 1997, p. 24).

Many schools have instituted safe-school programs emphasizing respect for self and others. The continued decline in violent crimes committed by juveniles will require public awareness and continued political and community support of programs already in place.

In other innovative efforts, schools and the court system have instituted programs to help kids deal with their anger. Designed to help kids who respond in a volatile manner to things that most of us would not give a second thought, these programs teach kids to keep a journal of what made them angry, how they felt about it and what they did, to avoid that which triggers the anger, to walk away from potentially explosive situations and to think before acting (Callahan, 1997, p. 38).

TEEN PREGNANCY

In the United States, the mid-1970s marked the beginning of a study increase in the proportion of out-of-wedlock births for all age groups (Glazer, 1993, p. 411). More recent statistics, however, show a national decline in the birth rate for American teens with the most dramatic decrease among African American girls. According to Secretary of Health and Human Services Donna Shalala, the decline represents the success of various programs and initiatives to curb sexual activity among teens and an increase in the use of birth control precipitated by an heightened awareness of AIDS (Meckler, 1998).

Between 1991 and 1996, the birth rate for African American teens fell by 21 percent. Based on 1996 statistics, the birth rate for African American teenagers was 9.2 percent, reflecting the lowest rate since the government began compiling such data in 1970. With this significant decline, Hispanic teens are now more likely than their African American counterparts to give birth. However, even this group showed a decline in the birth rate from 10.7 percent in 1995 to 10.2 in 1996. Despite the decline for both African American and Hispanic teens, their birth rate is still more than double that of white teens at 3.9 percent (Meckler, 1998, p. 55). Based on 1996 statistics, one of every twenty girls between the ages of fifteen and nineteen gave birth, reflecting a decrease of 11.9 percent since 1991. Today, approximately a half million teenagers give birth each year.

While the figures for the United States were higher during the 1950s, the social consequences were quite different for a number of reasons. During the 1950s, mothers were more likely to marry the fathers, fathers assumed responsibility for the child, more babies were put up for adoption, and there was social stigma attached to giving birth outside of wedlock. Today, there is a different reality. There is virtually no social stigma attached to giving birth out of wedlock. No longer are girls required to quit school or, if allowed to stay, banished to placement outside of the regular school setting. In general, fathers do not claim responsibility for the child or contribute to the child's care. The vast majority of teenage mothers (95 percent) choose to raise their child (Turbak, 1991, p. 21).

Another disturbing phenomenon is the number of girls entering high school as ninth graders who are already mothers and those who will have a second child before their scheduled graduation date. As many as 70 percent of teen mothers will become pregnant again within two years, without some type of pregnancy prevention assistance (Turbak, p. 50).

Despite the decline in the teenage birth rate between 1991 and 1996, there is still the reality that children unequivocally change the course of the teen mother's life. The teenage mother's lifestyle and life chances are drastically altered. On the average, they earn less money and are more likely to perform menial labor ("Single-parent kids," 1997). For most, prospects for a brighter future that come with a good education dissolve with childbirth. Only half will complete high school and just 2 percent will graduate from college. This is a dismal picture compared to their nonparent peers where 96 percent will graduate from high school and 20 percent complete college. The sad reality is that welfare dependency will become a way of life for many of these young mothers. A survey of teenage mothers in New York City between the ages of fifteen and seventeen revealed that nearly three-fourths were welfare dependent. This virtually ensures a life of poverty (Turbak, p. 22; Sander, 1991).

Not only do teenage mothers and their offspring exact a price for this phenomenon, society also is left with a heavy debt. These families will require health care and other social services for their survival, and taxpayers must pay the bill. In 1985, the United States spent approximately $21.5 billion dollars a year providing such services (Turbak, 1991; Sander, p. 187). With inflation, despite the decline in the birth rate, costs will remain high. There are those who would take the hard-line approach and say, "You made your bed, now lie in it," but at what cost? Without providing these teen mothers with the necessary support, everyone pays in terms of welfare cost, special education services, health care, juvenile detention facilities, etc.

Many of their children will enter school handicapped by the circumstances of their birth. Compared to their peers, children born to teenage mothers will experience more illness and injuries, are more likely to suffer birth defects and mental disabilities, are physically smaller, more easily distracted and frustrated, and more likely to spend some part of their lives in foster care (Turbak, 1991; Sander, 1991).

Clearly, not having themselves reached the level of physical, social, and emotional maturity to successfully handle the rigors of parenting, these mothers before their time inadvertently stifle the development of their offspring. Studies conducted by the Contingency Response Intervention for Infants of Adolescent Parents in Athens, Georgia, found that teenage mothers lack the skills to properly bond with their offspring. Teenage mothers are less responsive to their children. They do not talk to, look at, or engage in cuddling them as much as mature mothers. Virtually everything the teen mother does, as part of childrearing, will have long-term repercussions for the child. For example, many teen mothers lack proper knowledge regarding nutrition and subject their offspring to their own poor eating habits. Teen mothers were found to begin feeding their babies solid foods before the recommended time, to use food as a pacifier, and to feed the child a diet of pizza, hamburger, and candy. This coupled with the fact that many teen mothers do not receive proper prenatal care can retard the child's mental and physical development (Turbak, 1991).

Social workers at the Johns Hopkins Center for Teen-aged Parents and Their Infants found that children of teenaged mothers showed language deficiencies stemming from a lack of consistent contact with the mother. These children are more likely to be shuffled between grandparents, other relatives, or day care providers, thereby limiting contact with the mother from whom they learn complex language skills through imitation. These deficiencies will come to bear heavily on these children as they enter school. Compared to their peers, these children score lower on intelligence tests, are more likely to have to repeat a grade and exhibit behavioral and emotional problems (Turbak, p. 22).

As these children enter the system, schools must be prepared to meet their special needs, and the school's reach must extend beyond the classroom. Teachers must understand that many of the problems and behaviors these children manifest are endemic to their social circumstances and organic causes and are beyond the child's control. Therefore, teachers must be trained to identify the cause and respond appropriately. Without this preparation, teachers can become overwhelmed with frustration and the goal of educating children is replaced with simply attempting to maintain order in the classroom.

There are also educational consequences for the teen mother. What about the teen mother who struggles to stay in school while attempting to raise a child?

The world of the teen mother is one of contradictions. On the one hand she is saddled with adult responsibilities of providing care for a dependent child. On the other, she is usually dependent upon her own parents for her survival, and as she is still a minor subject to obey their rules. This sometimes carries over to the school setting when a teen mother says to a school official who attempts to reprimand her that she is grown. There is no doubt that she has adult responsibilities that set her apart from her peers, but the contradiction lies in her ability to carry out those responsibilities.

Nevertheless, having attained the status of mother, many of these adolescents may resent being treated as children. Additionally, there is the stress produced in attempting to balance the responsibilities of motherhood, school, home, and sometimes a part-time job, and still enjoy the trappings of youth—dates, parties, hanging out (Turbak, p. 22). Managing multiple responsibilities is a formidable challenge for mature adults; imagine the toll this takes on an adolescent ill-equipped with the necessary emotional, intellectual, and physical maturity to cope.

In effect, bearing a child does not make one a mother, no more than fathering a child makes one a father. They are still adolescents whose youthful propensities do not automatically dissipate with parenthood. Consequently, many relate to their children more as siblings and peers. They grow up with their children. The problem is exacerbated in families where the problem of teenage pregnancy is generational (Sander, 1991). Consider that today, if a girl gives birth at age fifteen and the pattern of out-of-wedlock births is repeated for each successive generation, she will be a grandmother at age thirty, a great grandmother by age forty-five and a great-great grandmother by age sixty. Here lies the problem that school officials often face when attempting to meet the needs of children, that is, dealing with parents and grandparents who are still attempting to live out the idiosyncrasies of their own life stage. It is as if each generation is being propelled through space, arriving at a place before their appointed time, and lacking the skills and life experiences that would adequately prepare them for the new realm in which they find themselves. How can you discipline a student about his/her dress when the parent appears for the conference, a mirror image of the student? How can you discipline a student for substance abuse when the parent is an abuser?

Consider the following scenarios that clearly affirms the magnitude of the problem. A popular music group was featured at a program held immediately after school. One of the chaperones pointed out a student in the crowded stands with a baby of just a few months old. The student was called down. It was discovered that the baby was hers. She had left school, as she was expected to pick the baby up from the sitter at a specified time, and returned to school with the baby so as not to miss the concert. When she was told she could not bring the baby into that environment, she became very defiant. A staff member held the baby while she made a call for a ride home. After completing the call, she jerked the baby from the staff members arms with such force that the baby was startled. The student was reprimanded, and the incident was reported to the school social worker, as it clearly raised concerns about the well-being of the child. As the mother feels increasingly deprived of her youth because of childrearing responsibilities, is the child at risk of becoming a victim of abuse? In another incident, a parent reported a teen mother at a football game on a cold and wet day in the stands with her improperly dressed baby who was just a few months old. One of the mothers intervened, counseled the student as to the health risk to the baby, and convinced her to take the child home.

Many young mothers, in fulfilling their own desires, fail to act in the best interest of their children. In some cases, the child is protected and cared for by the grandparents or even great-grandparents, or at the very least these family members are available to monitor the teen mother as she fulfills her duties. This opens the door to a whole new phenomenon. According to a 1993 Census Bureau survey, approximately 3.4 million children live with their grandparents. This represents a 50 percent increase since 1970. While the mother is present in most of these households, in about one-third neither parent is present. Based on these figures, over a half million grandparents provide total custodial care of their grandchildren (Jones, 1997).

Age and financial considerations exacerbate the problem. The median age of grandparents is fifty-seven; however approximately 36,000 are over the age of seventy-five. Their median income is $18,000, half that of traditional households. According to one survey, 65 percent receive no state aid to assist with the care of the child. Those receiving government financial assistance received $109 per month per child, while foster parents received $371. In effect, children who are officially wards of the state receive more benefits than those who are cared for by relatives and not classified as wards of the state (Jones, 1997, p. 43). How can we account for this growing phenomenon? According to one grandmother, "You reap what you sow, and as a country, we're reaping our value system. There's a lack of responsibility on a lot of people's part" (p. 43).

This phenomenon also has widespread consequences for educators, as they attempt to work with grandparents who are already overburdened with caring for grandchildren and often their own elderly parents. Social trends do not give reason for optimism, if divorce rates and substance abuse continue at their present level. A survey of five hundred grandparent caregivers revealed that in only 20 percent of the cases were children placed in the care of grandparents as a result of death, divorce or illness, while 44 percent lived with grandparents because of the parent's substance abuse and 28 percent as a result of abandonment, neglect, or abuse. Schools must assume the dual responsibility of helping these children and their grandparents cope with the circumstances thrust upon them (p. 43).

Parenthood presents a formidable challenge to even mature adults. The mental, physical, financial, and time commitments invoke all of one's reserves to come into play. In the majority of instances where parenthood is a conscious choice and not an accident of nature, the joys of parenting far outweigh the personal sacrifices. However, when the parent is a child, nature's most wonderful gift, the ability to produce something of one's self, to perpetuate one's self through time, can become a devastating force that forever changes the course of a life, often leaving in its wake a frustrated, angry adolescent who feels deprived and cheated of her youth and a child who will suffer the consequences of being born before its time.

The picture darkens. For many young mothers, motherhood presents such emotional turmoil that they are brought to the brink of suicide. Teenage mothers are seven times more likely to attempt suicide than their nonparent peers (Turbak, 1991, p. 20). The demands of motherhood are exacerbated by financial concerns. Judy Musick, a developmental psychologist and founding director of the Illinois Ounce of Prevention Fund, notes that "from conception to adulthood, the children of teenage mothers often face physical, mental, social and economic disadvantages" (Turbak, p. 20)

At the most fundamental level, we must address the causal factors of teenage pregnancy. We must answer the fundamental question why so many adolescent girls, despite the availability of birth control, sex education, and, in many cases, the hardship of welfare dependency that characterize their own lives, choose to become mothers before their time. The problem can be addressed from two levels, proactive and reactive, with obvious concentration on proactive measures to continue the decline in the teen birth rate. Proactive measures are driven by an examination of the variables that give rise to the problem. Through detailed case studies, Sander (1991) journeys into the lives of four generations of women in one family who were teenage mothers. This unique study places in historical perspective the reasons that led each successive generation to follow the same path. In so doing, she addresses such issues as the search for the ideal family that evolves from parental loss through mental illness or abandonment, dysfunctional families, low self-esteem, lack of positive role models, failed educational systems, feelings of hopelessness, and lack of job opportunities (pp. 177-184).

Home, school, and community—individually and collectively—can effect change. Parents must make their children their first priority, understanding the necessity of being an active participant and positive influence in the life of children. Schools must actively strive to provide services and programs that help teen mothers stay in school and complete their education. Communities too can assist in this effort by making prenatal care available to pregnant teens, providing parenting classes that address such topics as nutrition, discipline, health care, child development, and, most important providing day care that will enable teen mothers to stay in school and further their education (Turbak, 1991).

However, not all children of teenage mothers are consumed by the pathologies that permeate their circumstance. Those mothers who are fortunate enough to have the active support and guidance of parents or some significant other, a friend or relative perhaps, are able to weather the storm and raise children who are able to successfully fashion a place for themselves in the world as well-adjusted and productive adults (p. 50).

TEEN SUICIDE

Teen suicide ranks as the third leading cause of death of young adults between the ages of fifteen and twenty-four, exceeded only by accidents and homicide. What is even more alarming is that the teenage suicide rate has tripled since the 1950s. Teens who commit suicide defy attempts to typecast them. Adolescent suicide victims represent a cross section of the general population. They hail from all social, ethnic, and economic classes. They may have all of the right social connections and be academically and athletically successful. In a word, they seem to have everything to live for. Yet, they are as likely to fall prey to the same emotionally debilitating issues as adolescents from broken homes who have few friends and are uninvolved in school activities (Worsnop, 1991). Many studies, including a 1986 government-commissioned survey that asked experts in the area of teenage suicide research and prevention to list the characteristics of teens most at risk of committing suicide, cited the following: (Chiles, 1986; Worsnop, 1991; Huard, 1997; Dwyer, 1998):

Family conflicts. Family discord created by divorce, desertion, separation, domestic violence, physical and sexual abuse, and drug abuse can have a devastating effect on children. These issues may be the source of or exacerbate the emotional turmoil suicidal teens experience. Moreover, teens from dysfunctional families where they become the emotional scapegoat are at greater risk of experiencing depression, anxiety, and suicidal propensities. Many experts concur that "drug abusing and suicidal teenagers often feel abandoned by parents who are themselves suffering from severe personal problems" (Chiles, 1986, p. 40). Research has revealed insecurity, anger, and hostility emanating from unstable living conditions as a common thread in the lives of drug-abusing, suicidal adolescents.

Alcohol or drug abuse. More so than a direct cause, alcohol or drug abuse may be symptomatic of the emotional turmoil that leads to suicide and may serve as a trigger. One study found that up to one-half of all suicide attempts involved individuals who were drinking at the time (Chiles, 1986, p. 37).

Social isolation. The dissolution of the nuclear family as a result of divorce, remarriage, single-parent homes, frequent changes in residences, and schools and child abuse are among the causes of social isolation for the teenager. In general the greater the degree of their social integration into a group, the less likely they are to commit suicide (Worsnop, 1991).

Sexual orientation. A study conducted by researchers at the University of Minnesota and the University of Wisconsin found homosexual teens were three times more likely to attempt suicide than heterosexual teens (Worsnop, 1991).

Depression. Some studies have produced evidence to suggest a genetic or biological link to suicide. In particular such research has noted significant differences in the brain chemistry of suicidal teenagers from nonsuicidal teens. This research finding supports other studies that have found a connection between depression and abnormalities within and between the brain's neurotransmitting systems (Worsnop, 1991).

A common misconception regarding depression is that children who are depressed are quiet or shy. While this may be the case for some children, it should be noted that "young males are more prone to externalize their depression through hostility. They may have an anti-authority attitude and put themselves in situations where they are going to be rejected or hurt by other people" (Dwyer, 1998, p. 24). These are the students typically identified as frequently engaging in acting out behavior. In dealing with these students caution is advised as the external behavior may belie deeper emotional issues.

Low self-esteem. Many suicidal teens are their own worst critics. They intensely scrutinize their actions. Because of the impossibly high standards they set for themselves, they may miss their mark. When this occurs, it sets off a domino effect in which they perceive themselves as failures, which gives rise to a lack of the self-confidence they need to cope with everyday problems and to overcome their fear of the cycles repeating itself. Hopelessness insidiously creeps in, propelling them down a path for which they cannot see an end. Ultimately, suicide seems to be the only realistic solution to the problem. The issue of self-esteem is exacerbated for adolescent girls. In a culture that judges females by their physical beauty, adolescent girls often become fixated on self-image and acceptance by others. If they perceive themselves as falling short of the societal standard for beauty or attractiveness and as incapable of achieving the standard, low self-esteem may be the result (Chiles, 1986; Huard, 1997). As educators we can assist these girls by placing more emphasis on ability than physical appearance and cultivating among students a sense of community that acknowledges the worth of every student.

Male-female relationships. Among other precipitating factors in teen suicide attempts are male-female relationships and school problems (Chiles, 1986).

Feelings of hopelessness. No one is immune to episodes of feelings of hopelessness and desperation. It is an emotional state that is not age specific. However, the physical and emotional issues that accompany adolescence tend to exacerbate such feelings and can be so invasive and overwhelming as to push some teens to contemplate suicide (Chiles, 1986).

Poor communication skills. For many teens the lack of skills to cope with stress is exacerbated by an inability to articulate troubling issues. This results in a feeling of being trapped with no means of escape, of feeling that their problems are interminable and intolerable. This mental state is conducive to suicidal thoughts. Providing troubled teens a forum in which they feel comfortable to express their problems and share with others who have a sympathetic ear, can lessen the anxiety that leads to suicidal tendencies (Chiles, 1986). The offer of friendship and a show of concern can be restorative, sending the message that their situation is not hopeless; there is a light at the end of the tunnel.

Impulsiveness. The exact number of adolescent deaths that can be attributed to suicide is unknown. The statistics may be skewed, as many car accidents, gunshot wounds, and self-poisonings among teens may in actuality be shield suicides (Chiles, 1986).

Unreasonable expectations. While the above traits are found with greater frequency among low achievers, they ironically may be applicable to high achievers, since they often set unrealistically high expectations for themselves and when unable to meet them view themselves as failures. Teens who define their self-worth in terms of achievement are particularly at risk. They may become perfectionists driven by the need to get it right to please family or peers. Their self-worth is garnered from the recognition they receive from excelling academically or socially (Chiles, 1986).

Next to parents, teachers may be the adult figures most likely in a position to note changes in adolescent behavior that may signal depression and or suicidal tendencies. Neither parents nor teachers should dismiss behavior changes as "passing through a phase," or take comfort in the fact that most suicide attempts are not successful. The behavior changes could be symptomatic of more serious problems (Chiles, 1986; Rhodes, 1998).

Suicide and suicide attempts increase with age, occurring rarely among those under age twelve. Over the past two decades, suicide attempts among adolescents have significantly exceeded completed suicides. While the suicide rate among adolescents has increased, they are more likely to be unsuccessful in actually completing the act. Only one out of every one hundred or one hundred and fifty suicide attempts result in death. There is a sharp drop in attempted suicides after age thirty, while completed suicides steadily increase with age. While more females attempt suicide, males are more likely to succeed in taking their lives (Chiles, p. 25). Additionally, males are more likely to choose more violent methods of committing suicide than females.

In the final analysis, teen suicide is an issue that should command our attention as educators and others who come into daily contact with teenages. The cry for help is not always audible. Therefore, responsible adults must be cognizant of changes in behavior and other conditions that signal the potential for trouble.

VALUES

"Emile Durkheim, one of the founders of modern sociology, held that common values are the bonds of social order, and that the loss of such values lead to social and individual instability, as well as to suicidal behavior" (Chiles, 1986, p. 53). Over the decades, there has been increased focus on liberalism and individualism both of which have merit and can advance the cause of social progress. However, taken to the extreme such ideologies can be counterproductive and negatively impact the moral fiber of society. When extreme liberalism, by eroding the basic structure of social traditions that safeguard human rights and promote social order, leads to anarchy, there is reason for concern. Similarly, when individualism is taken to such extremes that "I" rather "we" become the extant reality, we may soon find such values as respect for others and ethical behavior precariously perched on the edge of social order.

Kennedy-Townsend (1992) broached the issue of a growing concern regarding the deteriorating moral character of the nation's youth. She made the point that while traditionally teaching values was the province of parents, parents in general have fallen short of the mark. Statistics have shown an increase in problems such as theft, disrespect for others, fighting, vandalism, alcoholism, sexual misconduct, and substance abuse within the environs of schools.

These behaviors are inextricably tied to values. The question was raised as to whose values are to be taught and who should assume responsibility as many parents have either abdicated the responsibility because of physical or emotional absence or because their values are the antithesis of established social values. It is indeed disturbing to hear reports of parents who themselves engage in unethical behaviors and conscientiously, by direct instruction or by example, indoctrinate their children into a lifestyle governed by the same behaviors. Parents who allow their children to smoke pot, consume alcohol, bring obviously stolen goods into the home, condone violence as a means of resolving conflict, and/or engage in such activities with their children have clearly abdicated their responsibility (Herbert & Daniel, 1996). These students often come to genuinely accept such values as the norm. School officials, consequently, are faced with an additional challenge as they attempt to communicate with these parents in an effort to ameliorate or change student behavior.

However, the values of which Kennedy-Townsend speaks are of a universal nature, espousing such traits as honesty, responsibility, respect for others and volunteerism. The goal is not to sway students in their opinion of specific controversial issues such as abortion, religion, gays, etc. Its goal is to encourage those universal values that will ensure a society in which the worth of each individual and his or her property is respected. Ms. Kennedy-Townsend holds that values education consists of lessons in friendship, responsibility, being polite, respecting others, and helping others in need.

Schools teach values all of the time. Students are expected to attend school regularly, get to class on time, not cheat on exams; to say please, thank you, and excuse me and wait their turn in line, etc. Rules and expectations provide the structural framework for our value system. However, students seem not to be getting the message. Consequently, some school districts have instituted programs specifically aimed at inculcating values. Many have done this under the umbrella of required community service. Ms. Kennedy-Townsend relates that on a smaller scale schools can teach values study by incorporating it into their existing curriculum. The operative word here is incorporate into the existing curriculum. She suggests this can be accomplished simply by capitalizing on class discussions where lessons on value can be extracted and highlighted.

The issue of lack of socially constructive values has reached such proportions as to draw political attention. Both the Bush and Clinton administrations have recognized the need to restore values. While neither has proposed a clear-cut means of accomplishing this goal, each has nevertheless recognized the negative impact of the present trend on the moral fabric of our society.

In educational institutions from elementary to high school, the issue of safety and student conduct has produced alarming statistics. These are not just problems of the inner city. Reports of widespread cheating scandals and drug abuse involving top students have made local headlines. Sixty-one percent of high school students said they cheated on an exam during the past year; since 1978, nationwide, assaults on teachers have increased 700 percent and 282,000 students are assaulted each month. For the first time ever teenagers face a greater risk of violence in school than on the streets (Kennedy-Townsend, 1992). When one factors in verbal assaults and vandalism to the personal property of school employees from teachers to secretaries and their being harassed in public solely by virtue of their affiliation with the school, the problem becomes even more pervasive. Disdain for school that is transferred to its employees is yet another problem that is symptomatic of a lack of values and the need not only to find a socially acceptable means of venting frustration but to learn to accept responsibility for one's predicament.

These statistics attest to the need to specifically teach values. However, schools cannot do it alone. There must be a partnership between school, home, community, and government. The problem is exacerbated when those we herald as cultural heroes behave badly and betray the public trust. There are numerous accounts of such behavior that all too frequently make the national news, involving sports heroes, actors, politicians, business leaders, educators, etc. Adults, in general, must present themselves as exemplars if our schools are to remain institutions of learning rather than minefields of violence and dishonesty.

One teacher noted that teachers are in part to blame. Working in a school with a predominantly white faculty and African-American student population, he sensed a reluctance on the part of his peers to call students on inappropriate behavior. He attributed this to fear on the part of some, based on stereotypical perceptions, and for others, to not wanting to get involved in any situation with the potential to escalate. The same holds true in general. I think, nationally, there is a fear of teenagers, particularly when encountered in groups. So, rather than risk a confrontation, it is easier to look the other way. However, in doing so, we exact a high price, creating an educational climate in which our actions are governed by fear and values continue to erode. The problem will persist as long as teachers continue to view the teaching of values as not being their responsibility or too time consuming and until there is a political consensus that values education should be part of the curriculum. Political leaders and educators must join forces to fill the gap, to find ways to instill values in our children.

Teaching values, while initially met with resistance in some school districts that have instituted it, has been shown to effect positive changes in student attitudes and behavior. Kennedy-Townsend noted that a survey of 176 schools with a values curriculum reported a 77 percent decrease in disciplinary problems, 68 percent increase in attendance, 64 percent decrease in vandalism, and in one middle school in New Haven, Connecticut pregnancies dropped from sixteen to zero. Schools have had to assume other responsibilities once considered the family domain—driver education, sex education, etc. Why not values?

Raising a moral child has become more problematic as we attempt to cope with moral ambiguities created by alienation from or the questioning of traditional values embodied in church, school, and community (Herbert & Daniel, 1996). Nevertheless, we must continue our effort to instill in our children those universal values that sustain the culture.

Adverse environmental conditions can seriously compromise the academic potential of students. Consequently, educational institutions have had to broaden their scope to address not only the intellectual but the social, emotional, and physical needs of students. There is a need for support staff and ongoing staff development initiatives to assist teachers and administrators in identifying and developing strategies to meet the needs of students who have inherited social conditions that can compromise their future.

Summary

There are five underlying themes that have reoccurred throughout this book. They are: (1) education is a partnership, (2) perceptions and attitude dictate behavior, (3) knowledge creates understanding and understanding creates change, (4) there are different ways of knowing and educators must broaden their pedagogy to allow students to learn in ways amenable to their learning style, and (5) there are many extraneous variables that impact a student's educational experience. These underlying themes were woven through six chapters that engaged the reader in an in-depth discourse on primary issues in education— parental involvement, teacher attitude, student achievement, student motivation, discipline and social issues that impact the educational process.

The educational future of our children depends upon the successful partnership between home, school, and community. For too long, there has been a reluctance for each of these entities to collectively engage in a meaningful dialogue. Each group, to varying degrees, has addressed educational issues. However, when narrowly focused on the issues as they relate to one group as a separate entity, the dialogue fails to recognize the common interest and collective impact of each group in providing our children with the best possible educational experiences. Each must come to terms with the realization that what one does has a residual effect on the other. When parents fail to instill in their children the value of education, schools must deal with the consequences. If schools are unsuccessful in meeting this challenge, businesses will reap the consequences in the form of an inadequately prepared workforce, and we all will feel the impact in terms of level of productivity, quality of goods and services, and the general advancement of our culture. Home, school, and community must come together in a symbiotic relationship to offer our children the support necessary for academic success, ensure adequate educational funding to enable us to meet the needs of all children, provide staff development opportunities for teachers, and develop and maintain programs and curriculums so that our children can, at the very least, remain competitive in the world community.

The focus on student performance levels has propelled education into the national spotlight. Consequently, many state and local legislatures have responded with such measures as establishing academic standards and required proficiency tests. The residual fallout has been the tendency to place blame. Parents blame teachers, teachers blame parents, the business community blames the schools. In the final analysis, each must share responsibility for the state of education in our communities and the country as a whole. The role of each is addressed in this book.

Too often in our attempts to assess the reasons for the flagging academic performance of American students in comparison to students in Asian and European countries, teachers often factor themselves out of the equation. This may in part be attributed to how teachers define their role. If the role of teacher is narrowly defined as imparting knowledge, they are not likely to accept responsibility for low academic performance. The thinking tends to be that if one teaches, students should learn. In so narrowly defining the role of teacher, they have factored out many of the extraneous variables that impact student learning. Among these are teacher attitude. Attitude dictates behavior. Studies have shown that teachers' attitude toward students significantly influences their academic and behavioral expectations of students and that generally there is the tendency to teach to the level of expectation. Attitudes similarly influence the nature of their interaction with students.

Teachers must raise their level of consciousness of the affective side of teaching. They must be willing to engage in greater introspection to examine their underlying assumptions about the students they teach and what being a teacher means in the '90s. They must be flexible, willing to change their pedagogy to meet the needs of students rather than cling to the expectation that students must acquiesce to their methods. To reach students requires understanding them and refraining from defining them and their ability solely on the basis of test scores or other variables.

Master teachers see beyond student test scores, behavior, ethnic or socioeconomic background. Instead, they attempt to discover that special gift that we all possess but that for many students may be shrouded by circumstance. These teachers seek to build bridges to understanding rather than destroying them when motivated by social, and cultural differences or their lack of ability to step outside of their box to view the world from the perspective of another. They seek to bridge the gap rather than build a wall. Teachers must understand how loudly the unspoken language of the classroom reverberates through the educational experiences of children. Teacher body language, gestures, and voice inflection can create a social distance between teacher and student that can negatively impact learning. Similarly, something as seemingly innocuous as the way the teacher dresses may be interpreted by students as a manifestation of the way the teacher feels about them. In effect, teachers must understand the very powerful impact of the affective side of teaching on the efficacy of their practice.

Student achievement is the standard measure of the success of educational institutions in meeting their mandate to provide all students with an educational environment conducive to learning and to develop curriculums that will ultimately prepare students to be competitive in the marketplace and assume their role as informed consumers and citizens. It is the desire of the master teacher to instill in students an insatiable thirst for learning, to not only absorb knowledge but develop the intellectual curiosity that leads to the production of knowledge, to make a difference in the world. While there are many variables that impact student academic achievement, the student remains the nucleus. No matter the circumstance, in large measure their success or failure depends not upon the circumstance but how they choose to respond to it. History is replete with examples of individuals who have overcome adversity to claim a notable place in history. Then, there are those who cannot claim fame, yet were no less determined and courageous in their struggle, transcending their circumstance to fashion a place for themselves in the world as responsible and successful citizens.

There is much, however, that educators and members of the business community and government can do to assist students whose academic success is compromised by the social conditions they inherit. They can focus on educating the whole child, learn from successful business operatives such as Saturn and Wal-Mart strategies for creating positive and productive work environments. The business community can offer work/study opportunities and mentoring programs, revisit the definition of the role of teacher, and government agencies can commit to ensuring equitable education funding for all students. Students must also look inward, set realistic goals, and accept responsibility for their learning. As one teacher said, you can force them to the table but you cannot force them to eat. School attendance is mandatory in some states until age sixteen. This brings students into the school setting but the desire to learn cannot be legislated. This must come from intrinsic and extrinsic motivation buoyed by values that affirm the importance of education.

Motivation is predicated upon a goal or goals one aspires to achieve. Consequently, goal setting acquires added significance when framed within the context of academic achievement and success. Goals enable students to maintain their focus. They fulfill an emotional, physical, or spiritual need or desire. Goal aspiration is the driving force of motivation. Motivation emanates from many sources both intrinsic and extrinsic. Once again, parents, teachers, and the community can do much to motivate students, and they can start by reinforcing the value of education. From this vantage point, students can start by setting goals and making the right choices to ensure that their aspirations are met.

Teachers can motivate students by creating an environment that promotes learning, a sense of community in the classroom, discovering and capitalizing on each student's "gift," showing an enthusiasm for the subject matter, projecting a caring attitude, and setting high expectations for students. Parents can set the stage for educational success by exposing children to experiences that are intellectually stimulating and afford them an opportunity to explore their talents and interests. They can reinforce positive behaviors by offering praise, encouraging exploration, offering themselves as exemplars of the values they wish to instill, showing an interest in their activities by being present at performances, and clearly articulating expectations. The community can motivate students by providing incentives for exemplary performance, starting a mentoring program, providing work/study opportunities for students, and sending specific skill area professionals into the classroom to assist, lecture, or give special presentations. The more aggressively each of these entities engages in motivating students, the greater the potential for all students to be academically successful.

As discipline has increasingly become an area of concern in American schools at all grade levels, it has evolved as a significant factor in academic success. There is a direct relationship between behavior and academic success. For the most part, students who consistently find themselves at odds with their peers and authority figures do not perform up to their maximum academic potential. Behavior problems get in the way of learning. Students with even moderate behavioral problems can jeopardize their learning. As education is a partnership between home, school, and community, each can play a role in assisting students to cope with or resolve the issues that impede academic success. Parents are the first line of defense. They must instill in their children the value of education, respect for adult authority and the rights of others, and clearly articulate their expectations regarding proper decorum and academic achievement. Teachers can assist by examining how their behavior, attitude, and teaching methodology affect students. When students feel teachers are inflexible, unfair, and uncaring, it creates a dynamic for conflict. When teachers are reluctant to evaluate how their teaching style impacts learning and fail to develop strategies that accommodate the varied learning styles of their students, student frustration manifested in behavior problems may be a consequence. The community can assist by developing after-school programs for students of working parents, and, as is the case with many communities, curfew ordinances and other measures that hold parents accountable for their children.

There have been many societal changes over the decades that have had a direct impact on institutions of learning. These changes have impacted the scope of education (focus on the whole child), what we teach (a more inclusive core curriculum), and how we teach (technology in the classroom).

No longer can the educational process be defined in such simplistic terms as teaching reading, writing, and arithmetic. Changes in the family constellation and other social problems mean that many children come to school with a lot of baggage. Broken homes, poverty, physical abuse, sexual abuse, domestic violence, gangs, and alcohol and drug abuse are issues that can seriously compromise a child's potential and ability to take advantage of educational opportunities.

Consequently, educators must be cognizant of the many extraneous variables that impact student learning and behavior. They must be willing to defer judgment of a child's potential and prospects for the future by accepting them where they are and taking them to where they should be. From a more global perspective, schools must attend to the emotional and physical needs of children. They must work to break down the emotional and social barriers to learning. This necessitates an adequate and well-trained support staff consisting of a school nurse, social worker, psychologist, speech therapist, and substance abuse counselor, as well as school counselors and police liaisons, to provide support and to assist children with working through issues that impede their educational progress.

WHERE DO WE GO FROM HERE?

Start Early, Provide Preschool Opportunities

Recent polls have established that among concerns of Americans, education ranks number one (Diamond, 1998, p. 14). A major issue has been improving student academic achievement. O'Connell (1998) gives a brief summary of various trends in education built on the premise that early education is essential to improving academic performance. It appears that the goal is to ensure that by the time a child enters first grade at age six, he/she will possess the requisite academic and social skills to take full advantage of a formal education program.

Throughout the nation, various learning institutions are adopting innovative programs to achieve this goal. In over two hundred communities across the nation existing preschool programs are being linked. The network is called "Success By 6." Undergirding this effort is the belief that networking will have a greater positive outcome on preschool education. The network was started in 1989 by the United Way. Each local coalition is funded and operated by public and private sources and charities. The results of this effort are seen in programs like New Vistas, a high school in Minneapolis. New Vistas opened in 1990 as a public high school for teen mothers and pregnant teens. Its objective is to encourage the teen mother to stay in school by providing child care for their infants, toddlers, and preschoolers. The obvious success of the program resulted in two additional facilities being opened in 1994 and 1997. Community commitment to the concept is evident as the facilities are housed in a corporate office and two hospitals.

In Charlotte, North Carolina, the focus was on inner-city children. These children received quality developmental day care under the auspices of the Child Development Center. The program in Salt Lake City, Utah, is designed to penetrate the very core of problem. Their Home Visitor program sends volunteers into the homes of at-risk families, providing in-home instruction on parenting skills and becoming self-sufficient, as well as making referrals to other community service organizations. The state of Georgia has taken the quantum leap of offering free preschool. This initiative delivers a double punch, giving students an education advantage prior to formally starting school while providing quality child care for parents at no cost (Diamond, 1998, p. 14).

Establish Education Partnerships

Schools struggling with low student achievement could be linked to local universities and education consultants (Bey 1996, p. 13). Universities could place students in their education program in these schools as part of an internship program, long before the more formalized student teacher placements that characterize teacher education programs.

Assess Past Practices, Current Programs and Needs

Among the questions that might be asked in such an assessment are:

- How effective is the school tutoring program? Is the program taking full advantage of all available resources, that is, peer tutors, before- and after-school labs to assist students who need more assistance outside of class, Saturday tutoring sessions, student study groups, parents and other professionals who volunteer as tutors, etc.
- What is the status of social promotions? Are they effective? Is there mandatory summer school for students who are performing below grade level?
- What kind of articulation is there between elementary, junior high, and high school? Does the left hand know what the right-hand is doing?

Make Education a Family Matter

The United States Department of Education, Partnership for Family Involvement in Education program proposes Seven Good Practices for Families. They are:

Take the time. Encourages families to spend time together by eating meals together or take family field trips to the zoo, museum, or library, etc.

Read together. Read to children, have children read to you, share a book on an interesting topic with your teen.

Use TV wisely. Limit TV viewing to no more than two hours during the week. TV does have educational value, contingent upon thoughtful program selection that parents can monitor and control.

Maintain contact with the child's teachers. Encourage children to stretch the limits of their ability. Parents should check homework and inquire what the student learns in school each day.

Know the school staff. Meet with teachers and the principal. Inquire about the curriculum and academic standards.

Monitor the child's activities. Know where your children are, especially teens. To ensure that the child is involved in wholesome activities that will provide a social outlet as well as enhance physical and emotional development, parents should promote participation in school- or community-sponsored groups.

Teach family values. Engage children in straight talk about expectations and values. Discuss the dangers of alcohol and substance abuse.

Keep education on the national agenda. President Clinton, in his nationally televised State of the Union Address on January 27, 1998, shared with the American public his school reform agenda. Heralding the Chicago school reform program as a national model, the President stated, "I will promote a national effort to help schools that follow the lead of the Chicago system."(Sweet, 1998, p. 3). He added substance to his commitment with the promise of federal funding to promote the implementation of various reform measures.

President Clintons school reform agenda called for:

- Academic standards for students and teachers
- The end of social promotions
- Reduction in class size to eighteen—especially for first, second, and third graders
- Extension of after-school care services to an additional half million children

The future of our society depends in part upon the success of educational institutions in producing citizens capable of engaging in higher level thought processes to not only assimilate and disseminate knowledge but to produce knowledge that will take us into the twenty-first century and improve the quality of life for all. This discourse has shed light on the complexity of the process and has shown that the responsibility does not fall upon the shoulders of this institution alone. Each of the major social institutions—family, government, economic, religious—plays a vital role in the process.

Children are the door to the future, and the nature and level of our collective investment in them is the mirror to what that future holds. When you touch the life of a child, you touch eternity, for the sense of self and the legacy that each successive generation leaves behind evolves from the core of the relationships each builds with its children.

Bibliography

A nation at risk: The imperative for educational reform. The National Commission on Excellence in Education. (1983). Washington, D.C.: Government Printing Office.

Ahern, Mi-Ai. (1998, February 4). Learning customs of other lands bridges cultures. *Chicago Sun-Times*, p. 56.

Ashton, A. (1991, August 3). Community involvement important. *Chicago Sun-Times,* Back-to-School Supplement, p 6.

Atkins, A., & Schlosberg, J. (1996, August). Dressed to learn: Are schools better when kids are in uniform. *Better Homes and Gardens*, p. 42.

Baldacci, L. (1997, July 29). Too many drivers running on anger. *Chicago Sun-Times*, p. 19.

Bauer, W. D., & Twentyman, C. T. (1985). Abusing, neglectful, and comparison mothers' response to child-related and non-child-related stressors. *Journal of Consulting and Clinical Psychology, 53*, 335-343.

Becker, H. S. (1963). Outsiders: Studies in the sociology of deviance. New York: The Free Press.

Bellah, R. N. (1985). *Habits of the heart.* Berkeley: University of California Press.

Bennett, W. J. (1992). *The de-valuing of America.* New York: Simon & Schuster.

Bettelheim, B. (1960). *The informed heart.* New York: Free Press.

Bey, L. (1996, October 10). When kids fall short. *Chicago Sun-Times*, p. 13.

Bing, L. (1991). *Do Or Die.* New York: HarperCollins, 1991.

Bloom, B. (1985). *Developing talent in young people.* New York: Ballantine.

Boomers out of touch with kids' drug use. (1998, April 13). *Chicago Sun-Times*, p. 20.

Brooks-Bonner, L. (1997 Spring). Responding to aggressive parents. *School Safety*, pp. 20-22.

Browne, A. (1986). Assault and homicide at home: When battered women kill. In Saks, M. J., and Saxe, L. (Eds.), *Advances in Applied Social Psychology*. Hillsdale, NJ: Erlbaum.

Brownlee, S., & Miller, M. (1997, May 12). Lies parents tell themselves about why they work. *U. S. News & World Report*, pp. 58-73.

Brownstein, R. (1997, July 23). Middle-class exodus from cities persists. *Chicago Sun-Times*, p. 14.

Bruner, J. (1996). *The culture of education*. Cambridge, MA: Harvard University Press.

Byrne, D. (1997, July 31). Standards not exactly golden. *Chicago Sun-Times*, p. 27.

Callahan, S. (1997, July 20). Angry teens turn cool. *Chicago Sun-Times*, p. 38.

Campbell, J. R. (1972). *In touch with students: A philosophy for teachers*. Missouri: Educational Affairs.

Carpenter, J., Rossi, R. & Lawrence, C. (1998, February 5). Help didn't reach killing suspect, 12. *Chicago Sun-Times*, p. 10.

Cassell, J. (1997a, June 27). Grown-ups in survey fault kids. *Chicago Sun-Times*, p. 14.

Cassell, J. (1997b, July 31). Jackson hails school reforms. *Chicago Sun-Times*, p. 10.

Chapman, C. (1993). If the shoe fits: How to develop multiple intelligences in the classroom. Palatine, IL: IRI/Skylight.

Cheyney, L. , Fine M., & Ravitch, D. (1987). American memory: A report on the humanities in the nations's public schools: National Endowment for the Humanities. In C. Kuykendall (Ed.), (1992), *From rage to hope: strategies for reclaiming black and Hispanic students*. Bloomington, IN: National Educational Service.

Chiles, John (1986). *The Encyclopedia of Psychoactive Drugs: Teenage Depression and Suicide*. New York: Chelsea House.

Clark, Reginald (1983). *Family life and school achievement: why poor black children succeed or fail*. Chicago: The University of Chicago Press.

Clifford, M. N., & Walster, E. (1973, Spring). Research note: The effect of physical attractiveness in teacher expectations. *Sociology of Education, 46*, 248-59.

Coffey, R. (1997, June 12). Mom says schools treat parents as enemy. *Chicago Sun-Times*, p. 8.

Coffey, R. (1998, April 23). Fulton school teachers take on their principal. *Chicago Sun-Times*, p. 8.

Coleman, G. (1996). *African-American stories of triumph over adversity: joy cometh in the morning.* Westport, CT: Bergin & Garvey.

Coleman, J. (1990). *Quality and achievement in education.* Boulder, CO: Westview Press, Inc.

Coon, D. (1992). *Introduction to psychology: exploration and application* (6th ed.). New York: West.

Cooper, H. M., et al. (1975). Understanding pygmalion: The social psychology of self-fulling classroom expectations. Alexandria, VA: ERIC Document Reproduction Service, ED 182 642, 1979.

Cotliar, S. (1997, March 21). Drug has designs on suburbia: Ecstasy lures young, affluent. *Chicago Sun-Times*, p. 3.

Diamond, David. (1998, January 23-25). Want to send your child to free preschool? Move to Georgia. *USA Weekend*, p. 14.

Diaz, C. (1992). *Multicultural education for the 21st century.* Washington, DC: National Education Association.

Deerin, M. (1997, July 26). School standards Ok'd: Rules cover what, when a child learns. *The Daily Southtown*, pp. 1, 5.

Denbo, S. (1986). Improving minority student achievement: Focus on the classroom. Washington, DC: Mid-Atlantic Equity Center, American University. In C. Kuykendall (Ed.), (1992), *From rage to hope: Strategies for reclaiming black and hispanic students*, p. 10, 12. Bloomington, IN: National Educational Service.

Dewey, J. K. (1916). Voluntarism in the Roycean philosophy. *Philosophical Review*, pp. 245-254.

Dodge, S. (1997, March 16). Plain talk about the hard stuff. *Chicago Sun-Times*, pp. 24-25.

Dodge, S. (1998, January 29). Schools like smaller classes, wary of cost. *Chicago Sun-Times*, p. 2.

Dwyer, K. (1998, January). The lowdown on depression. *NEA Today*, p. 24.

Egeland, B., Jacobvitz, D., & Stroufe, L. A. (1988). Breaking the cycle of abuse. *Child Development*, *59*(4), 1080-1088.

Fine, M. (1986, Spring). Why urban adolescents drop into and out of public high schools. Princeton, NJ: *Teacher College Board.*

Fischer, D. (1997, March 3). Taking on tenure. U.S. New & World Report, p. 60.

Fiske, E. (1991). *Smart schools, smart kids—why do some schools work?* New York: Simon and Schuster.

Forbes, M. S. (1991, July 22). Humanitarian move. *Forbes*, p. 23.

Fordham, S., & Ozbu, J. (1986). Black students' school success: Coping with the burden of acting white. *The Urban Review*, *18*(3), 176-206.

Forward, S. (1989). *Toxic parents: Overcoming their hurtful legacy and reclaiming your life.* New York: Bantam Books.

Fox, P., & Oakes, W. (1984). Learned helplessness: Non-contingent reinforcement in video game performance produces a decrement in performance on a lexical decision task. *Bulletin of the Psychonomic Society, 22*, 113-166. In Coon, D. (1992). *Introduction to psychology: exploration and application* (6th ed.). New York: West, pp. 346-347.

Franchine, P. (1998, February 17). School wades in, cuts student fights: Surveys play a role in reducing conflict. *Chicago Sun-Times*, p. 4.

Fried, P. A., & Watkinson, B. (1990). 36- and 48-month neurobehavioral follow-up of children prenatally exposed to marijuana, cigarets, and alcohol. *Journal of Developmental & Behavioral Pediatrics, 11*(2), 49-58.

Gamoran, A., & Mare, R. (1989, March). Secondary school tracking and educational inequality: Compensation, reinforcement or neutrality? *American Journal of Sociology*, 1146-83.

Gardner, H. (1983). *Frames of mind: The theory of multiple intelligences.* New York: Basic Books.

Gardner, H. (1991). *The unschooled mind: How children learn and how schools should teach.* New York: Basic Books.

Gardner, H. (1995, November). Reflections on multiple intelligences: Myths and messages. *Phi Delta Kappan, 77*(3), 200-209.

Gest, T. (1996, March 25). Crime time bomb. *U.S. News and World Report*, pp. 29-36.

Giovannoni, J. M., & Becerra, R. M. (1979). *Defining child abuse.* New York: Free Press.

Glasser, W. (1990). *Quality schools: Managing students without coercion.* New York: Harper & Row.

Glasser, W. (1984). *Control theory: A new explanation of how we control our lives.* New York: Harper & Row.

Glazer, S. (1993, May 14). Preventing teen pregnancy. *Congressional Quarterly, 3*(18), 411.

Good, T. L. (1981, February). Teacher expectations and student perceptions: A decade of research. *Educational Leadership*, Vol. 38, February 1981, pp. 415-22 . In C. Kuykendall (Ed.), *From rage to hope: Strategies for reclaiming black and Hispanic students.* Bloomington, IN: National Educational Service.

Goodlad, J. I. (1984). *A Place Called School.* Institute for the Development of Educational Activities.

Grossnickle, D. R. (1989). *Helping students develop self-motivation.* Reston. VA: The National Association of Secondary School Principals.

Grossnickle, D. R., & Sesko, F. P. (1985). *Promoting effective discipline in school and classroom: A practitioner's perspective.* The National Association of Secondary School Principals.

Gutloff, K. (1997, October). Make it happen: Five strategies for reaching the hard-to-reach parent. *NEA Today, 16*(3), pp. 4-5.

Gutloff, K. (1998, February). Moving targets. *NEA Today, (16)*6, pp. 4-5.

Hale-Benson, J. (1982). *Black children: Their roots, culture and learning styles.* Provo, UT: Brigham Young University Press.

Half of nation's children live in non-traditional families. 1995 Information Please (TM) Almanac, Annual 1995, Houghton Mifflin, 1995, p. 841.

Hancock, L. (1998, January). When teacher gets an F. *Good Housekeeping,* pp. 100-101, 143-144.

Hatty, M. (1998, May 1-3). Ten ways to a healthy self-image. *USA Weekend,* p. 10.

Hazler, R. J., Hoover, J. H. & Oliver, R. (1993, March). What do kids say about bullying? *The Education Digest, 58*(7), 16-21.

Headden, S. (1997, October 20). The hispanic dropout mystery. *U.S. News and World Report,* pp. 64-65.

Henderson, A. (1998, January). Parent involvement: More thank kids' play. *NEA Today, 16*(5), p. 14.

Herbert, W. & Daniel, M. (1996, June 3). The moral child. *U.S. News & World Report,* pp. 52-59.

Herrnstein, R. J. & Murray, C. (1994). *The bell curve: Intelligence and class structure in American life.* New York: The Free Press.

Hetter, K. (1996, March 25). A Pittsburgh court battles the tide: Can judges succeed where parents have failed? *U.S. News and World Report,* pp. 37-38.

Hewitt, B. (1991, January 21). Hope for the hopeless. *People Weekly,* pp. 43-47.

Hill, H. D. (1989) *Effective strategies for teaching minority students.* Bloomington, IN: National Educational Service.

Holt, J. C. (1967). *How children learn.* New York: Pitman.

Howard, J. (1998, January). Expecting the best. *NEA Today, 16*(5), p. 14.

Huard, C. (1997, August 3). Girls need extra boost to counter teen pressures. *Chicago Sun-Times,* Back-to-School Supplement, p. 7.

Huffington, A. (1997, August 3). Missing the point on education. *Chicago Sun-Times,* p. 34.

Ihejirika, M. (1997, February 26). Educators address money gap between rich, poor schools. *Chicago Sun-Times,* p. 11.

Ilsley, P. J. (1990). *Enhancing the volunteer experience.* San Francisco, CA: Jossey-Bass.

Jaeger, R. M., & Hattie, J. A. (1995, November). Detracking America's schools: should we really care? *Phi Delta Kappan, 77*(3), 218-220.

Jakes, T. D. (1994). *Can you stand to be blessed? Insight to help you survive the peaks and valleys.* Shippenburg, PA: Treasure House Destiny Image.

Johnson, D. W., & Johnson, R. T. (1993, April). Implementing cooperative learning. *The Education Digest, 58*(8), 62-67.

Jones, A. (1972) *Students: Don't push your teacher down the stairs on Friday.* New York: Quadrangle Books.

Jones, R. (1997, January 5). Grandparents raising kids. *Chicago Sun-Times*, p. 43.

Karl, B. D. (1984). Lo, the poor volunteer: An essay on the relation between history and myth. *Social Services Review, 54*(4), 493-552.

Kaufman, J., & Zigler, E. (1987). Do abused children become abusive parents? *American Journal of Orthopsychiatry, 57*(2), 186-92.

Keeping kids in focus: Ten ways to help kids who have trouble paying attention. (1998, March). *NEA Today, 16*(7), 4-5.

Kennedy-Townsend, K. (1992, December). Why Johnny can't tell right from wrong. *Washington Monthly*, pp. 29-32.

Kleinman, R. E. et al. (1998, January). Hunger in children in the United States: Potential behavioral and emotional correlates. *Pediatrics, 101*(1), 3.

Knight, H. (1997, August 1). Hispanic dropout rate 30% nationwide. *Denver Post*, p. 12A.

Kochman, T. (1983). *Black and white styles in conflict.* IL: University of Chicago Press.

Kronholz, J. (1997, June 15). Schoolwork hits home: Programs get parents more involved in education. *Chicago Sun-Times*, p. 39.

Kuykendall, C. (1992). *From rage to hope: strategies for reclaiming black and Hispanic students.* Bloomington, IN: National Educational Service.

Ladson-Billings, G. (1994). *The dreamkeepers successful teachers of African American children.* San Francisco, CA: Jossey-Bass.

LaPoint, V., Holloman, L. & Alleyne, S. (1993, March). Dress codes and uniforms in urban schools. *The Education Digest, 58*(7), 32-34.

Lawrence, C., & Houlihan-Skilton, (1998, May 20). Execs get principal's inside look at schools. *Chicago Sun-Times*, pp. 1 & 2.

Lee, R. T., & Ashforth, B. E. (1990). On the meaning of Maslach's three dimensions of burnout. *Journal of Applied Psychology 75*(6), 743-747.

Leland, J. (1998, June 1). Savior of the streets. *Newsweek*, pp. 22-25.

Lenz, L. (1997, May 4). Can tests help kids to learn? *Chicago Sun-Times*, p. 30.

Lerman, P. (1998, May 1-3). Valuing God is cool. *U.S.A. Weekend*, p. 12.

Main, M., & George, C. (1985). Responses of abused and disadvantaged toddlers to distress and agemates: A study in day care. *Developmental Psychology, 21*, 407-412.

Malone, G., & Bowser, P. (1998, March). Can retention be good for a student? *NEA Today, 16*(7), p. 43.

Manning, S., & Hardy, J. E. (1991, January 25). A world of pain. *Scholastic Update*, pp. 6-9.

Marcus, L. (1998, January 6). Admissions exams losing points with more colleges. *Chicago Sun-Times*, p. 6A.

Marshall, R., & Tucker, M. (1992). *Thinking for a living: Education and the wealth of nations*. New York: Basic Books.

Maslach, C. (1982). *Burnout: The cost of caring*. Englewood Cliffs, NJ: Prentice-Hall.

Matarazzo, J. D. (1984). Behavioral immunogens and pathogens in health and illness. In B. L. Hammonds & C.J. Scheirer (eds.), *Psychology and Health*. Washington, DC: American Psychological Association, 5-43.

Math, science exam scores don't add up. (1998, February 25). *Daily Southtown*, pp. A-1, A-2.

Matthews, D. B. (1990). A comparison of burnout in selected occupational fields. *Career Development Quarterly 38*(3), 230-239.

McBrien, J. L., & Brandt, R. S. (1997). *The language of learning: A guide to education terms*. Alexandria, VA: Association For Supervision and Curriculum Development.

McNamee, T. (1997, January 26). Jobs don't always help teenagers. *Chicago Sun-Times*, p. 19.

McNichol, T. (1997, February 14-16). Computers in class: A waste of $50 billion? *USA Weekend*, p. 10.

McNichol, T. (1998, February 6-8). The power of touch. *USA Weekend*, p. 22.

McWhinnie, C. (1998, March 23). School zooms in on security. *Chicago Sun-Times*, p. 8.

Meckler, L. (1998, May 1). Fewer teens having babies, *Chicago Sun-Times*, p. 55.

Mendler, A. N. (1993, March). Discipline with dignity in the classroom. *The Education Digest*, *58*(7), 4-10.

Michie, G. (1997, November/December). The story of their lives: Three Hispanic girls bond over a book. *Teacher Magazine*, pp. 43-47.

Mitchell, M. A. (1996, October 13). Kids just don't take the tests seriously. *Chicago Sun-Times*, p. 18.

Mitchell, M. A. (1996, October 21). Schools must finish job parents start. *Chicago Sun-Times*, p. 9.

Mitchell, M. A. (1998, May 7). A kid's best friend. *Chicago Sun-Times*, p. 33.

Mitchell, M. A., & Bey, L. (1996, October 13). Attendance on the skids without truant officers. *Chicago Sun-Times*, p. 18.

Mones, P. (1991). *When a child kills: Abused children who kill their parents*. New York: Pocket Books.

Most juveniles crimes committed after school. (1997, September 29). *JET*, p. 24.

Murray, H. B., Herling, B. B., & Staebler, B. K. (1973). The effects of locus of control and pattern of performance on teacher evaluation of a student. *Psychology in the Schools, 10*, 345-50.

Nale, R. F. (1997, June 1). In education, accountability counts. *The Star*, p. A-7.

Noonan, P. (1998, January). Looking forward, what makes kids happy. *Good Housekeeping*, p. 160.

O'Connell, B. (1998, January 23-25). New routes to success by 6. *USA Weekend*, p. 14.

O'Donnell, M. (1997, July 29). Teens play hooky in school. *Chicago Sun-Times*, p. 10.

Olsen, G., & More, M. (1982). *Voices from the classroom*. Oakland, CA: Citizens Policy Center.

Overmier, J. B., & Seligman, M.E.P. (1967). Effects of inescapabale shock upon subsequent escape and avoidance learning. *Journal of Comparative and Physiological Psychology, 63*, 23-33. In Coon, D. (1992). *Introduction to psychology: exploration and application* (6th ed.). New York: West, pp. 346-347.

Palladino, J. (1993, March). Single-parent students: How we can help. *The Education Digest, 58*(7), 47-53.

Papert, S. (1993). *The children's machine*. New York: Basic Books: A Division of Harper Collins.

Parents remain major influence on children's behavior well into their teen years: Study. (1997, September 29). *JET*, p. 23.

Pearlman-Debelak, J. (1995, April 9). Girls in gangs: their power trip leads to a dead-end street. *The Star*, p. B-1, B-3.

Psychology profession fails to meet needs of blacks say black psychologists. (1998, May 25). *JET*, p. 22.

Ragland, R., & Saxon, B. (1985). *Invitation to Psychology*, Glenview, IL: Scott Foresman Co.

Raymond, B. (1990, December). Rescued by love: Forgotten Romanian babies. *Redbook*, p. 116.

Recer, P. (1997, September 26). Reading aloud to babies aids language skills. *Chicago Sun-Times*, p. 3.

Relin, D. O. (1991, January 25). Lost to the streets. *Scholastic Update*, pp. 10-13.

Rhodes, S. (1998, May 1-3). When depression turns deadly. *USA Weekend*, p. 16.

Rhule, P., & Soriano, C. G. (1998, May 1-3). Teens tackle their identity crisis. *USA Weekend*, pp. 6-7.

Rodriguez, A. (1997, March 24). What reform taught Michigan. *Chicago Sun-Times*, p. 6.

Rosen, L. E. (1997, Fall). Wanted: Alternatives to suspensions and expulsion. *School Safety*, pp. 8-11.

Rosenthal, R. (1973, September). The pygmalion effect lives. *Psychology Today*, pp. 56-63.

Rosenthal, R., & Jacobson, L. (1968). *Pygmalion in the classroom: Teacher expectations and pupil's intellectual development.* New York: Holt, Rhinehart and Winston.

Rossi, R. (1996, October 7). Make kids attend school from ages 5 to 17-Vallas. *Chicago Sun-Times*, p. 7.

Rossi, R. (1997a, February 25). Study says many kids lack exposure to math. *Chicago Sun-Times*, p. 8

Rossi, R. (1997b, March 25). School reform tradeoffs–academics may be tied to funding. *Chicago Sun-Times*, p. 4.

Rossi, R. (1997c, July 1). School's in session for 150,000. *Chicago Sun-Times*, p. 22.

Rossi, R. (1998, February 8). The discipline debate: Killings fuel doubts about out-of-school suspensions. *Chicago Sun-Times*, p. 11.

Rotzoll, B. W. (1998, March 25). Kids ambush kids. *Chicago Sun-Times*, pp. 1, 2.

Rotzoll, B. W., & Dodge, S. (1998, March 26). Adults often miss signs of trouble from distressed kids, experts say. *Chicago Sun-Times*, pp. 6, 7.

Rozek, D. (1997, September 28). Technology as teacher. *Chicago Sun-Times*, p. 6.

Rubovits, P. C., & Maehr, M. L. (1973). Pymalion in black and white. *Journal of Personality and Social Psychology, 25*, pp. 210-218.

Ryndak, H. (1997, April 10). Needy schools push for change. *Chicago Sun-Times*, p. 6.

Sadler, M. & D., & Long, L. Gender and educational equality. In Banks, J. and C.A., (eds.), Multicultural Education—Issues and Perspectives. Boston: Allyn and Bacon, 1989.

Sander, J. (1991). Before their time: Four generations of teenage mothers. New York: Harcourt Brace Jovanovich.

Saul, S. (1997a, January 3). Agony, not joy. *Newsday*, p. A-6.

Saul, S. (1997b, January 3). Broken dreams. *Newsday*, p.A-5.

Schools vow to 'suspend' unruly parents. (1998, April 8). *Chicago Sun-Times*, p. S-39.

Schrof, J. (1996, April 1). What kids will have to know. *U.S. News and World Report*, pp. 57-60.

Schurr, S. L. (1993, April). 16 proven ways to involve parents. *The Education Digest, 58*(8), 4-9.

Seligman, MEP (1974). Submissive death: Giving up on life. *Psychology Today, 7*, 80-85. In Coon, D. (1992). *Introduction to psychology: exploration and application* (6th ed.). New York: West, pp. 346-347.

Seligman, MEP (1989). Helplessness. New York: Freeman. In Coon, D. (1992). *Introduction to psychology: exploration and application* (6th ed). New York: West, pp. 346-347.

Shapiro, J. P., & Wright, A. R. (1996, September 9). Can churches save America? *U.S. News & World Report*, pp. 47-52.

Shaugnessy, J. G., Coughlin, M. & Smith, K. (1997, June/July). Dealing with disruptive behavior in high school classrooms. *The High School Magazine, 4*(4), 44-47.

Shepard, L., & Smith, M. (1989). *Flunking grades: Research and policies on retention.* Philadelphia, PA: Farmer Press.

Shields, C. J. (1996, December 12). Reading success tied to strong parental support. *The Star*, p. A-7.

Siegel, L. (1997, August 5). New York school turns troubled teens in new direction. *Chicago Sun-Times*, p. 15-A.

Silberman, C. E. (1970). *Crisis in the classroom: The remaking of American education.* New York: Random House.

Single-parent kids fare better if parent is divorced rather than never married: Census data show. (1997, December 8). *JET*, p. 48.

Slavin, R. E. (1995, November). Detracking and its detraactors: Flawed evidence, flawed values. *Phi Delta Kappan, 77*(3), 220-222.

Small classes hold long-term benefits. (1998, March). *NEA Today, 16*(7), 17.

Smith, B. (1997, August 11). Girl gang members tell why. *Chicago Sun-Times*, p. 6.

Smith, R. P., & Denton, J. J. (1980, Spring). The effects of dialect ethnicity and orientation to sociolinguistics on the perception of teaching candidates. *Educational Research Quarterly* (3), pp. 70-79.

Smith-Maddox, R., & Wheelock, A. (1995, November). Untracking and students' futures: Closing the gap between aspirations and expectations. *Phi Delta Kappan, 77*(3), 222-229.

Sowell, T. (1993). *Inside American education: The decline, the deception, the dogmas.* New York: The Free Press.

Sowell, T. (1997, June 28). Without criticism, there is no chance for growth. *Chicago Sun-Times*, p. 20.

Spielman, F., & Rossi, R. (1997, March 11). Expulsion policy to stiffen: Off-campus arrest could boot kids. *Chicago Sun-Times*, p. 3.

Stevenson, H. W., & Stigler, J. W. (1992). *The learning gap—Why our schools are failing and what we can learn from japanese and chinese education.* New York: Simon and Schuster.

Stiggins, R. J. (1995, November). Assessment literacy for the 21st century. *Phi Delta Kappan, 77*(3), 238-245.

Streissgut, A. P., Barr, H. M., Sampson, P. D., & Darby, B. L. (1989). IQ at age 4 in relation to maternal alcohol use and smoking during pregnancy. *Developmental Psychology, 25*(1), 3-11.

Students see jump in gangs, crime. (1998, April 13). *Chicago Sun-Times*, p. 21.

Study reveals most juvenile crimes committed after school. (1997, September 29). *JET*, p. 24.

Sun, R. C. (1996). *The family math companion: Arithmetic—the foundation of math.* U.S.: Stoneridge Books.

Survey reveals teens say drugs more common in schools than on streets. (1997, September 29). *JET*, p. 22.

Sweet, L. (1998, January 27). City makes Clinton's agenda. *Chicago Sun-Times*, p. 3.

Taylor, D. B., & Taylor, P. M. (1990). *Coping with a dysfunctional family.* New York: Rosen .

Teen crime takes plunge in 1996. (1997, October 3). *Daily Southtown*, pp. 1, 10.

The learning lag: you can't blame TV (1996, December 2). *U.S. News and World Report*, p. 16.

Thomas, R. (1997, September 18). Teen substance abuse target of symposium. *The Star*, pp. 1, A-4.

Tobias Ulrich, C. (1994). *The way they learn: How to discover and teach to your child's strengths.* Colorado Springs, CO: Focus on the Family.

Tobias Ulrich, C. (1995). *The way we work.* Colorado Springs, CO: Focus on the Family.

Touch, T. et. al. (1996, April 1). The case for tough standards. *U.S. New and World Report*, pp. 52-56.

Touch, T., Bennefield, R. M., Hawkins, D., & Loeb, P. (1996, February 26). Why teachers don't teach. *U.S. News and World Report*, pp. 62-71.

Tresemer, D. W. (1977). Fear of success: An intriguing set of questions. New York: Plenum. In Dennis Coon (Ed.) 1992, *Introduction to psychology: Exploration and application* (6th ed.). New York: West p. 316.

Turbak, G. (1991, May). When children have children. *Miwanis Magazine*, 20-22, 50.

Vandegrift, J. A., & Greene, A. L. (1993, April). Involving parents of the at-risk: Rethinking definitions. *The Education Digest 58*(8), 18-22.

Wagner, B. (1996, December 2). Where computer do work. *U.S. News & World Report*, pp.83-93.

Weinberg, G., & Catero, H. (1971). How to read a person like a book. New York: Hawthorn Books. In Kuykendall, C. (1992). *From rage to hope:*

Strategies for reclaiming black and Hispanic students. Bloomington, IN: National Educational Service.

Wilberg, E. (1997, August 5). Alternative school gives kids second chance. *Chicago Sun-Times*, p. 14-A.

Wisnewski, C. (1997, April 6). Beyond the classroom: counselors take on more than guiding students to best careers. *The Star*, p. E-1.

Worsnop, R. L. (1991, June 14). Teenage suicide. *Congressional Quarterly Researcher*, *1*(6), 371. In Social Issues Resources Series, YOUTH, *4*(9).

Yednak, C. (1997, December 29). Changing the look of learning: Teachers tap into multiple intelligence theory. *Daily Southtown*, pp. 1, 4.

Index

About the Author

GERALDINE COLEMAN is a High School Associate Principal in Illinois and the author of *African American Stories of Triumph Over Adversity* (Bergin & Garvey, 1996).